T0381791

SMARTPHONES WITHIN PSYCHOLOGICAL SCIENCE

Psychologists can now quantify behaviours beyond the laboratory using a mass-adopted, unified system that is primed for data capture a.k.a. smartphones. This is the first book to bring together related areas of smartphone research and point towards how psychology can benefit and engage with these developments in the future. It critically considers how smartphones and related digital devices help answer and generate new research questions for psychological science. The book then guides readers through how smartphones are being used within psychology and social science more broadly. Drawing from examples of both good and bad practice within current research, a new perspective is brought to major themes and debates across behavioural science. In the digital age, smartphones and associated devices will be able to accomplish much more in the near future. Psychology has a key role to play when it comes to balancing this monumental potential with carefully considered research.

David A. Ellis is an Associate Professor of Information Systems at the University of Bath and holds an Honorary Research Fellowship at the University of Lincoln. His research to date has been published in psychological, medical, and computer science journals with results regularly appearing on TV and Radio.

SMARTPHONES WITHIN PSYCHOLOGICAL SCIENCE

DAVID A. ELLIS

University of Bath

CAMBRIDGE UNIVERSITY PRESS

CAMBRIDGE
UNIVERSITY PRESS

University Printing House, Cambridge CB2 8BS, United Kingdom

One Liberty Plaza, 20th Floor, New York, NY 10006, USA

477 Williamstown Road, Port Melbourne, VIC 3207, Australia

314–321, 3rd Floor, Plot 3, Splendor Forum, Jasola District Centre,
New Delhi – 110025, India

79 Anson Road, #06–04/06, Singapore 079906

Cambridge University Press is part of the University of Cambridge.

It furthers the University's mission by disseminating knowledge in the pursuit of
education, learning, and research at the highest international levels of excellence.

www.cambridge.org
Information on this title: www.cambridge.org/9781108497954
DOI: 10.1017/9781108671408

© Cambridge University Press 2020

First published 2020

A catalogue record for this publication is available from the British Library.

Library of Congress Cataloging-in-Publication Data
NAMES: Ellis, David A, 1986– author.
TITLE: Smartphones within psychological science / David A Ellis.
DESCRIPTION: New York : Cambridge University Press, 2020. | Includes index.
IDENTIFIERS: LCCN 2020018183 (print) | LCCN 2020018184 (ebook) | ISBN 9781108497954
(hardback) | ISBN 9781108671408 (ebook)
SUBJECTS: LCSH: Technological innovations – Psychological aspects. | Smartphones. |
Human-computer interaction. | Emotional intelligence.
CLASSIFICATION: LCC QA76.9.P75 E45 2020 (print) | LCC QA76.9.P75 (ebook) |
DDC 004.16701/9–dc23
LC record available at https://lccn.loc.gov/2020018183
LC ebook record available at https://lccn.loc.gov/2020018184

ISBN 978-1-108-49795-4 Hardback
ISBN 978-1-108-70934-7 Paperback

To Mum, Dad and Brittany

Contents

Figures

Tables

xii

Preface

It often feels like the rate of technological change is accelerating, but advances in computing and communications have been transforming society since the advent of the printing press. Today, the smartphone has democratised computational power to billions of people across the world by bringing together many technologies that existed separately. Providing a means of communication first, smartphones have replaced the need to carry a separate camera, video recorder, radio, MP3 player, television and laptop computer. Human–computer interaction has become a cornerstone of life as people rely on ubiquitous technology to meet everyday obligations. These realities, coupled with the fact that the smartphone remains in close proximity, provide new opportunities for psychological science.

Such developments come at an interesting time for the social sciences as they face a number of methodological and conceptual challenges, including issues of replicability, transparency and measurement. Many researchers also continue to have reservations about the applicability of laboratory-based research. For example, Tajfel once described the typical laboratory experiment as 'a temporary collection of late adolescent strangers given a puzzle to solve under bizarre conditions in a limited time during their first meeting while being peered at from behind a mirror' (Tajfel, Fraser and Jaspars, 1984, p. 474). While this is a slightly dated view of modern experimental psychology, there remains a tension between ecological validity and experimental control. New technologies, however, can help reduce if not eliminate that tension, and opportunities afforded by advances in electronic sensors, reduction in battery sizes and developments in computational data analysis are ideally suited to understanding the complexity of psychological processes as they unfold in everyday contexts. Mobile and wearable devices, specifically, can record multiple measurements every few seconds, including a person's location, activity levels and patterns of communication. These technologies provide a prima facie case for a more applicable psychology because understanding what happens outside the lab allows one to ask detailed questions and provide answers that cannot be gleaned from other methods.

Despite this promise, this book grew from equal measures of academic curiosity and frustration. While a large body of research has focused on developing new methods to help answer specific questions, psychologists have spent far more resources investigating how smartphones and other digital technologies (e.g., video games, social media) might cause harm. There is considerable uncertainty in both camps. Therefore, this book is the first to document how developments in mobile technology feed into research avenues traditionally associated with psychology and behavioural science. It also aims to provide guidance on how psychological research might capitalise on the capabilities of smartphones and mobile computing in the future. In this respect it is often a tale of two halves.

Throughout, I provide explicit advice, opinions and suggestions on the quality of research and how it might be improved. I do not claim that every point of view is correct or universally accepted – but it should provoke discussion. This book is certainly not an explicit 'how to' guide when it comes to conducting research with smartphones. Other people have already curated excellent books that cover related topics (e.g., Mehl and Conner, 2012). Nor is this a book that considers which theory can be applied to a specific question. However, one overarching theme concerns how psychology might position itself going forward as part of a larger interdisciplinary effort. Disciplinary isolation has done us few favours, and the content reflects psychology's natural ability to transcend across multiple specialities. As a result, the material is accessible by those who sit outside the discipline.

Smartphones perhaps illustrate the problems and struggles faced when scientific progress appears to be moving faster on paper but slower in practice. In line with the United Kingdom Research and Innovation's (UKRI) current priorities, new ideas and technologies are critical to addressing the complex challenges facing society. However, at many levels we do not yet fully know how to leverage technology in order to support positive social and economic changes. The technical and analytical challenges faced, particularly when working with government and industry partners, have probably had a considerable influence on my views about research. That said, contributions from social science are essential if new technologies are to have a positive impact on people and society.

The digital age has opened a Pandora's box of opportunities and challenges. Provided psychology can avoid past mistakes, and break free from unproductive cycles of research, the discipline is well placed to make some impressive contributions.

Acknowledgements

Several funding awards supported the development and preparation of this book, including:

- The Centre for Research and Evidence on Security Threats (ESRC Award: ES/N009614/1)
- GetAMoveOn: leveraging technology to enable mobility and transform health (EPSRC Award: EP/N027299/1)
- Faculty of Science and Technology research grant (PSA7866) from Lancaster University
- Research Investment Grant (RIF2014–31) from the University of Lincoln.

Many people have contributed to my personal and professional development. While I have not always followed advice to the letter, I owe a great deal to those who have allowed me to explore ideas without fear of failure. This type of environment can be hard to work in when you are looking for direction, but it breeds independence and creativity. I would also like to specifically acknowledge the many helpful discussions and opportunities provided by students, colleagues and friends, including Sally Andrews, Stacey Conchie, Brittany Davidson, Kris Geyer, Rob Jenkins, Niklas Johannes, Adam Joinson, Linda Kaye, Mark Levine, Sally Linkenauger, Kirk Luther, George Mather, Neil McLatchie, Ross McQueenie, Gregg Neagle, Jared Piazza, Lukasz Piwek, Nicola Power, Michael Reynolds, Jet Sanders, Heather Shaw, Paul Taylor, John Towse, Thomas Wilcockson, Andrea Williamson and Philip Wilson.

Finally, I would also like to give formal acknowledgement of permissions to reprint some of the following material:

Elsevier Publications (Introduction, 1 and 3)

Piwek, L. & Joinson, A. (2017). Automatic tracking of behavior with smartphones: Potential for behavior change interventions. In

L. Little, E. Sillence, & A. Joinson (eds.), *Behavior Change Research and Theory* (pp. 137–165). Academic Press: Elsevier.
(Figure 1.2 reproduced with permission.)
Ellis, D. A. (2019). Are smartphones really that bad? Improving the psychological measurement of technology-related behaviors. *Computers in Human Behavior, 97*, 60–66.
Ellis, D. A., Davidson, B. I., Shaw, H., & Geyer, K. (2019). Do smartphone usage scales predict behavior? *International Journal of Human-Computer Studies, 130*, 86–92.
Wall, H. J., Taylor, P. J., Dixon, J., Conchie, S. M., & Ellis, D. A. (2013). Rich contexts do not always enrich the accuracy of personality judgments. *Journal of Experimental Social Psychology, 49* (6), 1190–1195.

Sage Publications (Chapter 2)
Ellis, D. A. & Piwek, L. (2018). Failing to encourage physical activity with wearable technology: What next? *Journal of the Royal Society of Medicine, 111*(9), 310–313.

Mary Ann Liebert (Chapters 4 and Conclusion)
Shaw, H., Ellis, D. A., Kendrick, L. R., Ziegler, F., & Wiseman, R. (2016). Predicting smartphone operating system from personality and individual differences. *Cyberpsychology, Behavior, and Social Networking, 19*(12), 727–732.
Ellis, D. A., Davidson, B. I., & Kaye, L. K. (2019). Should smartphones be banned for children or does cyberpsychology have a bigger problem? *Cyberpsychology, Behavior, and Social Networking, 22*(7), 508–509.

American Association for the Advancement of Science (Chapter 6)
Jenkins, R., & Burton, A. M. (2008). 100% accuracy in automatic face recognition. *Science, 319*(5862), 435–435.
(Figure 6.1 reproduced with permission.)

BMJ Publishing Group (Conclusion)
Davidson, B. I. & Ellis, D. A. (2019). Social media addiction: Technological déjà vu. *BMJ, 365*, l4277.

Introduction

The history of psychological science appears short when placed alongside physics, chemistry and biology. Nevertheless, the field has consistently evolved in response to new challenges. For example, one of the crucial features of scientific psychology in the twentieth century was grounding itself in objectivity. By changing the subject to the study of behaviour, psychology could be based on scientific laws of behaviour. In contrast, introspection relied exclusively on an observation of one's mental state. Behaviourism initially helped psychologists better understand learning and behavioural change, but motivations and other mediational processes (e.g., thinking) remained hidden because they were not directly observable (Skinner, 1971). Despite academics arguing that the scientific assessment of behaviour can be yoked to cognition and emotion, behaviourism was never universally accepted, especially in Europe or Canada, because it could only provide a partial account of what it means to be human (Baddeley, 2018; Watson, 1913). These gaps in knowledge became crystallised further following rapid advances in technology during the Second World War, which led to a new approach that brought together computer science, psychology, linguistics and philosophy (Miller, 2003). Psychology became a key player of what has frequently been referred to as the cognitive revolution (Miller, 2003). Some scholars have even attempted to mark the exact date when cognitive science was conceived (11 September 1956). The day included presentations from IBM, which demonstrated how a computer could test a psychological theory, that aimed to explain how the brain might operate (Miller, 2003).

Baddeley (2018) points out that progress was only possible as several disciplines became closer after reaching similar conclusions. Many at the time expected that the events of the 1950s might lead to a new discipline that included linguistics, psychology, anthropology and computer science, but this never happened. Each academic area brought different priorities and while some have become increasingly intertwined with each passing decade, this was not sufficient at the time to create a new integrated field. While these methodological transitions are often portrayed as a revolution, almost every new development can be described as a gradual evolution of the discipline with the benefit of hindsight. In the present day, interdisciplinary research that brings ideas and methods from multiple fields, while not revolutionary, has become the norm. As with the cognitive evolution, computer science, engineering and psychology have allowed research involving other new technologies to prosper (Lazer et al., 2009; Mazzucato, 2013). The modern-day equivalents of IBM are Apple, Amazon and Google. Similarly, the smartphone has become the latest mass-adopted technology to drive the modern economy.

However, long before industry started to drive the notion of a 'new' digital age, the development of tools to measure behaviour or underlying cognitions often involved modifying or adapting existing technologies. In many cases, these provided new empirical measurements and helped establish entire bodies of research that continue to the present day. Despite a number of journals documenting some of these developments, information is scattered widely across psychology and beyond. At the same time, many of the debates and challenges within psychological science today echo arguments of the past. Therefore, while this introduction is not a complete history of methodological development in psychology, it is important to understand and appreciate our history within and beyond the laboratory in the first instance (Baddeley, 2018).

Analogue to Digital

The development of digital computers provided a new way of thinking, measuring and understanding a variety of psychological processes. Originating with the British mathematician Alan Turing's proof that a 'simple machine' could, in principle, carry out any possible computation, this led to the notion of programmable machines (Turing, 1937). These and related developments were forerunners to the digital age in which we currently reside. However, modern micro-computers that were even remotely recognisable as the ubiquitous computers of today only started to become readily available in universities from the mid 1970s onwards (Weinberg, 2019). As a result, many psychologists throughout the 1960s and early 1970s had limited access to digital technology. The majority of methodological innovation remained grounded in an analogue domain. This included the use of simple machines to measure key press responses.

Those who wanted to go beyond simple behavioural responses and study social or biological processes had to innovate with materials that were readily available. For example, tracking eye movement across a scene involved behavioural observations in the first instance. Early observers noticed that reading does not involve a smooth sweeping of the eyes along text but a series of several stops (called fixations) and quick saccades. The first eye tracker to track such observations automatically and with increased precision used a lens connected to the pupil and an aluminium pointer that moved in response to movement (Huey, 1908/1968). This was extremely unpleasant for participants.

Improving or adapting such processes became important as psychologists sought to enhance the accuracy and reliability of such measures. Daniel Kahneman describes the development of a set-up that could capture pupil dilation. He and colleagues theorised at the time that these changes may reveal different processes involved with cognitive processing. Previous work had suggested that the pupils respond distinctly to mental effort and emotional arousal (Kahneman, 2011). Beatty and Kahneman developed an experimental set-up to measure this behavioural response more accurately. This involved a participant placing their head on a chin-and-forehead rest while staring at a traditional film-based camera. Participants listened to recorded information and answered questions while the audio of a metronome clicked. Each beat triggered an infrared flash, whereby a picture was captured to film. When pictures were developed, the researchers projected images of the pupil onto a large screen and used a ruler to measure the width of the pupil. Modifying existing technologies of the day, Kahneman and colleagues discovered that the pupil varied in response to changing demands of a specific task. Their methods advanced to the point where a video-camera system would project a participant's pupil onto a screen in another room. This removed the need to wait for the film to be developed. Kahneman writes that the development of these methods had a large impact on both his own and Beatty's careers.

Such an approach may still appear clunky and prone to considerable measurement error by today's digital standards, but it paved the way for others to develop eye-tracking systems that would eventually measure both pupil dilation and eye movement using digital computers running specialised software. Portable and head-mounted eye-trackers are now being used routinely within and beyond the laboratory (e.g., Mele and Federici, 2012; MacDonald and Tatler, 2018; Pérez-Edgar et al., 2020) and may transmit data to smartphones in the near future. Alternatively, technology within inexpensive desktop trackers that allow for basic eye-tracking could be integrated into cameras placed on the front of most smartphones. This might lead to self-contained eye-tracking systems that are synchronised with experiments running on the same device (Wilcockson, 2017).

Like eye-tracking, early versions of existing methods relied on analogue technologies until digital computers allowed the field to expand. Throughout the 1960s and 1970s psychologists developed, often in colla-boration with engineers and computer scientists, a number of other new tools. These helped capture a variety of social and physiological responses, including social interactions from audio records captured to analogue tape (Azrin et al., 1961), heart-rate variability using small portable recorders (Holter, 1961) and devices to assess sexual responses (Freund, 1963, 1965; Hanson and Bussière, 1998; Rachman, 1966; Simon and Schouten, 1992). Similarly, slide or overhead projectors that presented stimulus, for exam-ple, were eventually replaced by computers, but only when it became possible to present high-resolution graphics or photographs.

Innovative methods of the time became more established when they could be applied to multiple research questions across multiple disciplines. As with social and personality psychology today, cognitive science has benefited enormously from advances in physics, computer science and industry. This includes the development of functional magnetic resonance imaging (fMRI) that can detect changes in blood flow in the brain. As with all new methods, however, it takes time to develop best practices. Misunderstandings can have serious consequences. Specifically, larger volumes of data allow researchers to conduct more statistical tests, and some of these will always produce significant results (the multiple compar-isons problem). In fMRI, each brain scan is divided into around 40,000 cubic units (voxels). The majority of analysis treats each voxel indepen-dently and compares them accordingly many thousands of times (Uttal, 2001). Many techniques have been developed for dealing with these problems, including Gaussian random field theory to calculate the prob-ability of falsely 'finding' activated areas just by chance and to keep this acceptably low (Chumbley and Friston, 2009). However, the majority of fMRI research in the past did not control for these comparisons. In 2008, a dead salmon was placed in an MRI scanner and shown a series of photo-graphs of humans in social situations and asked to determine the emotional response of each person in the photo (Bennett, Miller and Wolford, 2009). Without correcting for multiple comparisons, it would be possible to conclude that the salmon was in fact reacting to the photographs. To be clear, this study does not show that fMRI is in itself problematic, but it demonstrates the importance of understanding how to correctly process and interpret data from data-intensive methods. Research in this area now often reports corrected and uncorrected comparisons as a result.

The methodological developments outlined earlier involve tools or devices that are only suitable for use in the laboratory. This includes presentation software and hardware to measure a variety of behavioural (e.g., reaction time) and physiological responses (e.g., heart rate). Today, these often sit within integrated systems that have become easier to use and less susceptible to error. As a result, psychologists have access to a variety of tools that can assist with quantitative and qualitative investigations. However, these developments alone have struggled to address ongoing concerns associated with conducting research in a laboratory environment.

Limitations of the Laboratory

Psychological science has historically held onto the notion that data obtained from strictly controlled laboratory settings, where the effect of single variables can be observed, remain the apex of research practices. As a result, the majority of psychologists run experiments, but these are often not particularly naturalistic. Welcomed into a testing room, participants are asked to perform tasks in return for money or course credit.

Lab-based research remains vulnerable to a range of biases and participant effects can be an artefact of an experiment rather than natural response to a manipulation. These are often referred to as demand characteristics (Hogg and Vaughan, 2005). The dynamic between an experimenter and participant can also impact responses. While these can be controlled statistically to an extent, contextual differences that occur within a lab environment, which is naturally less anonymous, are far reaching and can also change how participants express themselves and respond to psychometric assessments (Joinson, 1999).

Laboratory studies may be ideal when it comes to understanding perceptual or cognitive process, but they are less than perfect when it comes to understanding other everyday behaviours. For example, attempting to examine how people use personal technology in a lab will provide little new knowledge when life largely unfolds around these devices throughout the day. This is also difficult to experimentally manipulate for long periods of time. Many other behaviours or thought patterns that are presented in a lab are simply not reflective of what happens in the real world. For example, laboratory results suggesting conformity to authority go against what we know about how people behave when faced with conformity outside the laboratory (Francis, 2012). Within developmental psychology, similar challenges have, until recently, faced researchers who wish to study related phenomena (Nielson et al., 2015). Emotional regulation, for example, is a central process that underpins adaptive social and emotional development. However, this area of research has struggled with conceptual and methodological challenges in operationalising and investigating effects over time, in different contexts and with multiple measures (Cole, Martin and Dennis, 2004). Specifically, how someone responds to negative emotional events in their everyday life, especially during development, cannot be simulated ethically in a laboratory.

Another example concerns a renewed interest in how individuals interact in spaces where intergroup contact takes place (McKeown and Dixon, 2017). Specifically, not only is intergroup contact a way to improve attitudes towards outgroups, it has also been argued as equally important when it comes to informing people about how social systems are regulated and can improve problem-solving, enhance cognitive flexibility and generate creativity (Hodson et al., 2018). Methodological barriers have previously made it difficult to examine intergroup contact in real life (Thai and Page-Gould, 2018). As a result, the literature is either reliant on aggregated data across individual contact interactions or uses laboratory environments to study interactions between strangers. Current methods are simply unable to capture the dynamics of group behaviour, and this will almost certainly lead to additional discrepancies between experimental and more ecologically valid approaches in the future (Keil, Koschate-Reis and Levine, 2020). Methodological choices that determine how contact is measured, however, already go beyond issues pertaining to ecological validity. Opposing methods have been shown to change the direction of results, whereby intergroup contact appears to undermine support for social change that leads to greater equality (Hässler et al., 2020; Saguy et al., 2009). Understanding when and why these inconsistencies occur is important and will likely involve the combination of lab-based methods and large-scale secondary data analysis (Ellis, 2012).

While many experimental results across psychology have not replicated or held up to closer inspection, the same issues likely afflict a variety of other methodological practices (Open Science Collaboration, 2015). Any carry-over effects for those who place a high value on more ecologically friendly methods are important to understand because there are many other circumstances across all areas of science where it is not possible to conduct an experiment. Replication alongside methodological pluralism is important, however, if we are to ever establish a general evidence base for psychological phenomena. Regardless, there remains an ongoing tension between those who wish to maintain ecological validity and those who wish to focus on experimental controls and the removal of extraneous variables. This has continued to fuel a long-standing debate; however, recent developments, largely derived from applied psychology, can help reduce that tension.

Beyond the Laboratory

Methodological advances that attempt to bring the best elements of the scientific method, while avoiding the ecological limitations of the laboratory, have historically been less prominent within psychology. However, a variety of technologies that can help researchers observe people inside and outside the laboratory are both readily available and comparatively inexpensive. These have evolved across multiple disciplines, including medicine, computer science and sociology. For example, early digital systems helped researchers collect observational data using portable devices that have many attributes in common with modern smartphones. However, perhaps due to the disparate nature of early micro-computer systems, many early opportunities were either poorly advertised or never widely available (Farrell, 1991). This remains a challenge in the digital age. Therefore, in the following sections I trace some of these developments, which have eventually provided psychologists with a new set of research tools following the widespread adoption of mobile technology.

Direct Observation

Prior to the advent of computer-assisted systems that helped researchers record observational data, social scientists were limited to using a clipboard and timer to log and record events. Computers here made a researcher's job easier by ensuring data was captured accurately and in real time. Timestamps could be automatically logged with each event (Kahng and Iwata, 1998). In addition, the number of events that could be recorded also allowed for more complex statistical analyses. PROCODER, for example, was a software system that could be used to code video data (Tapp and Walden, 2000). Time codes on VHS tapes allowed researchers to find events or sections of tape very quickly. The enormity of software available for coding and analysing such observations at the end of the 1990s was reviewed by Emerson, Reeves and Felce in 2000. However, these methods only started to gain popularity as portable computing became more readily available. Indeed, some of the software discussed ran on an Apple Newton, which could be considered a very early, albeit commercially disastrous, incarnation of a smartphone. Palmtop computing, as it was referred to at the time, was a precursor to the development of smartphones, but rather than being used by participants, these were used by researchers to record behaviour directly. While smaller than a laptop, they were functionally identical. To use a description of the Epson HX20 from Emerson et al. (2000):

> The Epson HX20 was one of the first truly portable, battery driven computers. Approximately the size of a closed laptop computer, it was relatively robust, with a small liquid crystal display mounted above a QWERTY keyboard, rather than a hinged screen. It also had a microcassette drive for the storage of programme and data files and a small integral printer similar to those in supermarket cash registers. (Emerson et al., 2000, pp. 48–49)

Many palmtop computers were developed during the 1990s by a variety of manufacturers who unlike Apple never went on to develop smartphones, including Casio, Sharp and Philips. Some of these systems were used in health-care settings to study patient behaviour and improve treatment. This included predicting, for example, self-injury on a mental health ward based on previous context to reduce the risk of self-harm in the future (Emerson et al., 2000). They appeared less frequently in psychological science, demonstrating that not every methodological development or new technology will facilitate subsequent research. Recent failures also include Google Glass, which from research potential may have been extremely useful for observation, but concerns around security meant that as a product it was quickly discontinued (Hofmann, Haustein and Landeweerd, 2017).

Mass Communication (Pre-Smartphone)

The adoption of mass-communication technologies has continued to transform psychological science. Before the internet became popular, psychologists in the 1990s relied on television, radio and print media to investigate if the public could detect lying through different communication channels. For example, a previous body of work had considered what cues people use to detect lying, but the majority of this research had been carried out in a laboratory with small numbers of university students (Wiseman, 1995). In one study, Wiseman wanted to see if similar findings would generalise across the general population. Working closely with the BBC, a well-known celebrity was interviewed twice. In one interview, he consistently told the truth, but consistently lied in another. Transcripts of these interviews were printed in the *Daily Telegraph* (verbal cues only), broadcast on BBC Radio 1 (verbal and vocal cues) and shown on television (verbal, vocal and visual cues). For each medium the public were asked to report via telephone which of the two interviews they thought contained lies. Over 40,000 members of the public responded. Visual clues appeared to reduce individuals' ability to detect lying. Of course, this could tell us something specific about the listeners of radio versus television, but nevertheless, the results replicate previous laboratory findings. Such research also helped initiate the idea of citizen science, whereby the public are both involved with collection and directly linked back into dissemination activities that take place on a larger scale (Wiseman, 1996, 2007).

Wisemen and others went on to develop similar innovations using books and the internet. This included a real-world experiment that demonstrated how people are often unconsciously influenced by the size of another individual's pupils. Specifically, men tend to rate pictures of women with large pupils as more attractive (Tombs and Silverman, 2004). Using his own book, Wiseman requested that the publisher produce two slightly different front covers (Wiseman and Watt, 2010). Both included a photo of a smiling woman, but the woman's pupils on one cover were digitally enlarged. Those books also had unobtrusive marks on the back cover to distinguish them. A final page of the book asked readers to visit a website where respondents could indicate if they were male or female, the mark on the back of the book, and whether they had purchased the book in a shop or online. Data from high-street purchases confirmed that a significantly greater percentage of readers had chosen the cover with the large pupils. Through the use of online purchasing data, Wiseman and Watt (2010) were also able to demonstrate the absence of an effect, which confirms that their result was not driven by a participant's decision to take part in the experiment. This demonstrates how consumer behaviour can be unconsciously influenced by subtle cues.

Before the work of Wiseman and others, most psychologists initially used the internet to collect small quantities of survey data within university campuses or in specific populations after developing custom web-pages (e.g., Joinson, 1999). However, twenty years later, the internet has become a standard data collection tool for psychological science (Musch and Reips, 2000; Reimers and Stewart, 2015). By avoiding pen and paper, not only can this approach reduce participant and researcher errors, but the internet has allowed psychologists to generate additional statistical power by increasing sample sizes without the need for additional lab space (Buchanan and Smith, 1999; Sassenberg and Ditrich, 2019).

Crowdsourcing to recruit large numbers of participants to complete surveys online previously involved working with traditional media (e.g., the BBC) that also provided a dissemination platform (Chamorro-Premuzic et al., 2009; Reimers, 2007). For example, Reimers (2007) collected data from around 255,000 participants to investigate sex differences. The impact on individual differences/personality research has been particularly prominent as research designs placed online allow for the presentation of personality assessments alongside other media (Chamorro-Premuzic et al., 2009). In recent years, cognitive experiments can also be developed online using HTML5 or freely available tools, including PsychoPy (Peirce et al., 2019; Reimers and Stewart, 2015, 2016).

Recruitment has also become more researcher-focused as commercial systems like Amazon Mechanical Turk and Prolific Academic now act as integrated participant compensation systems and provide access to large, diverse participant pools (Buhrmester, Kwang and Gosling, 2011). Critics have argued that these may still not be representative of the general population and continue to generate new challenges associated with data quality; however, many solutions have been developed to address these issues (Chandler, Mueller and Paolacci, 2014; Paolacci and Chandler, 2014; Peer, Vosgerau and Acquisti, 2014). Nevertheless, while the 1990s were characterised as a decade of behaviour because these were viewed as societally important (Fowler, Seligman and Koocher, 1999), recent years have witnessed the dominance of survey-based research, which often aligns poorly with actual behaviour (Baumeister, Vohs and Funder, 2007). The internet has, at least in the short term, increased our reliance on self-report, which cannot address every research question.

In contrast, experience sampling can also be conducted using web-pages or via mobile text-messaging systems (Conner and Lehman, 2011; Reimers and Stewart, 2009). Originally appearing in the 1970s, experience sampling allows for 'real time', in situ assessments of behaviour temporally close to the moment of enactment. Early attempts involved participants carrying beepers. These small devices would remind a participant at intermittent intervals to write down something about themselves or their environment. Using the internet, participants can dispense with pen and paper and log on to specific pages (usually daily) and provide information about the previous 24 hours or complete specific tasks (e.g., a cognitive test). Perhaps one of the major discoveries in this area concerns the importance of social interaction for well-being (Killingsworth and Gilbert, 2010). Such methods are becoming increasingly more valuable in combination with other sensor technologies that enable the real-time measurement of physiology and the delivery of behaviour change interventions, which aim to improve health (Pursey et al., 2014).

Sensor Technology

Given that many of the developments associated with empirical measurement outside the laboratory have taken place in relatively quick succession, an outsider might speculate that research practices have changed at a rapid pace. However, new methods appear to take several years and false-starts to become readily integrated into current psychological practices. Experience sampling, for example, is not a new development. Several scholars during the nineteenth century used diaries to reconstruct daily lives of individuals in various social classes and occupations – this became a staple toolkit for sociologists, but was largely ignored by psychologists (Mehl and Conner, 2012; Sorokin, 1950). Advances in electronic measurement, reduction in battery sizes and developments in computational data analysis, however, appear to have re-ignited interest in this area (Arute et al., 2019). Like neuroimaging, these tools can often reveal what was previously invisible. For example, it was until recently impossible to record everyday conversational patterns and physiological measures, including heart rate in natural settings, with a high level of precision over time.

Recent decades have therefore witnessed considerable progress in the development of sensor technologies, many of which were adapted from commercial applications in the first instance (McGrath, Scanaill and Nafus, 2014). While accelerometers can detect movement in a variety of automated factory processes, they are also used in laboratory-based motion capture systems. This includes research that aims to understand what information people use when determining intentions in others, through to deception and emotion detection (Poppe et al., 2014). Beyond purpose-built commercial systems, the DIY sentiment of the analogue age continues as researchers have taken existing technologies and customised these for research purposes to create inexpensive alternatives. For example, video-game controllers, including balance boards developed by Nintendo, have been used to demonstrate links between the motor system (approach avoidance) and perceptions of facial attractiveness whereby participants unconsciously lean towards more attractive faces (Kramer et al., 2020). Similarly, Microsoft's Xbox Kinect video-game controller has been frequently re-deployed as a cost-effective motion capture system (Zhang et al., 2013).

Many other sensors were originally intended to monitor people, but their form factor has reduced over time. The measurement of heart rate, for example, was available in the laboratory long before it became portable and battery powered (Boccia and Roberts, 2000). Beyond physiology, other specialised devices that contain small microphones have been around for a number of years. Specifically, an electronically activated recorder (EAR) provides a method for the naturalistic observation of daily social behaviour. These portable audio recorders intermittently record snippets of ambient sounds while participants go about their lives and have recently been used to better understand differences between trait and state changes in the perception of the self across days and weeks (Mehl, 2017; Sun and Vazire, 2019). These have become incrementally more powerful after transitioning from analogue to digital domains (see Mehl (2017) for an overview of the EAR). Small cameras and microphones, when worn by multiple participants, also allow for the analysis of speech including speech overlap (i.e., interruptions), speech mimicry and influence.

The development of other wearable technology has further expedited the ability of researchers to capture social behaviour outside the laboratory. A wearable accelerometer can measure the degree and direction of movement. Similarly, Bluetooth sensors allow for the detection, classification and prediction of group behaviour and social interaction. The Global Positioning System (GPS), in addition, provides contextual information about the environment and also assists with determining patterns of movement (Geyer, Ellis and Piwek, 2019). Radio frequency identification (RFID) can specifically quantify face-to-face interactions (Elmer et al., 2019). For example, if two devices are running identical software, it is possible to determine if the two sensors (or individuals) came into close contact with one another. This can also be extended to determine whether a person is in the presence of many people (or alone). However, while some approaches use close contact as a proxy for social interaction, inferences can be improved further with some additional experience sampling or sensor data (e.g., via a microphone).

Combining multiple sensors into smaller form factors has led to the development of integrated systems (Choudhury and Pentland, 2002). A sociometric sensor, for instance, is a small cigarette-box-sized device that is worn around the neck in the same way as a lanyard. It measures individual and interpersonal behaviours by way of four sensors: (i) a microphone that records speech; (ii) an accelerometer that measures the degree and direction of movement; (iii) a Bluetooth transmitter that measures the proximity of multiple sensors; and (iv) an infrared transmitter that measures when two sensors (i.e., sensor wearers) are facing one another. Once activated, the sensors provide a time-synchronised recording of all four outputs. The data recorded from these sensors can be translated into useful measures of social behaviour. Specifically, measures can help researchers capture both aspects of individuals' behaviour, such as the wearer's speaking frequency (Kim et al., 2012), and aspects of the social dynamic, such as who amongst interacting wearers has a dominant or influential role (Kim et al., 2008). Similarly, data recorded from the accelerometers in a badge can be used to examine a wearer's nonverbal behaviour. A researcher can not only tell how animated the individual acts during a period of interaction, but, by comparing data across synchronised badges, he or she can determine the degree to which wearers' movements are coordinated with one another (nonverbal mimicry) (Hung, Englebienne and Cabrera-Quiros, 2014; Kalimeri et al., 2011).

Using sociometric badges, we previously examined the data provided from these and other wearable devices that recorded heart rate and galvanic skin response. Individually or collectively, these could reliably distinguish between stressful and relaxed states, which were manipulated in a laboratory (Mozos et al., 2017). However, these devices have been used in a variety of other innovative studies outside the laboratory, including occupational settings (Chaffin et al., 2017). For example, Bernstein and Turban (2018) examined the effect of open office environments on employees' face-to-face, email and instant messaging patterns. This is an area of research where prior theory is divided. Sociological theory would argue that removing barriers should increase collaboration by removing social barriers (Festinger, Schachter and Back, 1950). On the other hand, social psychological theory would suggest the opposite effect (Ireland and Garnier, 2018). Following two field studies, they observed that the volume of face-to-face interactions decreased by around 70 per cent when moving from traditional to open-plan office space.

As these sensors are integrated into more and more devices, psychologists have started to further validate these digital traces accordingly (Matusik et al., 2018). The line between consumer wearables and medical devices has blurred and many devices can monitor a range of environmental, social and physiological indicators (Figure I.1). This includes watches that can track physical activity or sleep patterns via an

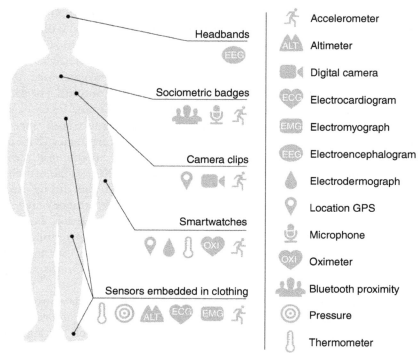

Figure I.1 Examples of wearable sensors that can measure a variety of behaviours and
physiological responses that are of particular interest for both medicine
and psychological science
Piwek, L., Ellis, D. A., Andrews, S., & Joinson, A. (2016b). The rise of consumer
health wearables: promises and barriers. *PLOS MEDICINE*, *13*(2), e1001953.

accelerometer (Jean-Louis et al., 2001; Yang and Hsu, 2010). In addition, a
female's most fertile period can be identified with detailed body tempera-
ture tracking, while levels of mental attention can be monitored with a
small number of non-gelled electroencephalogram (EEG) electrodes
(Poltavski, 2015; Rollason, Outtrim and Mathur, 2014). The exponential
number of Bluetooth- or Wi-Fi-enabled devices also allows for the mapping of large social networks and social interactions based on proximity
detections alone (Eagle, Pentland and Lazer, 2009).

Exactly how some of this new wearable technology might best serve
psychological science is fragmented at present (Piwek et al., 2016a).
Regardless, while sensor development and the continual miniaturisation
of technology have specific standalone applications, these have become

essential for mobile computing, including the smartphone. Therefore, when aligned with hyperconnectivity, this has helped establish an entirely new sub-discipline: computational social science.

Computational Social Science

Advances in computational power and the availability of user-generated data provide a variety of new opportunities for psychology and social science more generally (Schmidt and Cohen, 2013). The majority of the population interact with digital devices and services. For example, in the United Kingdom, 87 per cent of people now access the internet or related services. Those who do connect spend on average 24 hours a week online (OFCOM, 2018). As more amenities come online, a growing number of people rely on the internet to shop, bank, gather information, manage utilities, seek entertainment and make new friends. Psychological traits can be readily inferred from digital records of these behaviours. For example, spending patterns predict personality factors and materialism (Gladstone, Matz and Lemaire, 2019). This is sometimes referred to as computational social science, but is also considered a strand of behavioural analytics in other contexts (Lazer et al., 2009). Specifically, this refers to an ability whereby researchers can collect and analyse streams of data that reveal patterns of individual and group behaviours.

Beyond internet-enabled services, other research has continued to rely on secondary sources of data generated by governments and private companies, which were previously difficult to locate (Ellis, 2012). Many large organisations now have dedicated members of staff who deal specifically with research data requests. These informal exchanges also cover ethical and related data-protection issues. Cherry-picking should, in theory, be less likely because a solid case has to be made for any data to be released. However, this is frequently not what happens in practice (Weston et al., 2019), and overly flexible practices can become an even larger problem (Simmons, Nelson and Simonsohn, 2011). At the same time, this reusability of existing data has been emphasised by funders who often mandate that data collected is available for future research purposes.

Secondary data analysis, when conducted in line with best practices, can be particularly useful for extrapolating experimental findings beyond the laboratory. It can also give hints as to whether an idea is worth pursuing further. For example, health-care systems across the world generate large volumes of data about patients, including information about their age, sex and medical history. This also captures information on how patients interact across multiple points of care (e.g., hospitals, dentists and general practice). Much of this data can therefore be leveraged for social good. This ranges from the use of behavioural analytics to better predict service demand through to understanding the impact of behaviour change interventions. In my own research, we were able to map mental representations associated with days of the week to real-world behaviour. Specifically, appointments at the beginning of the week were more likely to be missed than appointments at the end of the week. As a result, non-attendance rates could be significantly reduced by preferentially loading appointments onto high-attendance days (Ellis and Jenkins, 2012; Ellis, Wiseman and Jenkins, 2015).

Secondary sources also extend outwards from digital records curated by governments and health-care systems directly to other public systems that have helped provide valuable insights regarding human conflict. For example, the micro-dynamics of human conflict resolution can be studied in public space using closed-circuit television (CCTV) surveillance. Beyond the proliferation of digital cameras in other devices, there are more than 4.2 million CCTV cameras in the United Kingdom – 1 for every 14 members of the population – and almost every town and city centre has a system (Murakami Wood et al., 2006). Levine, Taylor and Best (2011) specifically examined episodes of public aggression and observed that third parties were more likely to take conciliatory actions than to escalate violence. This tendency increased as group size increased, demonstrating the importance of collective third-party dynamics in understanding conflict resolution.

There has never been more data available to scientists (Weston et al., 2019). Ironically, while this capacity might have benefited social science first instead, physics and biology were transformed long before this reached psychological science. This is surprising because it is generally well acknowledged that conclusions regarding behaviour drawn from the lab do not always replicate in the real world, which has become of particular concern for social psychology. It is also important for the discipline as a whole that we can develop models of behaviour that confirm, improve or reject existing theory derived from lab-based experiments alone.

Leading psychology journals have only recently started to show evidence of this new field. Much progress however has been made elsewhere; for example, Google arguably holds an astonishing amount of data about individuals' location and sporadic thought processes. Secondary sources of data and systems like Amazon Mechanical Turk and Prolific Academic discussed previously are the tip of the iceberg as the social sciences are being rapidly exposed to new methods involving social media (Buhrmester, Talaifar and Gosling, 2018; Kosinski, Stillwell and Graepel, 2013) and portable computing (Piwek, Ellis and Andrews, 2016). In essence, mobile technology in the digital age allows researchers to unify almost every source of data discussed previously.

Smartphones: Promises and Barriers for Psychological Science

The smartphone has become a defining feature of the modern economy. By centralising an increasing number of digital services that were previously scattered, including finance, entertainment and communications, smartphones have transformed the way in which we can individually and collectively experience music, software and advertising. However, their existence and value for research relies on a host of other technologies that are hidden within the device itself.[1]

> Every technology that makes the iPhone a smartphone owes its vision and funding to the state: the internet, GPS, touchscreen displays and even the voice-activated smartphone assistant Siri all received state cash. (Mazzucato, 2013, p. 26)

This technological milestone has resulted in over two billion people across the world carrying small but powerful computers that can measure an ever-growing number of behavioural and environmental cues (Piwek and Joinson, 2017; Piwek et al., 2016a). Psychologists can therefore quantify behaviours beyond the laboratory using a mass-adopted, unified system that is primed for data capture. Data can be derived from the way a person relates to and interacts with their smartphone (e.g., via apps or experience sampling methodologies). Alternatively, psychologically relevant information can be gleaned from a growing number of embedded sensors (Figure I.2). Combining both approaches within individual differences research, for example, can provide psychologically relevant information about the individual behind the screen – frequently referred to as digital traces (Ellis and Piwek, 2016).

We therefore have the ability to conduct experiments and analysis at a scale which was never possible before. However, while psychology, and much of social science more generally, continues to struggle with issues around transparency and honest-reporting, other issues pertain to exactly how disciplines identify themselves within an increasingly digitised society.

---

[1] As with many scientific developments that founded our modern economy, scientists rarely appreciate or anticipate the impact their work might have on the future. For example, in 2019 the Nobel Prize for Chemistry was awarded for work on lithium-ion batteries. Such advances were essential for many devices including smartphones, but are also found in laptops and electric cars.

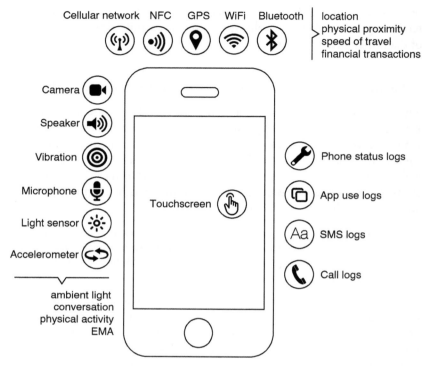

Figure I.2 Examples of sensors and tracking features commonly found in modern
smartphones.
Note: Ecological momentary assessment (EMA) allows for 'real time', in situ assessments temporally close to the moment of enactment. This can include measures of
self-report (e.g., mood), behaviour (e.g., physical activity) and physiology (e.g., heart
rate).
Piwek, L. & Joinson, A. (2017). Automatic tracking of behavior with smartphones:
Potential for behavior change interventions. In L. Little, E. Sillence & A. Joinson
(eds.), *Behavior Change Research and Theory* (pp. 137–165). Academic Press.

Digital technologies and digital data are legitimate topics of study in their
own right. They are central to the making of worlds in which inequality,
prejudice, social justice and social change are consolidated and challenged.
At the same time, an ever-growing number of computer scientists are now
conducting research that would traditionally be associated with social
science, with many using mobile electronic devices, including smartphones, to gather data for around the last 20 years. Like cognitive science,
computational social science and related areas have not become new fields

in their own right. Multiple disciplines are, however, often without realising, converging. The increasingly availability of digital data has also recently been heralded as 'the new digital age' (Schmidt and Cohen, 2013), but this has to be balanced against ethical challenges and the reduced resources available to the social sciences when compared to engineering and computer science (Lazer et al., 2009).

Transcending disciplinary norms remains challenging. While interdisciplinary teams often produce higher-quality research, progress can sometimes be slower when compared to single disciplinary work due to the variety of perspectives and broad nature of discussions (Jones, 2010). Additional issues concern a lack of analytical tools and ethical frameworks associated with the long-term tracking and cloud storage of digital records. Research that applies smartphones to real-world research remains challenging (Orben and Przybylski, 2019), and data derived from smartphones directly also has the added problem of being more difficult to handle and interpret (DeMasi, Kording and Recht, 2017). Perhaps these issues explain why, in recent years, psychological research has tended to take advantage of the digital age by favouring larger sample sizes and self-report (Sassenberg and Ditrich, 2019). However, these reasons only explain part of the discrepancy. Psychology has often viewed mass-adopted technologies with suspicion. Specifically, the discipline has long been fixated on how new technology might harm people and society. This is also reflected in how smartphones are studied (Davidson and Ellis, 2019).

The ability to record digital traces of behaviour therefore comes at a time where concerns about new technology are widespread and behavioural measurement is often absent. For example, Doliński (2018) observed that only 6 per cent of articles in a recent volume of the *Journal of Personality and Social Psychology* examined behaviours. These concerns are not new, however (Baumeister et al., 2007), and the continual lack of validation and clarity regarding constructs and measurement is detrimental to the sound utilisation of measures used in research (Clark and Watson, 1995). This feeds into a growing consensus that while psychology has acknowledged a problem with replication, the discipline also needs to address similar issues within measurement and theoretical development (Ellis, 2019; Flake and Fried, 2019; Kornbrot, Wiseman and Georgiou, 2018; Open Science Collaboration, 2015; Yarkoni, 2019). Psychology has historically never reached an agreement on what constitutes a useful measure for example. Many will view qualitative descriptions as more valuable than any empirical measurement, while others are predominantly interested in the output of a functional brain scan or heart-rate monitor. This lack of consensus is

both a strength and a weakness. While providing a multitude of possibilities when it comes to answering a specific question, from an applied
perspective a lot of research can only speak to very local interests far
removed from the people or groups we wish to understand.

Despite these debates, many of which are not unique to smartphone-
related research, these devices are inspiring and changing the way psychologists conduct research across every major sub-discipline. This ranges from
studies that have analysed call records to the monitoring of behavioural
data from apps and wearable devices. Many designs also allow individual
and situational factors to be considered at the same time, which have
traditionally been studied separately (Mischel, 2004). These varied methodologies complement psychology's diverse measurement practices within
an applied context because research relies on a device that is already
integrated into daily life. Collectively termed the Internet of Things, the
future potential for data linkage that could further leverage real-world
research for psychological science remains an exciting prospect.

General Overview

The current situation is challenging for psychology as research tends to be split
with dual purposes. Like a plethora of other digital technologies, smartphones
have become psychologically interesting in themselves, with some arguing
that they are, by their nature, highly addictive (Ellis et al., 2018). Meanwhile,
very few groups have run large-scale studies using devices directly, and existing
research, in some areas, lags far behind what smartphones can actually
accomplish (Lathia et al., 2013; MacKerron and Mourato, 2013). However,
lessons learned from current work will resonate further as the digital age
expands. It also has to be remembered that smartphones and associated
devices will be able to accomplish much more in the near future (Miller,
2012). Psychology has a key role to play throughout when it comes to
balancing this monumental potential with carefully considered research.
Therefore, this is the first book to bring together related areas of smartphone
research and point towards how psychology can benefit and engage with these
developments in the future. It has two distinct but complementary aims: first,
to critically consider how smartphones (and related digital devices) can
simultaneously help answer and generate new research questions for psychological science; second, it provides guidance when it comes to integrating
smartphones into psychological science more broadly. While previous texts
have considered cyberpsychology and the psychology of the internet, less
attention has been paid to the incremental rise of smartphones. Other

technical outlets tend to focus on smartphone software development rather than the utility of smartphones for social science. Conversely, the remainder of this book is structured around core areas of psychological science and incorporates a variety of surrounding literature accordingly. Each chapter considers research and key theoretical viewpoints within a specific sub-discipline or area of research before providing guidance for future work. The chapters are largely independent and can be read in any order, but occasionally overlap. For example, the positive and negative impacts of smartphone usage have been considered in the context of both social interaction and cognitive development (Chapters 3 and 5). A final chapter draws key strands together and provides guidelines for future research. Chapter summaries are provided below.

Chapter 1: Smartphone Usage

Psychological concerns around the impact of smartphone use tend to overshadow all other threats and concerns around digital spaces. This chapter critically considers research that has associated smartphone use with negative traits and behavioural outcomes. In contrast to other areas of smartphone research, and while many prominent academics have argued that smartphone data have a great deal to offer as a research tool in psychology, comparatively little research utilises objective smartphone usage data in relation to potential harms (Andrews et al., 2015). For example, the majority of existing research tends to rely on self-report alone when quantifying 'addictive' behaviour. A frank discussion regarding similar issues of measurement would help the field move forward more quickly, improve its visibility and generate additional impact from a policy and practitioner perspective.

This chapter provides a timely narrative and critically considers where smartphone research within psychology has advanced in a variety of innovative ways, but also where it is has been slower to innovate both theoretically and methodologically. While some progress has been made regarding the genuine impacts of general technology use, this chapter will conclude by reminding readers that smartphone 'addiction' provides an excellent example of where the field has to embrace the abilities of other disciplines if it is to make additional progress.

Chapter 2: Health and Behaviour Change

Smartphones and associated wearable devices have gained a greater prominence directly within health psychology. Not only can such devices track health and answer a variety of research questions in relation to physical and mental health, but real-time feedback can also be augmented to support subsequent behaviour change interventions. There are literally thousands of smartphone health apps that aim to change behaviour. Hence, health psychologists have been heavily involved with the design and testing of interventions (Ellis and Piwek, 2018). In addition, there are increasing numbers of interdisciplinary groups who focus on such interventions. However, while the research landscape is now littered with many well-publicised successes and failures, very little is known when it comes to understanding why such results are occurring even for users who engage with a long-term smartphone/wearable intervention. Despite having plenty of scope for development, progress has stalled somewhat because existing adaptations continue to be poorly designed from theoretical and patient perspectives.

With these issues in mind, this chapter points towards where psychological research is using smartphone sensing methods that can quantify health-related behaviours on a larger scale. It also considers how psychology can make a key contribution in the future. For example, while the process of behaviour change remains complex, additional research is urgently needed to understand how individuals, devices and related technologies can be designed and implemented if interventions are to become widespread across health-care systems in the future (Ellis and Piwek, 2018; Piwek et al., 2016b).

Chapter 3: Social Interaction and Interpersonal Relationships

Social interaction and the development of interpersonal relationships appear to be inherently linked to emotional well-being. Smartphones have increased an individual's social footprint while remaining the primary way in which people communicate with each other via social media, phone calls and text messages. However, many researchers have questioned if the same technology is simultaneously preventing us from developing meaningful relationships.

At the same time, other research has started to focus on a variety of popular smartphone apps that have changed the way modern relationships are formed and maintained (e.g., Tinder, Snapchat). This work typically considers a participant's own experience or data derived directly from apps themselves (Davidson, Joinson and Jones, 2018). However, it is also possible to explore real-wold social interaction via the variety of on-board sensors, which can also reveal group dynamics within the real world (Piwek et al., 2016a). For example, Bluetooth and location data derived from appropriate sensors can be used to infer when someone is meeting with others who are also running similar software on their device. This has also been referred to as Social fMRI whereby researchers can quantify social mechanisms in the real world (Aharony et al., 2011).

While smartphones have dramatically changed how large sections of society form and develop new relationships, this chapter points towards how the same technology can be leveraged further to understand how relationships and groups rapidly shift between offline and online contexts in the digital age.

Chapter 4: Personality and Individual Differences

While psychologists agree that individuals differ from each other on a variety of traits (e.g., personality), the theoretical and methodological assumptions used to develop pen-and-paper psychometric tests have failed to keep pace with recent computational developments that utilise digital traces to infer information about individuals and the world around them. For example, while self-report assessments are designed to predict behaviour in the absence of any real-world measure, digital devices (e.g., smartphones) have facilitated the measurement of many real-world outcomes (Piwek et al., 2016a). Even the purchase of a specific device can reveal something about the individual behind the screen (Shaw et al., 2016). Smartphones could therefore lead to a step change in how we study and conceptualise a variety of individual differences. This is particularly pertinent when it comes to understanding personality traits (e.g., levels of extraversion – a measure of sociability) that are automatically deployed in new situations seamlessly and non-consciously (Roberts and Hill, 2017).

A number of studies using smartphones have correlated data from these devices with traditional psychometric tests. However, following a brief review of this work, this chapter will question how much progress has been made in this domain. There remains a general consensus among many social scientists that, while traditional psychometric measures are far from perfect, they are the only option available. This chapter will challenge that assumption; however, data derived from smartphone sensing may ultimately support the notion that existing psychometric tools remain valuable and reinforce traditional models of personality.

Chapter 5: Cognition

Cognitive science has often considered the impact of new technology on childhood development and the ability of digital devices to disrupt attention and learning. Psychologists to date have also spent a great amount of resources attempting to understand how digital technology can disrupt basic and higher-level cognitive processes in adults, which in some cases can have fatal consequences. For example, the relationship between smartphone use and distracting driving has been well documented. However, beyond cognitive impacts, the same sub-discipline has also successfully implemented smartphones into existing research practices, which perhaps reflects the methodological training many psychologists working within cognition and perception receive as part of their doctoral studies. For example, standard psychophysical experiments and reaction time tasks have been ported to a variety of smartphones using their built-in web-browser. This has been extended to include the large-scale gamification of traditional cognitive tests (Wilmer, Sherman and Chein, 2017). Combining advanced graphical abilities, a number of cognitive tasks have been validated to assess working memory, attention and decision-making abilities (Paletta et al., 2014).

This chapter points towards a future whereby cognitive psychology could become the first sub-discipline within psychology to develop a complete portable laboratory. This would, in turn, reveal any causal links between technology use and cognitive functioning which continues to elude existing research paradigms.

Chapter 6: Safety and Security

The majority of smartphone research relies on participants consenting to have data collected from their device. However, these devices continue to pose an inherent security risk within and beyond research. Despite the majority of devices holding large quantities of personal information, many people continue to ignore advice when it comes to securing their device. This is particularly problematic when it comes to carrying out tasks on unsecured networks. Malware developed by criminal groups can also gain access to a smartphone and compromise its function. At a more general level, mobile technologies provide new avenues for illegal activities and the distribution of misinformation. Similarly, groups can straightforwardly collaborate and communicate across larger networks while avoiding detection.

The popularity of smartphones provides another digital outlet for illegal data capture, and this chapter will consider why, despite multiple security concerns, the majority of smartphone users and even large organisations are unable to recognise the importance of developing sound security practices. A second strand considers how psychologists and software developers are attempting to improve the security of existing devices and encourage security-focused behaviours. While data in the digital age can be tremendously valuable for research purposes, facilitating good practice remains essential when developing software that collects sensitive data from smartphones and associated devices.

Conclusion

Psychology as a discipline has much to gain from the digital age, especially following the mass adoption of smartphones. Software development is an entire discipline within itself, but even comparatively simple smartphone apps that collect minimal data can be highly revealing of everyday behaviour. However, we face numerous challenges that go beyond technological development. Some of these issues pertain to theorising and replication, while others concern the scientific climate in which we operate. Most of these issues are not unique to research involving new technology, but they become more apparent as the speed of innovation accelerates. As a result, we appear to carry very little understanding forward to the next mass-adopted innovation.

While progress to date has varied between sub-disciplines, this final chapter will touch on common themes throughout. By reflecting on past successes and failures, I provide guidance on how psychological research can become more productive and break free from broken cycles of research. More importantly, if the study of a multi-purpose, ubiquitous device can re-calibrate how psychological science approaches new technology, the discipline will, as a result, remain relevant in the digital age.

Useful Resources and Further Reading

Baddeley, A. (2018). *Working Memories: Postmen, Divers and the Cognitive Revolution*. Routledge.
Partly autobiographical, Professor Baddeley traces the development of his own career alongside theoretical and methodological advances in cognitive science.
Schmidt, E., & Cohen, J. (2013). *The New Digital Age: Reshaping the Future of People, Nations and Business*. Hachette UK.
Considers the future impact of technology on people and society. Slightly idealised in places, the book postulates both challenges and opportunities that new technology provides.
Uttal, W. R. (2001). *The New Phrenology: The Limits of Localizing Cognitive Processes in the Brain*. The MIT Press.

A still relevant critique of a popular method used to infer information about neuronal activity. Many criticisms serve to remind readers that new methods are often portrayed as a superior solution at the expense of more established and validated alternatives.

Thompson, T., Felce, D., & Symons, F. J. (2000). *Behavioural Observation: Technology and Applications in Developmental Disabilities.* Brookes.

Published in 2000, this book provides a fascinating snapshot of several (often obsolete) technologies that could record behavioural observations. The authors also point towards the potential for touch screens and voice recognition as a way of improving data entry, both of which are now a modern-day reality for participants and researchers.

CHAPTER I

Smartphone Usage

Historically, each new technology brings concerns associated with the consequences of a constantly connected society (Sas, 2019). These come in the form of personal experiences (Lucero, 2018), widespread media coverage focusing on 'negative consequences' (Black, 2018) and decades of scientific research that considers how technology might negatively impact on well-being (Bisen and Deshpande, 2018). Smartphones are no exception as they have ensured that human–computer interaction is now a cornerstone of everyday life (Mihajlov and Vejmelka, 2017; Thompson and Thompson, 2017; Widdicks et al., 2018). Specifically, much has been written in the last few years concerning how excessive screen time can reduce well-being and lead to a form of digital dependency. Of course, at face value and given societies' reliance on digital technology to shop, bank, gather information, manage utilities, seek entertainment and make new friends, one could argue that any form of digital dependency is a component of everyday obligations.

Regardless, this is an area where psychological science has, to date, focused much of its efforts. It's also where the discipline has had a considerable influence that stretches far beyond academic circles. However, the majority of existing research tends to rely on self-report when quantifying behaviours associated with technology use. Even without any contextual data (e.g., what apps are being used), visualising human–computer interaction appears infinitely more complex when contrasted with the information provided by a single duration estimate or survey score (Figure 1.1). This chapter will focus on the abundance of research that has typically correlated smartphone use with negative outcomes in teenage and adult populations.[1] The notion of smartphone 'addiction' provides a direct example of where the field has to develop clearer thinking and embrace the abilities of other disciplines if it is to make additional progress.

---

[1] The potential impacts on childhood development and adult cognition are considered in Chapter 5.

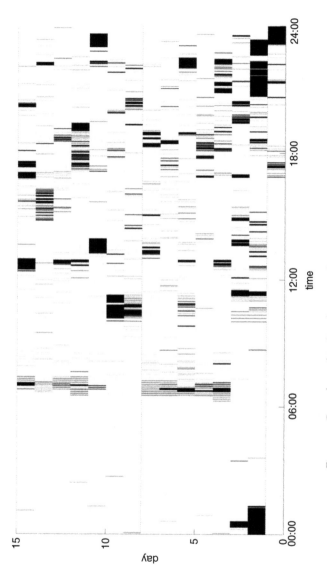

Figure 1.1 Barcode graphic that plots smartphone uses over a two-week period.

Note: Black areas indicate times where the phone was in use. Saturday is marked with a dashed line. Examining how much people actually use their smartphone can be useful for a variety of applications. For example, all except one participant in Andrews et al. (2015) used their phone as an alarm clock, and most reported that they always use their phone last thing before sleeping. Weekday alarm clock times (and snoozing) are clearly evident in the above example. These usage patterns can therefore provide a non-invasive indication of sleep length, which has the potential to augment sleep diary data (Andrews et al., 2015). My own lab has developed several methods that sample and visualise the frequency of smartphone usage behaviours. However, these developments have struggled to change how many psychologists operationalise human interactions with technology (Ellis et al., 2019).

Andrews, S., Ellis, D. A., Shaw, H., & Piwek, L. (2015). Beyond self-report: Tools to compare estimated and real-world smartphone use. *PLOS ONE*, *10*(10), e0139004.

1.1 The Dark Side

Behavioural science has spent many years attempting to understand how our interactions with technology might impact on numerous psychological outcomes (Shaw, Ellis and Ziegler, 2018). This lends itself to a wide variety of research questions from problematic use (e.g., do smartphones cause depression or anxiety?) to the effects of engaging with feedback as part of a behaviour change intervention (e.g., does monitoring physical activity improve health?) (Ellis and Piwek, 2018). Approaches within psychology have almost exclusively focused on correlational research that involves asking people to consider their personal experience with a technology rather than measuring their actual behaviour (Ellis et al., 2018). This reflects a general trend within social psychology as a whole (Baumeister, Vohs and Funder, 2007; Doliński, 2018) but remains surprising when considered alongside automated systems (e.g., smartphones (Miller, 2012)) that can record human–computer interactions directly (Piwek, Ellis and Andrews, 2016). For example, behavioural interactions can be measured 'in situ' with apps. However, this is not an avenue explored by the majority of research concerning usage, despite having spent over a decade attempting to define 'problematic' or 'addictive' smartphone behaviours (Panova and Carbonell, 2018). Conclusions surrounding use have therefore been largely negative, and smartphones have repeatedly been associated with depression (Elhai et al., 2017), anxiety (Richardson, Hussain and Griffiths, 2018), disrupted sleep (Rosen et al., 2016), cognitive impairment (Clayton, Leshner and Almond, 2015) and poor academic performance (Lepp, Barkley and Karpinski, 2015). This repeats a pattern of research priorities, which previously focused on the negative impacts of many other screen-based technologies, systematically moving from television and video games to the internet and social media (Rosen et al., 2014).

While some research has reported many beneficial associations with increased technology use (e.g., Barr et al., 2015; Przybylski and Weinstein, 2017; Ward, Dill-Shackleford and Mazurek, 2018), ominous results have had a far greater impact on public opinion. This has recently led to a UK government inquiry concerning the effects of screen time on health (UK Parliament, 2018). However, regardless of whether research aims to focus on narrow or broad definitions of technology use, our current understanding is based around a set of popular measures that present several methodological shortcomings (Ryding and Kaye, 2018; Shaw et al., 2018). This has become particularly pertinent as methods of investigation have remained static despite exponential changes in the availability and processing power afforded by modern technology (Shaw et al., 2018).

1.2   Capturing Usage from Self-Report

Historically, time has been the primary focus when attempting to quantify experiences with technology. Respondents are often asked to report their frequency or duration of use, but even simple self-reported estimates concerning mobile phone use (e.g., number of calls made or text messages sent) have been described as 'sub-optimal' when compared to phone operator data (Boase and Ling, 2013). Nevertheless, many studies continue to rely on estimates alone when making links between technology use and other psychological constructs (Butt and Phillips, 2008). When such estimates are scaled to larger samples, these often explain very little of the variance when predicting health or subsequent behaviour (Przybylski and Weinstein, 2017; Twenge et al., 2018). The use of multiple technologies simultaneously (e.g., a smartphone and a laptop) also makes such estimates problematic due to the level of cognitive burden required to quantify many different types of automatic behaviour (Boase and Ling, 2013; Doughty, Rowland and Lawson, 2012; Jungselius and Weilenmann, 2018).

Perhaps in response to this criticism, a growing number of prominent self-report instruments have been developed in an attempt to quantify smartphone-related technology experiences (Figure 1.2; Table 1.1). Traditional

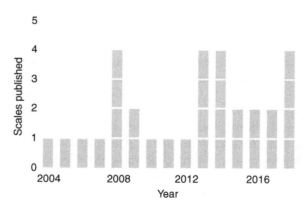

Figure 1.2 Publication of self-report instruments between 2004 and 2018 (extracted from Table 1.1), which aim to assess a variety of constructs associated with smartphone use in the general population

Ellis, D. A. (2019). Are smartphones really that bad? Improving the psychological measurement of technology-related behaviors. *Computers in Human Behavior, 97*, 60–66.

Table 1.1 *Examples of psychometric tools developed to assess general smartphone usage (translations to other languages are not included)*

Reference	Items	Scale
Bianchi and Phillips (2005)	27	Mobile Phone Problem Use Scale (MPPUS)
Billieux, Van der Linden and Rochat (2008)	30	Problematic Mobile Phone Use Questionnaire (PMPUQ)
Chóliz (2012)	22	Test of Mobile Phone Dependence (TMD)
Chóliz et al. (2016)	12	Brief Multicultural Version of the Test of Mobile Phone Dependence Questionnaire (TMD brief)
Csibi et al. (2018)	6	Smartphone Application-Based Addiction Scale (SABAS)
Ehrenberg et al. (2008)	3	Mobile Phone Addictive Tendencies Scale (MPAT)
Foerster et al. (2015)	10	Mobile Phone Problem Use Scale: short version (MPPUS-10)
Ha et al. (2008)	20	Excessive Cellular Phone Use Survey (ECPUS)
Jenaro et al. (2007)	23	Cell Phone Overuse Scale (COS)
Kawasaki et al. (2006)	20	Cellular Phone Dependence Tendency Questionnaire (CPDQ)
Kim et al. (2014)	15	Smartphone Addiction Proneness Scale (SAPS)
King et al. (2014)	29	Mobile Phone Use Questionnaire (MP-Use)
Koo (2009)	20	Cell Phone Addiction Scale (CAS)
Kuss et al. (2018)	16	Problematic Mobile Phone Use Questionnaire Revised (PMPUQ-R)
Kwon et al. (2013a)	33	Smartphone Addiction Scale (SAS)
Kwon et al. (2013b)	10	Smartphone Addiction Scale (SAS short version)
Lee et al. (2017)	28	Smartphone Overuse Screening Questionnaire (SOS-Q)
Leung (2008)	17	Mobile Phone Addiction Index (MPAI)
Lin et al. (2014)	26	Smartphone Addiction Inventory (SPAI)
Lin et al. (2017)	10	Smartphone Addiction Inventory: short-form (SPAI-SF)
Lopez-Fernandez et al. (2014)	26	Mobile Phone Problem Use Scale for Adolescents (MPPUSA)
Lopez-Fernandez et al. (2018)	15	Short Version of the Problematic Mobile Phone Use Questionnaire (PMPUQ-SV)
Martinotti et al. (2011)	10	Mobile Addiction Test (MAT)
Marty-Dugas et al. (2018)	20	Smartphone Use Questionnaires (SUQ-G & A)
Merlo, Stone and Bibbey (2013)	22	Problematic Use of Mobile Phones Scale (PUMP)
Rosen et al. (2013)	9	Media and Technology Usage and Attitudes Scale (MTUAS) (smartphone items only)
Rozgonjuk et al. (2016)	18	Short version of Estonian Smartphone Addiction Proneness Scale (E-SAPS18)

Table 1.1 *(cont.)*

Reference	Items	Scale
Toda et al. (2004)	20	Cellular Phone Dependence Questionnaire (CPDQ)
Walsh, White and Young (2010)	8	Mobile Phone Involvement Questionnaire (MPIQ)
Yen et al. (2009)	12	Problem Cellular Phone Use Questionnaire (PCPU-Q)
Yildirim and Correia (2015)	20	Nomophobia Questionnaire (NMP-Q)

Note: Many of these are conceptually similar to those that assess internet, social media or video-game 'addiction' (e.g., Kwon et al., 2013a). Validation typically relies on duration estimates, which are themselves poorly aligned with related behaviours (Boase and Ling, 2013) or by demonstrating a relationship with other constructs that are assumed to be related with increased technology use (e.g., impulsivity). Some measures (not listed) are built entirely around duration-based estimates or frequencies of use via Likert scales (e.g., Elhai et al., 2016). Others (not listed) ask about specific mobile functions (e.g., text messaging (Rutland, Sheets and Young, 2007)). Many non-peer-reviewed scales are simply adapted directly from measures used to assess other technology behaviours (e.g., video games) without any subsequent reliability or validation checks (e.g., Hussain, Griffiths and Sheffield, 2017).
Ellis, D. A. (2019). Are smartphones really that bad? Improving the psychological measurement of technology-related behaviors. *Computers in Human Behavior, 97,* 60–66

methods associated with scale development tools are reported to be reliable, but their validity remains highly questionable (Table 2.1). Scale development is normally a lengthy process, but, in the vast majority of instances, the empirical data and level of detail are simply not available to determine if these measures are psychometrically sound. Broadly speaking, technology usage assessments, which vary from television to internet, online gaming and, more recently, smartphones, rely on extraordinarily similar scales or estimates – substituting device for device as required (Rosen et al., 2014). This similarity problem has become especially prominent within smartphone usage scales as their development is detached from this recent history. Despite being developed years apart and around different frameworks or conceptualisations of use (e.g., fear, attachment or problematic use) several appear to measure almost identical constructs (Ellis et al., 2019). This all stands in stark contrast to other papers that have developed scales from the ground up in related areas (e.g., Buchanan et al., 2007).

While measures are framed around 'smartphone behaviours', the language used to describe subsequent results becomes misleading. Paper titles including the words 'smartphone use' are inaccurate when this has simply not been measured, causing confusion for casual readers, policy makers and even those who work within the field (Ellis et al., 2018). This vagueness resonates further as readers are left unclear as to whether usage in each instance refers to negative behaviours that could become addictive like gambling, or positive alternatives including those that can support and maintain a healthy lifestyle (Ellis and Piwek., 2018; Panova and Carbonell, 2018). There is also little evidence to support the existence of the constructs under investigation (e.g., technology 'addiction'), yet many papers and scales continue to use language associated with a specific diagnosis (see Panova and Carbonell, 2018, for a recent review).

These measures generally assess a respondent's attitudes and feelings towards their smartphone or technology usage. While no less important, the constructs under investigation may be fundamentally different to the very behaviour they seek to explain. To date, current self-report measures do not align well with or predict simple objectively measured smartphone behaviours (Table 1.2). It would appear that objectively measured time spent on a device may correlate with some self-report scales or duration estimates, but this relationship appears patchy. When testing the predictive ability of several psychometric scales, we found that every scale correlated with at least one smartphone objective measure (total usage, pickups or notifications). However, the strength of these relationships was far from convincing (Figure 1.3). As these scales struggle to capture simple behaviours, it remains questionable as to how they could effectively measure habitual, atypical and more complex behavioural patterns. Combining multiple scales did not assist in the identification of participants with high usage patterns derived from behaviour alone. As a consequence, these results have implications for studies that attempt to understand the impacts of smartphones and other screen-based technologies on health and well-being. These issues extend to research that has attempted to link a variety of individual differences (e.g., personality) with technology use (e.g., Butt and Phillips, 2008; Horwood and Anglim, 2018; Takao et al., 2009).

Even if current measures do correlate with behaviour, there is still reason to question the extent to which they measure constructs as expected. First, given the range of activities that can be performed on a smartphone, scores will have little bearing on a person's overall experience with that technology. One may speculate that active versus passive use will be an important mitigating factor when quantifying outcomes. For example, engaging in positive conversation online can bring many health benefits, with passive consumption likely to be less valuable (Day, Ong and Perry, 2018). Second, scales present leading questions that focus on worries surrounding a participant's relationship with their smartphone, which may be more representative of general traits. The majority of smartphone usage scales by their very nature likely overlap with higher levels of anxiety and depression rather than smartphone usage, as the items' wording tends to be conceptually similar to that of depression and anxiety scales. People who are, for example, depressed may simply apply this self-schematic structure to a related measure of technology use (Dozois and Rnic, 2015). Items that ask participants about levels of impatience associated with reduced use may instead reveal a general impulsivity that is not smartphone specific and could apply to any other personal product used on a regular basis (Belk, 2013). Indeed, how unique these results are to a specific technology and not a globalised behaviour that filters into other daily activities (e.g., exercise, coffee consumption) remains unknown.

Much of our current understanding is therefore based around a set of measures which struggle to capture and understand the subsequent impact of technology. However, this has not prevented the development of theoretical models that are based entirely around data generated from these psychometric tools (Billieux et al., 2015). Of course, and as with any psychological phenomenon, several of these scales and the constructs they aim to measure are likely to go beyond behaviour. However, the scales are routinely used without this broad conceptualisation in mind and are framed as an assessment of usage alone. In recent years, these problems have become magnified further as theoretical and methodological advances have allowed for dynamic and fluid approaches to data collection. These can provide greater specificity and flexibility when exploring our relationship with technology (Jankowska, Schipperijn and Kerr, 2015).

1.3   Objective Measures of Smartphone Usage

If technology use cannot be controlled experimentally, then exposure to general (e.g., hours of smartphone use) or specific use (e.g., hours of Facebook use on a device) provides an alternative source of objective data (Scharkow, 2016). This removes issues concerning social desirability and cognitive burden. However, while those in computer science have been measuring such interactions with smartphone technology since around 2010, these developments have had very little impact on how

Table 1.2 *Research that has attempted to validate single estimates or
smartphone usage scales against objective behaviours.*

Reference	N	Time (days)	Findings
Andrews et al. (2015)	23	14	Estimated time spent using a smartphone correlated moderately with actual usage. Estimates concerning the number of times an individual used their phone did not correlate with actual smartphone use. Neither estimated duration nor number of uses correlated with the MPPUS.
Elhai et al. (2018)	68	7	No overall relationship between Likert estimations of use and average daily minutes. Weak overall relationship between average daily minutes and SAS short version. Likert estimates and SAS scores predicted weekend but not weekday averages.
Ellis et al. (2019)	238	6	Weak relationships observed between objective smartphone measures and a variety of self-report measures (including single duration estimates).
Foerster et al. (2015)	234	*	Weak relationships observed between short version of MPPUS-10 and phone calls/sent SMS messages. Moderate correlation between MPPUS-10 and data traffic volume. *Objective data was available for up to six months.
Lin et al. (2015)	66	30	Estimated time spent using a smartphone correlated moderately with actual usage. Note: Duration estimates were generated with assistance from psychiatrists.
Rozgonjuk et al. (2018)	101	7	Weak relationship between SAS and minutes of screen time in a week (Spearman). No relationship between SAS and the number of times an individual used their smartphone (Spearman).
Wilcockson et al. (2018)	27	14	No relationship observed between MPPUS and actual usage or the number of interactions with a smartphone lasting less than 15s (Spearman).

Note: This only includes papers that have used peer-reviewed, unmodified versions of the scales listed in Table 1.1
Ellis, D. A. (2019). Are smartphones really that bad? Improving the psychological measurement of technology-related behaviors. *Computers in Human Behavior, 97*, 60–66

psychology attempts to quantify, explain and understand technology use more generally (Oliver, 2010). For example, only a handful of papers have attempted to validate existing scales against behaviour, with mixed results (Table 1.2; Figure 1.3).

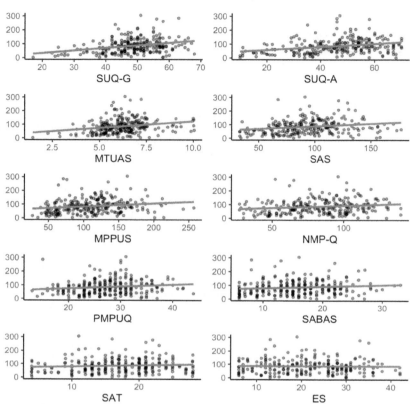

Figure 1.3 Data from Ellis et al. (2019) illustrating weak associations between objective data – in this case smartphone pickups and smartphone usage scales. Note: These are ordered in magnitude of effect size from strongest (*r* = 0.31) to weakest (*r* = –.01)

Abbreviations: ES = Possession Incorporation in the Extended Self and SAT = Smartphone Attachment (Sivadas and Venkatesh, 1995). See Table 1.1 for other acronyms.

These objective-based studies confirm that people use devices like smartphones and associated apps frequently and habitually (Andrews et al., 2015). However, this alone does not equate to any form of problematic usage. It may seem reasonable to assume that those who spend a long time in front of a screen have problematic use; however, heavy users are not necessarily the same as problematic users (Andrews et al., 2015; Oulasvirta et al., 2012). Many research designs using related methods also challenge the notion that mobile technology use is becoming more prevalent. For example, the quantity of short-checking behaviours observed in research conducted in 2018, for example (Ellis et al., 2018), is remarkably consistent with those recorded in 2015 and 2009 (Andrews et al., 2015; Oulasvirta et al., 2012). Some objective research has certainly supported the notion that younger people use their smartphone more; however, patterns of usage are similar across social economic strata (Christensen et al., 2016). In addition, while smartphone use often appears high, within-participant patterns are consistent and establishing a baseline of typical usage for an individual appears possible (Fullwood et al., 2017; Wilcockson et al., 2018).

In recent years, objective studies have also started to focus on the potential negative impacts of smartphones on mood; however, their conclusions are dramatically different from previous findings, which rely on self-report alone. For example, Rozgonjuk et al. (2018) observed that depression and anxiety severity were not associated with total smartphone usage. In addition, higher depression scores correlated with less phone checking over a week, suggesting that periods of low mood may lead to less engagement with technologies that primarily enable social interaction. This supports the notion that a sudden lack of smartphone use may be an early warning sign of social withdrawal (Mou, 2016).

Machine-learning and data-intensive approaches have also demonstrated that smartphone use alone does not predict negative well-being. Specifically, ecological momentary assessment (EMA) methods can allow for a better understanding of within-person relationships between usage and mood over time. Katevas, Arapakis and Pielot (2018) combined an experience sampling methodology with 23 objective measures of behaviour, including phone unlocks, calls received, and battery drain. In one of the largest studies of its kind, participants who reported lower levels of well-being tended to use their smartphones more at night. However, these differences were less convincing when mood assessments were repeated at regular intervals throughout the day over several weeks. In support of this research, led by computer scientists, psychological studies using similar methods that again involve smartphone logging and experience sampling have yielded similar results (Jensen et al., 2019; Johannes et al., 2019).

While these results and methods are compelling, they remain difficult to place in context because the majority of psychological research continues to rely on a very different methodological framework. They are also largely exploratory, consider a very limited definition of technology use and remain correlational in nature. However, objective studies often challenge the notion that smartphones are problematic for a large percentage of the population.

1.4 Conceptual and Methodological Challenges

Research that attempts to develop methods which can quantify smartphone and related technology use often aligns with a conceptual framework that problematises usage without considering how typical these behaviours are in the general population. Conceptually, the field appears to have taken this approach with video games, the internet and social media; however, smartphones may finally be the point where psychologists consider going beyond these clinical definitions (Ellis et al., 2018). Similarly, while psychology now has access to new technologies that would improve current practices, a number of methodological challenges also remain if new data collection methods and analytical routines are to prosper.

1.4.1 Conceptual

Conceptual misunderstandings may, in part, help drive research that focuses on the negative implications of technology, despite many obvious benefits (Days, 2018; Surrat, 1999). For example, the idea that problematic technology use can be framed as a behavioural addiction is widely accepted despite being poorly defined (Van Rooij et al., 2018). As before, the enormity of activities that can be performed on a smartphone immediately makes this definition difficult (Doughty et al., 2012; Ellis et al., 2018; Ryding and Kaye, 2018). This has, in turn, led to the proliferation of 'treatment' programmes that lack empirical support. Based on associations between reduced objective use and social withdrawal, such programmes could result in unintended negative consequences (Stieger and Lewetz, 2018). Of course, some forms of use could satisfy a diagnostic criterion, but the evidence base required to support such a claim has yet to appear and existing smartphone 'addiction' scales do not correlate with the rapid checking behaviours one would associate with a behavioural addiction (Andrews et al., 2015; Rozgonjuk et al., 2018). It therefore remains difficult to classify something as a behavioural addiction without actually measuring behaviour. A growing body of evidence now supports the notion that psychology should start to move away from a behavioural addictions framework when studying technology use (Panova and Carbonell, 2018).

The repeated tendency to problematise technology behaviours can also be explained by considering how little work in psychology has attempted to conceptualise technology use in a broader context. There is some overlap with models which emphasise the formation of habits and planned behaviour. Specifically, repeating a technology interaction behaviour in response to a cue over time will quickly lead to the automaticity of that behaviour (Lally et al., 2010). Other recent attempts have considered everyday smartphone use in the context of attentional lapses and mind wandering, which arguably are of greater concern to public health and include phone use that can demonstrably interfere with driving or walking (Ioannidou, Hermens and Hodgson, 2017; Marty-Dugas et al., 2018). However, other models derived from computer science, information systems, marketing and management provide several high-level constructs that also attempt to explain impacts associated with continued use. These range widely from the measurement of individual differences to specific features of the technology under investigation (Shaw et al., 2018).

Perhaps before considering the impact of technology on our psychology, more resources need to be devoted to defining what we mean by usage itself. Does the use of a smartphone, for example, only register when actively creating something with the device (e.g., writing a tweet), or would this also include time spent passively viewing content (e.g., reading the news)? Some research hints that this might be an important distinction regarding Facebook, but as before relies on self-reported usage (Verduyn et al., 2015).

Current definitions of use may be too narrow, particularly when online and offline identities are intertwined. Much of the population are now permanently online (Vorderer, Krömer and Schneider, 2016), and smartphones have become a core part of a person's digital identity. Qualitative accounts often reflect the ability of these devices to help support existing social activities. This in part explains why many people develop strong psychological attachments to them (Belk, 2013; Bodford, Kwan and Sobota, 2017; Fullwood et al., 2017; Shaw et al., 2016). This 'individualised' perspective of smartphone usage fits well within the framework of the Uses and Gratifications model and reflects consistent yet individualised patterns of behaviour (Katz, Blumler and Gurevitch, 1974; Wilcockson et al., 2018). Therefore, people appear to often use the affordances of technology in order to gratify very personal needs (Kaye, Malone and Wall, 2017). However, such conceptualisation is very much at odds with the majority of research, which focuses on technology as a problem, rather than on a device which supports everyday activities (Shaw et al., 2018).

1.4.2   Methodological

The use of duration estimations in isolation no longer seems suitable when contrasted directly with how people describe their usage patterns, especially when this involves multiple devices (Doughty et al., 2012). Recent studies attempting to correlate technology use with brain development illustrate the gulf in methodological development further. Specifically, the psychometric resources devoted to understanding technology use pale in comparison to brain-imaging techniques that quantify white matter in the brain (e.g., Hutton et al., 2019). Once a technology has become intertwined with daily life, people are less able to accurately report on these behaviours, particularly when it comes to estimating the number of single interactions in a 24-hour period (Andrews et al., 2015). At the same time, research that aims to improve our understanding of technology use has become increasingly more technical, which poses a number of methodological challenges for psychologists (Jensen et al., 2019; Johannes et al., 2019; Piwek et al., 2016). Standard measurements produce small data sets and rarely go beyond interviews and psychometric assessment. However, smartphone apps can measure both where and how a device is being used, allowing for distinctions to be made between active (e.g., typing/photo taking) and passive (e.g., reading tweets) use. It is also possible to distinguish between spontaneous use and response-based usage patterns, the latter of which involves responding to a specific notification (Piwek et al., 2016). This leaves many new methodological avenues open to exploration whereby a variety of human–computer interactions can be assessed longitudinally (Shaw et al., 2018).

Accordingly, it is essential that results and research materials are openly available for all researchers to scrutinise and build upon. Generally, research that focuses on the effects of technology are single studies that do not engage with preregistration or the sharing of data. Recent attempts to validate self-report measures (Table 1.2) also make replication very difficult (McKiernan et al., 2016). Commercial apps, for example, have not been robustly validated to ensure that they are measuring behaviours reliably, storing data securely and complying with ethical guidelines (Elhai et al., 2018; Rozgonjuk et al., 2018). On the other hand, source code, data sets and related materials are available from Andrews et al. (2015) and Wilcockson et al. (2018). However, the smartphone framework originally used to collect data is no longer actively maintained (Piwek et al., 2016). Therefore, smartphone apps and associated analytical tools that have been developed specifically for the purposes of research are now urgently required. Apple and Google are now providing more objective data that can be used directly by researchers, but these high-level approaches alone will not capture the complexity of psychological processes associated with everyday technology use (Ellis et al., 2019). An alternative but more elaborate proposition might focus on the development or adaption of hardware attachments that capture behaviours outside of a technology ecosystem (Liu et al., 2018). For example, small sensors which measure light can be attached to screens directly. The reverse side could simultaneously measure movement or detect a face to confirm, in addition to a measure of screen activity, if someone is actively using the device (McGrath, Scanaill and Nafus, 2014). Regardless of the research direction, linking computer science with psychology via interdisciplinary frameworks is vital if we are to overcome existing technical barriers (Orben and Przybylski, 2019; Orben, Dienlin and Przybylski, 2019b).

1.5   Conclusion

Results concerning the negative impact of general smartphone use on psychological well-being may surprise rather than worry many psychologists. Smartphones are primarily used to facilitate social interactions, and psychology has spent many years convincingly arguing that social support and integration have many positive health benefits (Day et al., 2018; Haslam et al., 2018; Jao et al., 2018; Pachucki et al., 2015). Even priming topics associated with smartphones appears to make relationship concepts more accessible (Kardos et al., 2018). New technology also offers a host of new possibilities to improve physical and mental health (Ellis and Piwek, 2018). Many conclusions from psychological science are therefore completely at odds with what might be expected in the general population. Given our current understanding, one might argue that the biggest threat facing those who engage regularly with a smartphone is that these interactions take up time which might have been traditionally spent elsewhere. For example, a lack of physical activity is of a far greater demonstrable risk to young people, with previous research highlighting clear links between technology use and childhood obesity (Chekroud et al., 2018; Costigan et al., 2013; Lee et al., 2012; Vioque, Torres and Quiles, 2000).

When it comes to understanding the impact of technology more generally, there has historically been an intrinsic lack of high-quality evidence (Ellis et al., 2018). Policy and advice to parents have become decoupled from current understanding. Some notable exceptions include advice from the Royal College of Paediatrics and Child Health (RCPCH) and recent reports from the British government (UK Parliament, 2018; Viner, Davie and Firth, 2019). Following these publications, large data sets and pre-registered designs have started to challenge current knowledge concerning the potential negative impacts of social media and smartphone use (Hall et al., 2019; Heffer et al., 2019; Orben and Przybylski, 2019; Orben, Dienlin and Przybylski, 2019a; Stronge et al., 2019). Longitudinal evidence has also failed to observe any causal link between depression and screen-based media (Coyne et al., 2020; Houghton et al., 2018). However, this debate is certainly not definitively settled when contrasted with cohort-based designs (Khouja et al., 2019). While recent studies are not objective in nature and tend to rely on duration estimates or single survey items, short measures like these may actually get closer to objective usage at a very general level (Ellis et al., 2019). This confirms a distinct lack of progress when contrasted with decades of inappropriate scale development.

Some revised psychometric tests may hold value in the future, provided they are grounded in relevant theory and validated accordingly. This may require careful consideration of how we can ask better questions after understanding existing limitations in more detail (Baranowski et al., 2008; Ernala et al., 2020; Vanden Abeele, Beullens and Roe, 2013). A future study may also wish to compare how self-report measures correlate with both anxiety assessments and objective behaviour. Recent research suggests that the correlation would be far stronger with the former than the latter (Ellis et al., 2019). However, psychological science should be in a position to go beyond these, particularly as social psychology appears to be acknowledging the limitations associated with a lack of behavioural measurement and validation of self-report measures across the field (Doliński, 2018). Perhaps more importantly, a frank and open debate is required regarding how psychologists might conceptualise, measure and understand general technology usage, which has long since become a core component of daily life (Shaw et al., 2018).

Finally, aligning technology use with an addictions framework has done the discipline a considerable disservice. This often provides a sheen of false clinical validity that diverts attention away from areas where clear harm is more likely. Issues that pertain to unequal access (Chapter 4) and privacy (Chapter 6) are bigger threats to digital spaces.[2] Even if smartphone 'addiction' were ever to be included as part of the World Health Organization's ICD-11 (International Classification of Diseases, 11th revision, 2018) alongside gaming disorder, any diagnostic criteria will almost

---

[2] It is worth considering how negative impacts from any new source are generally understood. This often involves converging evidence from observation, population-level studies, and experimentation to reveal causal links. For example, establishing that cigarette smoking was the leading cause of lung cancer started with observations from medical practitioners (Proctor, 2012). The initial suggestion that mass-adopted technology is typically problematic comes from social scientists first, not the medical community.

certainly have to focus on objective behaviour, clinical observations as well as thoughts, attitudes and feelings towards a technology (Lin et al., 2016). However, despite gaming disorder appearing as part of the ICD-11, it has done so with a comparatively weak evidence base (Aarseth et al., 2017; Van Rooij et al., 2018). Improved methods suggest that this was a mistake (Przybylski and Weinstein, 2019). While other authors tout the 'milestones' in this related area based on the quantity of papers, their conclusions appear detached from the quality of current evidence (Pontes and Griffiths, 2019).

One wonders what drives this pathologising of technology usage. Do psychologists feel that their work is taken more seriously when it suggests a clinical manifestation (Haslam, 2016)? Exactly why this continues to loop within current research is worthy of further discussion, and I return to these issues in the Conclusion. Indeed, many concerns reappear at various points throughout this book. The way in which psychology sometimes approaches technology, including smartphones, may tell us more about researchers themselves than the underlying science.

Useful Resources and Further Reading

Markey, P. M. & Ferguson, C. J. (2017). *Moral Combat: Why the War on Violent Video Games is Wrong.* BenBella Books, Inc.

Written by Pat Markey and Chris Ferguson, the book offers a comprehensive overview of the scientific research on gaming and critically considers the misplaced concern surrounding the impact of video-game violence on real-world violence. Much of the concern around smartphone and related technologies follows a similar narrative.

Przybylski, A. K. (2019, July 10). *Is Technology Addiction a Myth?* www.bbc.com/ideas/videos/is-technology-addiction-a-myth/p07ggx85

A short video produced by BBC Ideas where Professor Andrew Przybylski argues that 'digital addictions' are a myth.

CHAPTER 2

Health and Behaviour Change

Despite concerns about their regular use, smartphones, wearable trackers and associated devices have gained a greater prominence across health and related areas of psychological science (Figure 2.1). Piwek and Joinson (2017) are quick to point out that smartphones are much more than simply 'smart-phones' and could also be described in this context as

> a digital camera, a photo book, a video recorder, a music player, a radio, a voice recorder, a GPS navigator, a handheld games console, a digital television, an Internet browser, an email manager, a weather forecaster, a watch, an alarm clock, a calendar, a calculator, and so much more (Miller, 2012). This ingenious device continuously records numerous variables every few seconds; from location and levels of movement to the number of calls we make, the number of letters we type when sending text messages, or the proximity to other similar devices that we pass on our way to work. (Piwek and Joinson, 2017, p. 137)

While mobile devices can track health and answer a variety of associated research questions, streams of data can also become feedback to augment and support behaviour change interventions. Specifically, a growing number of smartphone health apps now aim to track physical activity or improve well-being. This includes psychological interventions to support patients with mental health concerns (Donker et al., 2013; Gravenhorst et al., 2015; Grünerbl et al., 2012; Ly et al., 2015; Puiatti et al., 2011), assist with behaviour change to increase exercise levels (Bort-Roig et al., 2014; Glynn et al., 2014) and facilitate weight loss (Allen et al., 2013; Carter et al., 2013). In conjunction with psychology, an increasing number of interdisciplinary groups are also starting to focus on how digital technology might improve health. However, while the research landscape is now littered with many well-publicised successes and failures, less is known when it comes to understanding why such results occur even for users who engage with a long-term intervention.

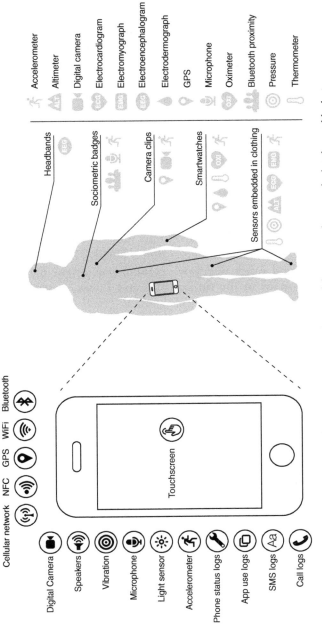

Smartphone sensors

Piwek & Joinson (2017) *Behaviour Change: Research and Theory*

Cellular network   NFC   GPS   WiFi   Bluetooth

Digital Camera
Speakers
Vibration
Microphone
Light sensor
Accelerometer
Phone status logs
App use logs
SMS logs
Call logs

Touchscreen

Consumer wearables

Piwek, Ellis, Andrews & Joinson (2016) *PLoS Medicine*

Headbands
Sociometric badges
Camera clips
Smartwatches
Sensors embedded in clothing

Accelerometer
Altimeter
Digital camera
Electrocardiogram
Electromyograph
Electroencephalogram
Electrodermograph
GPS
Microphone
Oximeter
Bluetooth proximity
Pressure
Thermometer

Figure 2.1 Examples of digital traces that can be harvested from smartphones and related wearable devices

Note: Left panel illustrates sensors and tracking features found in the majority of modern smartphones. Many sensors in smartphones also appear in a variety of other consumer wearable devices (right panel). These include devices that can measure several health metrics, including heart rate, muscle activity and cognitive function. Collectively, such systems can also deliver personalised, immediate and goal-oriented feedback based on specific tracking data obtained via sensors and provide long-lasting functionality without requiring continual recharging. Their small-form factor makes them easier to wear continuously.

Considering health care more broadly, digital technology is often viewed as the perfect solution that can meet the needs of patients, clinicians and managers (Department of Health and Social Care, 2018). Smartphones can also provide a centralised hub where researchers and participants can connect wearable devices (e.g., activity trackers) and augment secondary sources of data (e.g., electronic health records). In countries such as Africa and Australia there is already a considerable reliance on telemedicine and online care to support remote communities (Wykes, 2019). While this could allow patients and care providers to become fully informed about their current state of health across the globe, it can also bring new, unintended consequences for health-care provision.

With these issues in mind, this chapter will first consider how smartphones can help better understand health on a grand scale by quantifying a growing variety of health metrics. Some of this research has already started to challenge or support existing psychological theory. A second discussion will then cover how these metrics are being used to support behaviour change interventions. Finally, I will focus on how smartphones and other disruptive technologies might help or hinder health-care systems in the future (Ellis and Piwek, 2018; Piwek et al., 2016b).

2.1 Ambulatory Assessment: Digitised Self-Report

One of the weaknesses associated with research across psychology concerns the emphasis placed on retrospective survey methods. This includes collecting self-report data from questionnaires or interviews. Within health, it remains difficult to measure everyday behaviours and dynamic metrics (e.g., mood) using laboratory-based methods alone (Trull and Ebner-Priemer, 2014). For example, while the benefits of physical activity on health are well documented, self-report measures of this everyday behaviour will struggle to capture subtle nuances that will improve our understanding of these effects further (Celis-Morales et al., 2012). While physical activity can be measured objectively, even when this is not possible, the accuracy of self-report can be improved by asking for responses in the moment. What is often referred to as ambulatory assessment (AA), for example, encompasses a range of methods that can be used to assess people in a natural environment. Smartphones have democratised these measurement tools, which have become more powerful. Collectively, these can provide scientists with a more representative and less biased understanding of an individual's emotions, thoughts and behaviour in real life (Table 2.1).

Table 2.1 *Trull and Ebner-Priemer (2014) note that ES, EMA and AA are often used interchangeably, but historically their original aims differ (Shiffman, Stone and Hufford, 2008)*

AA	Measures	Example Reference
Experience sampling (ES)	Momentary self-report	Csikszentmihalyi and Larson (1987)
Ecological momentary assessment (EMA)	Electronic diaries	Stone and Shiffman (1994)
Ecological momentary intervention (EMI)	Automated reminders to engage with intervention	Schueller, Aguilera and Mohr (2017)
Passive behavioural observation	Audio/video recording or tracking another digital trace (e.g., call records)	Lieberman, Pillsworth and Haselton (2011)
Physiological tracking	Cardiac, respiratory function or activity levels	Piwek et al. (2016b)
Environmental tracking	Location, ambient light, noise or temperature	MacKerron and Mourato (2013)

Note: AA is a broad term used to summarise all the methods outlined here. ES often relies on random sampling across a specific period of time, which can use pen and paper with beepers or smartphones in isolation. EMA is associated with using self-report in the form of electronic diaries. EMIs involve a participant taking some action following an instruction. These methods do not prevent all forms of bias as the number of responses collected across participants can vary, which can skew results. However, improvements are starting to appear that involve using contextual cues to improve response rate, including time of day, last phone usage and battery life (e.g., van Berkel et al., 2020).

Specifically, AA allows for 'real time', in situ assessments temporally close to the moment of enactment. Early attempts involved participants carrying purpose-built devices, which were expensive and bulky. These custom beepers would remind a participant at intermittent intervals to write down something about themselves or their environment. Example questions might include 'How happy do you feel right now on a scale of 1–10 with 10 being very happy?' or 'Are you currently engaging with any form of social interaction?' As smartphones have become a central part of people's lives – the average person checks their device around 85 times a day – the threshold for people when it comes to providing additional information throughout the day is lower (Andrews et al., 2015). Building on previous research that involved the use of web pages to collect information daily, smartphones allow participants to easily visit web pages without any additional development. Alternatively, customised apps or commercial systems can be used to elicit a variety of participant-generated data directly.

When it comes to understanding health in the general population, these methods can redefine and test dynamic psychological processes, including those which impact on physical health and mental well-being. Such methods include research that considers emotions, mood, behavioural patterns and physiological correlates of everyday functioning. For example, processes like emotion are dynamic and fluctuate over time, often in response to specific factors. This data can also be used to evaluate the effectiveness of an intervention or become part of an intervention in its own right. Within psychological science specifically, research concerning health can be split into active and passive approaches. Active approaches involve the generation of data from participants directly, which might include responding to specific questions about current activities or mood. Alternatively, passive approaches involve the continual collection of data automatically without any participant involvement. Physical activity or location is currently used more frequently in passive research, but the opportunities in this area continue to expand. Irrespective of whether the approach is active or passive, data can be transmitted to a variety of cloud servers so it can be easily accessed by a research team. However, it is also possible to store all data locally on the device itself.

2.1.1   Active Monitoring

Ecological momentary assessment methods that involve self-report alone have already had a considerable impact on health psychology. This has often challenged or suggested revisions to existing theories, especially those that aim to explain the reasons behind or associated with negative impacts on health. For example, the desire for sleep, sex and leisure activity in everyday life is far stronger than for addictive behaviours like using tobacco or alcohol (Hofmann, Vohs and Baumeister, 2012). However, binge eating specifically is both preceded and followed by increases in negative effect, counter to predictions by the affect regulation model (Haedt-Matt and Keel, 2011). Alcohol, on the other hand, is associated with both positive and negative effects in clinical samples (Jahng et al., 2011). Similarly, decisions to start or continue drinking by students are both more likely when surrounded by others who already drink, which might require a step change in interventions that aim to reduce risky drinking by intervening at multiple points in time (O'Donnell et al., 2019).

By contrast, a sizeable body of research confirms previous laboratory-based research. For example, recent findings have emphasised the role of positive emotions that can benefit creative thought more strongly than negative emotions and neutral states (Baas et al., 2008). Conner and Silvia (2015) observed that days which involve more creativity are characterised by greater emotional zest and engagement, but personality modulated this emotion–creativity link. Such studies can start to further unpick complex processes that drive positive effect, and their findings support the notion that creativity can be a means towards positive psychological functioning. This may have implications for treatment programmes that aim to treat depression and anxiety (Conner, DeYoung and Silvia, 2018).

Other attempts using similar methodologies have confirmed the contrast avoidance model (CAM), which aims to explain processes associated with worry. CAM suggests that 'worry increases and sustains negative emotion to prevent a negative emotional contrast (sharp upward shift in negative emotion) and increase the probability of a positive contrast (shift toward positive emotion)' (Newman et al., 2019, p. 794). Similar thought processes have been linked with a variety of negative physical health outcomes, including poor sleep and heart disease (Hamer, Batty and Kivimaki, 2011; Weise et al., 2013). Newman et al. (2019) adopted an experimental approach whereby they compared worry, thought valence and arousal responses between participants with generalised anxiety disorder and controls. In line with CAM, they observed, over several days, that everyday worrying appears to reduce the likelihood of a sharp increase in negative effect. It does this by increasing and sustaining anxious activation.

Opportunities for active monitoring that have existed for many years are starting to become key components of research. However, while methods have become more prevalent, possibly as a result of increased smartphone adoption, the specific technology is rarely mentioned in the methods or design sections of subsequent publications. For example, any smartphone can facilitate the uploading of photos and future research will benefit further as participants can now accurately record food consumption in the form of photographs or barcode scanning (Kato et al., 2016). However, specific frameworks or systems used to accomplish these tasks should be made available to other researchers. If code and materials are not freely available or appropriately referenced, issues pertaining to replication and transparency will limit progress. On the other hand, the analysis of related data has started to become somewhat standardised. This typically involves separating out between (trait) versus within (state) patterns as is typical with longitudinal data to understand changes and associations over time. Stone and Shiffman (2002) outline standard reporting guidelines for researchers and information that can assist replication in this area. Related issues however, become even more important when it comes to passive monitoring using on-board sensors.

2.1.2   *Passive Monitoring*

Even without any user-driven interaction, smartphones can automatically record traces of behaviour. Many have argued that the potential for passively collected information is considerably greater because this places less burden on participants, who quickly tire of entering any data into an 'app' (Piwek and Joinson, 2017). This passive data collection can take information from apps, embedded sensors and linked devices such as smartwatches. This can include location, battery life, usage, data from connected devices and even ambient light and noise (see Figure 2.1). Complex research designs can combine sensor data with experience sampling. For example, where a person spends time can provide numerous insights into their behaviour, personality and mood by aligning GPS data with self-reported mood (Chorley, Whitaker and Allen, 2015; Geyer, Ellis and Piwek, 2019; Sandstrom et al., 2017) (Figure 2.2).

Even before smartphones, health psychologists have further attempted to unpick processes associated with physical activity and psychological processes across a variety of populations using related methodologies. For example, Dunton et al. (2014) observed that children reported feeling more energetic before and after objectively measured physical activity in the natural environment. Similar relationships between physical activity and positive mood have been observed in large groups of adults ($N>$10,000) by combining smartphone accelerometer data with experience sampling (Lathia et al., 2017). The same authors were also able to describe activity patterns over time. Research with older adults specifically has linked physical activity with improved near-term cognitive function by combining accelerometry measurements with cognitive testing over five days (Phillips et al., 2016); however, other research using self-report alone has challenged this conclusion somewhat (Bielak, Mogle and Sliwinski, 2017). Another project, developed by geographers, determined which locations in the United Kingdom were 'happiest', as well as the times, days and situations when people were most happy (MacKerron and Mourato, 2013). Location data was augmented with self-report, and it was concluded that people were happier when outdoors in natural rather than urban environments. Similar survey findings have observed that well-being is reported as higher when people spent at

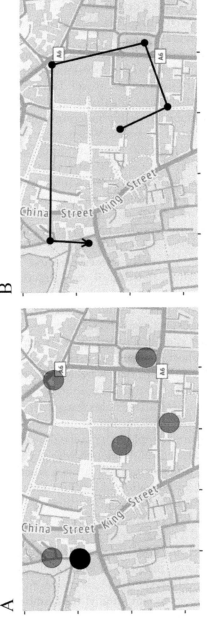

Figure 2.2 A simple visualisation derived from a short period of location tracking (Geyer et al., 2019)

Note: This includes a point map (A), which plots the individual location points (where darker points demonstrate repeated observations), and a path map (B), showing the directionality of the same participant's movement (Geyer et al., 2019). Location can be used to infer additional information about an environment (Müller et al., 2017), and related research in medicine has also sought to understand how environmental factors influence a variety of other health outcomes (James et al., 2016). It can also assist with the prediction of depressive symptoms and levels of social anxiety (Huang et al., 2016; Palmius et al., 2017; Saeb et al., 2016). Alternatively, trips between location points can quantify general levels of physical activity (Carlson et al., 2015; Jankowska et al., 2015).

least 120 minutes a week in nature (White et al., 2019). Considering future interventions, this suggests that a certain amount of time outdoors may represent a threshold for well-being, but this would require additional research to understand causality.

As before, comparing typical with clinical populations can help better understand how cognitive and physiological processes interact. Huffziger et al. (2013) collected momentary mood and cortisol data over a two-day period in remitted depressive patients and healthy controls. While cortisol plays an important role in a number of bodily functions, more cortisol is produced when the body responds to stress. When remitted depressed participants reported lower mood, this did not significantly affect cortisol levels. The authors conclude that there is a decoupling of affective and neuroendocrinological processes in these patients. While cortisol data was processed in a laboratory as part of this study, a number of researchers are developing systems that will allow participants to provide a variety of biosignals from saliva, blood and urine samples in the future using mobile laboratory devices that link directly with a smartphone (Choi et al., 2014; Roda et al., 2016; Zangheri et al., 2015). However, these and related developments will require careful validation if they are to be widely adopted (Wolf et al., 2013).

Passive methods remain powerful but do not feature as widely within health psychology as one might expect, and several of the above examples rely on web-based systems that can be accessed via a smartphone's web browser. Despite every smartphone containing a multitude of sensors, there remains a lack of suitable software that is freely available for those working within psychology and the social sciences more generally (Harari et al., 2017; Piwek et al., 2016a). Researchers also struggle to find appropriate alternatives from commercial application repositories – for example, via the Google Play or App stores (Apple, 2017; Google, 2017). This is largely because these apps have not been developed with psychologists in mind. Many commercial apps often struggle to strike a suitable balance between high levels of accuracy and duration of logging, which are methodologically important for sensor-based research (Palmius et al., 2017). Therefore, data collection can become completely under the jurisdiction of another application and beyond a researcher's control.

That said, it is unfair to level this criticism at psychology in isolation. Those who develop or propose new methods often struggle to explain or convince others to adopt them. However, there are moves to change this situation when it comes to experience sampling with a number of groups developing open-source frameworks (e.g., Hofmann and Patel, 2015;

Meers et al., 2019; Thai and Page-Gould, 2018). On paper at least, new sensor-tracking apps built for research appear equally as impressive as any expensive commercial solution (Geyer et al., 2019). Of course, even without these issues, AA methods still have limitations. Only participants with smartphones can engage with such methods (though most people today own such a device). Participants can still be strategic about what they report or share, yet using any form of ecological assessment will almost always improve the direction of travel when it comes to increasing the quality and validity of data collection, particularly when combining objective behaviour (e.g., physical activity) with self-report (e.g., emotion) (Ellis and Piwek, 2016).

Broadly speaking, AA is a promising methodology, especially for health psychology, because the data can shed light on dynamic processes as they unfold in daily life. When applied to health-related behaviours, data from smartphones and wearable devices may hold the key to understanding individual and global health. Combining multiple approaches is particularly valuable given the well-demonstrated yet debated links between self-reported physical health and mental well-being. Specifically, while mental health and physical activity are interrelated, when assessed longitudinally, some researchers have demonstrated that they do not appear to be causal but instead move together over time (Steinmo, Hagger-Johnson and Shahab, 2014).

In light of the above, and in the previous decade, similar data collection systems have been adapted in an attempt to improve health. Specifically, many researchers are asking how smartphone apps and wearable interventions might increase physical activity levels or improve well-being. The remainder of this chapter will therefore consider behaviour change interventions, before discussing how this knowledge might be applied across health-care systems in the future.

2.2   Physical Activity Interventions

Smartphones and related devices can characterise health-related behaviours and assist with a variety of behaviour change interventions that aim to encourage physical activity (Piwek et al., 2016b). The latter proposition is particularly pertinent, given that even small changes in behaviour could have far-reaching consequences for society as a whole. For example, if physical inactivity decreased by only 10 per cent, more than 533,000 deaths could be averted every year (Lee et al., 2012). Accelerometer and infrared LED sensors that measure heart rate have become increasingly valuable in this context as this technology can classify types of physical activity and daily activities (Case et al., 2015). A typical intervention provides participants with a smartphone app or wearable device in isolation or as a supplement to an existing behavioural intervention.

In the previous decade, some research has supported the notion that simply helping people to quantify their activity levels can change their behaviour (Lyons et al., 2017), and many systems are now fully integrated with smartphone operating systems. For example, Apple iOS contains inbuilt apps that can track physical activity. The most prevalent theoretical factors implemented into existing interventions (or apps) include concepts of self-monitoring and feedback (see Abraham and Michie, 2008, for a review). Both of these appear repeatedly across psychological and behaviour change literature (e.g., Bird et al., 2013; Kluger and DeNisi, 1996). Self-monitoring can increase self-efficacy[1] (Du et al., 2011) and reduce perceived barriers to start, or continue, an activity (Wilbur et al., 2003), which can facilitate positive behaviour change, including weight loss (Mateo et al., 2015; Womble et al., 2004). The majority of smartphone apps are therefore designed on the principle that self-monitoring provides people with insights into their everyday behaviour, including low levels of physical movement that correlate with poor health, which in turn motivates a change in behaviour (Sullivan and Lachman, 2016). In this manner, self-monitoring is inherently linked with feedback because a user has to review some aspects of the very behaviour that has been monitored. This feedback is typically related to performance (e.g., heart rate, steps taken, calories burned) (Forshaw, 2002; Kluger and DeNisi, 1996).

Early interventions focused on the utility of text messages to encourage physical activity recorded by activity trackers. However, thousands of apps are now available that aim to help people improve their physical and mental health by assisting with some form of behavioural change (Wiederhold, 2015). On the other hand, many success stories have come from apps which did not originally target users who want to be healthy (McCartney, 2016). Pokémon Go, for example, is a free app available for both Apple and Android devices. Players have to catch as many Pokémon characters as they can by physically navigating their city and viewing the world through their smartphone. This is an augmented reality game, where

---

[1] Self-efficacy is 'the belief in one's capabilities to organise and execute the courses of action required to produce given attainments' (Bandura, 1997, p. 3). People with high levels of self-efficacy for physical activity are also more likely to initiate, increase and maintain this activity, even in the face of obstacles and setbacks. Self-efficacy has previously been identified as one of the most consistent predictors of physical activity in adults of all ages (Bird et al., 2013).

characters appear superimposed over the real environment viewed through the camera. The game relies on gamification to encourage participants to move.[2] Walking increases the chances of catching new Pokémon characters and hatching their eggs. This translates to travelling 2, 5 or 10 km for a new character to be 'born'.

Early studies argued that Pokémon Go could have a large impact on public health if it could sustain the engagement of users over the long term, and Althoff, White and Horvitz (2016) were one of the first groups to quantify the impact of playing Pokémon Go on physical activity. They tracked data from physical activity trackers and observed that Pokémon Go led to significant increases in physical activity over a period of 30 days. These effects were present in men and women of all ages irrespective of height, weight or previous activity levels. However, challenges remain in sustaining engagement of users in the long term. For example, Howe and colleagues (2016) followed players and non-players for several weeks before and after playing Pokémon Go. As expected, players did walk further, but at the sixth week following installation, the number of daily steps had dropped back to pre-installation levels. Again, no other covariates moderated this effect.

Pokémon Go provides a somewhat mature research base. We know it can encourage physical activity, but struggles to sustain this long term for most people. It has also encouraged researchers to think carefully about potential new risks with these games, which include distracted driving and walking. However, these are comparatively lower given the risks of many other contact sports (e.g., football or rugby) (LeBlanc and Chaput, 2017). Perhaps part of the issue is that games like Pokémon target a very different type of motivation. The motivation therefore is based on a desire to not only become fitter or healthier but also win the game (extrinsic). This may not translate into long-term action as the game is unlikely to become part of daily life in the future (intrinsic). On the other hand, these changes in behaviour, even if short term, may carry over into other elements of physical activity, which are not tracked by the smartphone directly. For example, psychological studies concerning Pokémon Go have observed that daily time spent playing is associated with life satisfaction and increased levels of conversation with friends and strangers (Ewell et al., 2019). Of course, while the smartphone can be a motivator, as in the case of

---

[2] Gamification aims to make activities more engaging, including exercise. Activity-based games are frequently referred to as 'exergames' (Biddiss and Irwin, 2010; Chen et al., 2014). However, evidence supporting their ability to improve health and encourage long-term behaviour change is generally poor (Marshall and Linehan, 2017).

Pokémon Go, it can also act as a form of sedentary multitasking. In the previous decade, there has been a decrease in television consumption and an increase in smartphone- and video-game-related activities (OFCOM, 2018). Active video games are still not recommended as a strategy to help children become more physically active. This notion of failure or understanding the limits of such interventions is important if the field is to advance further.

2.2.1   The Importance of Failure

Mobile technology and the research methodology that underpins related interventions have a considerable distance to cover if they are to become standardised interventions that can help people become more active. Results from small pilots have often failed to replicate across larger samples that employ longitudinal designs. For example, one trial conducted over several years demonstrated a negative effect when patients were provided with a wearable intervention to help them lose weight (Jakicic et al., 2016). In addition to causing harm (e.g., reduced physical activity), other negative effects in this context would include interventions that provide no added benefit when compared to standard interventions or result in poor retention rates. Similarly, an effect that dissipates over time would also be classed as an overall negative outcome. This mirrors similar issues witnessed during the development of home telemonitoring interventions (Kitsiou, Paré and Jaana, 2013). For example, several trials in this domain have reported no benefit when patients were able to self-monitor blood glucose, with others demonstrating that these interventions led to increased levels of depression (O'Kane et al., 2008).

Nevertheless, these outcomes remain a key cornerstone in the literature because they emphasise the importance of understanding failures or unexpected results in order to capture the ideal functioning of a future device or intervention. Only then will it be possible to predict what physical activity interventions are more likely to show larger benefits at a population level.

In this context, we recently proposed and discussed a set of interdisciplinary guidelines that could assist in the development of future interventions that encourage physical activity with wearable technology, but this can also apply to smartphone-only interventions (Figure 2.3). While current research is at a relatively early stage, the consideration of failure across smartphone and wearable interventions warrants further discussion. It is also important to ensure that new research is mindful of current pitfalls and develops new paradigms accordingly.

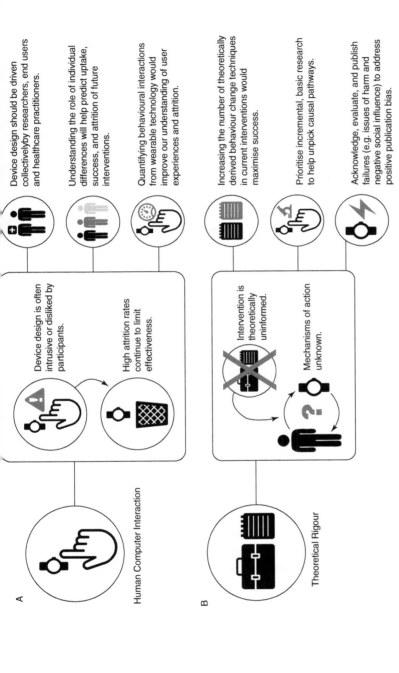

Figure 2.3 Guidelines that were developed following a review of papers that document failures in wearable interventions which aim to encourage physical activity. Note: These can also be applied to the majority of smartphone interventions. While not exhaustive, two key points of failure provide an avenue to develop future research priorities. (a) Outcomes from interventions may be set up to fail from the start, but subtle benefits (or harms) are likely to remain invisible with existing measures (human–computer interaction), and (b) many interventions are theoretically uninformed and mechanisms of action remain hidden (theoretical rigour).

Ellis, D. A. & Piwek, L. (2018). Failing to encourage physical activity with wearable technology: What next? *Journal of the Royal Society of Medicine*, *111*(9), 310–313.

2.2.1.1   Human–Computer Interaction: Falling at the First Hurdle

Wearables' and smartphone apps' design can often have an early negative impact to the point where a potential treatment effect may be thwarted from the outset. For example, one large clinical trial that provided wearable technology as part of a weight loss intervention observed that, over a two-year period, only 10 per cent of patients reported wearing a daily performance feedback device (Jakicic et al., 2016). Levels of engagement may be even lower for smartphone only interventions however, multi-functionality combined with frequent use throughout the day could instead result in increased levels of interaction. Regardless, many people continue to report that devices are unpleasant to wear and can make them feel uncomfortable around other people. Poor design that leads to low levels of comfort and social acceptability could reduce the impact of any similar intervention by limiting potential exercise opportunities (Patel, Asch and Volpp, 2015). Understanding the design issues that lead to high attrition rates within patients and consumers remains a key priority for future research. Specifically, where external devices are worn and how people engage with them on a daily basis are also likely to be fundamental to their success or failure. The wrist and upper arm have proven problematic despite their popularity and convenience (Finkelstein et al., 2016).

In addition, research concerning physical activity interventions has failed to include a measurement of behaviour that accurately quantifies how a participant interacts with their device (Jakicic et al., 2016). Subtle interactions with digital technology remain difficult to capture with self-report measures alone and are often inaccurate when it comes to health-related metrics (Ellis et al., 2018; Lichtman et al., 1992). Device usage, while straightforward to collect, has to date only been recorded in small samples of patients with pre-existing health conditions (e.g., hypertension) and not for devices used as part of a behaviour change intervention (Bloss et al., 2016). Therefore, while hardware development will continue to adapt and innovate, researchers are already in a position to capitalise on the quality and variety of data that can be captured from existing devices.

2.2.1.2   Theoretical Rigour

Technologies evolve more rapidly than traditional research models can evaluate them (e.g., Jakicic et al., 2016). While mobile technology itself has made great advances, its theoretical contribution towards behaviour modification has been considerably smaller (Ogilvie et al., 2007). For example, the popularity of an app does not correlate with the number of behaviour change techniques that have been shown to be effective in increasing physical activity. Allowing market forces to drive what is used by the public and possibly 'prescribed' or recommended by general practitioners (GPs) is not a suitable approach at present (Bondaronek et al., 2019). This also means that the public perception of digital health innovations is often driven by unsupported industry claims, which is similar to many other sport or lifestyle products that purport to have a large effect on performance (Heneghan et al., 2012).

Mobile and wearable systems could help to improve and develop new behavioural change techniques as part of a subsequent intervention (Mercer et al., 2016). It may, however, be more valuable to deliberately limit and control these techniques in order to test specific mechanisms of action. Otherwise, the mechanisms that underpin a specific change in behaviour are typically hidden. Even in larger research designs, there is frequently no control group (Jakicic et al., 2016). By contrast, trials within the life sciences that administer a new drug have well-established action pathways long before an intervention takes place.

Several theoretical avenues are worthy of further investigation. One causal pathway may involve the use of a device to make self-monitoring easier, which increases the frequency of self-monitoring over time. An alternative is that active self-monitoring increases the salience of behavioural choices more than passive self-monitoring, although a lack of engagement (e.g., not engaging with a device) across many interventions suggests that this is unlikely (Mercer et al., 2016). One simple approach could, for example, manipulate when feedback is provided between different participants. Subsequent results may challenge the widely held assumption that real-time feedback will optimise every intervention.

2.2.2   *Future Research*

Research programmes concerning physical activity should aim to strike a balance between controlled trials, with input from those working in applied contexts, and basic 'blue-sky' research. Without this equivalence, it will remain increasingly difficult to dismantle the elements of an intervention that drive or hinder an effect. A more extreme view considered later might argue that it is too early for large-scale trials when it comes to testing if mobile interventions can help increase physical activity levels, particularly when the vast majority of applied research struggles to change how decisions are made within public health (Ioannidis, 2016). One solution here may simply involve bringing public health-care professionals together with technology designers at the earliest opportunity.

On the other hand, it would be naive to assume that digital interventions concerning physical activity will be the silver bullet solution. Physical activity interventions that are a part of a larger programme (e.g., counselling) often appear to be more successful (Fukuoka et al., 2019). Current devices, interventions and research only reach a small part of the population that is interested in health or personal data capture or those who already lead a healthy lifestyle (Juniper Research, 2013; Sullivan and Lachman, 2016). While the line between assessment and intervention has blurred, the digital divide still exists, and one would question how these interventions can reach people who are most in need, especially children, older adults and low-socio-economic status (SES) populations. Considerable interdisciplinary progress is required if such interventions are to become commonplace, regardless of ability or personal goals. Even within the context of existing trials, the variation in patients' experience and behaviour is largely ignored. While many will abandon an app within a couple of months, others will persevere with these devices and will continue to track specific activities for several years. However, in the context of long-term behaviour change, strong evidence has yet to appear that supports these anecdotal observations or short-term effects following smartphones and wearable interventions (Dunton, 2018; Finkelstein et al., 2016).

2.3   Automated Tracking of Emotion and Mood

While at an earlier stage of development, related branches of work have focused on predicting an individual's emotional state, which can inform interventions that aim to improve well-being. This includes research that has explored how secondary data collected routinely from participants and expert observations could assist or predict future mental health concerns (Williamson, Darby and Fear, 2019; Williamson et al., 2020). Alternatively, the automatic detection or classification of emotions tends to focus on key emotions – including joy, happiness, sadness, surprise and fear – that provide a baseline for more complex expressions (Ekman and Friesen, 1978). However, other dimensional models argue that human emotion is far more variable in terms of both states and how they are expressed (Wilhelm and Schoebi, 2007). While the behavioural characteristics of an emotion can be expressed in the form of behavioural and physiological changes, this can vary across cultures, situations and even within an individual over a single day. To illustrate, when a person is angry, the pitch of their voice gets higher and their speech becomes faster. However, such a response could also mean a person is excited, anxious or frustrated. Similarly, when quantifying levels of stress, anxiety or general arousal can reveal huge overlaps when attempting to detect specific emotions automatically.

However, a number of studies, predominantly in computer science, have focused on the notion of classifying emotions from a variety of on-board smartphone sensors including the microphone and camera (Sandulescu et al., 2015; Suk and Prabhakaran, 2014). This often involves an element of self-report, which attempts to align patterns of behaviour with the emotion reported, and a variety of projects have considered how movement, location and audio signals alongside daily diary entries can predict a person's emotional state (Lathia et al., 2013; Rachuri et al., 2010). For example, how a person interacts with their smartphone, including typing speed, maximum text length and touch count, has been found to predict mood (Ellis and Piwek, 2016). Combining these with longitudinal measures of location changes can improve the accuracy of such predictions further (LiKamWa et al., 2013).

This trend in medicine is becoming increasingly popular and is often referred to as digital phenotyping. As with related definitions, researchers typically refer to the collection of individual data on a moment-to-moment basis, which can get closer to how a patient behaves outside a clinical setting (Insel, 2018). This can include feature-rich data collected from smartphones (e.g., location) and wearable devices (e.g., heart rate and galvanic skin response). Recent studies, for instance, have demonstrated that changes in activity levels can be an early sign of mania or depression (Reinertsen and Clifford, 2018; Torous et al., 2018). Similarly, passive smartphone data has also been used to predict relapses in schizophrenic patients, which could improve early warning systems and interventions that prevent hospitalisation in the future (Barnett et al., 2018).

Irrespective of hype, research in this area is still in its infancy. Specifically, selecting an appropriate statistical methodology remains challenging. Many researchers continue to use statistical approaches that have been applied to more traditional, less intensive data and/or different data structures (Marsch, 2018), and, for a variety of reasons, many algorithms tend to generate inflated optimism (DeMasi, Kording and Recht, 2017). On the other hand, while traditional machine-learning techniques may not be efficient enough to extract complex and non-linear patterns, new deep-learning techniques can work directly with raw data to automate feature extraction and selection (Kanjo, Younis and Ang, 2019). Despite computational potential, this remains difficult to enact within small clinical samples and the lack of consistency across findings means that further validation is essential on a grander scale (Cho et al., 2019; Torous et al., 2018). One wonders if an approach that considers sensor metrics alongside measurements of mood in non-clinical, larger samples would provide a more suitable approach in the first instance (Saeb et al., 2016). Results could then be extrapolated to clinical populations in future designs to reduce any risk to patients. Alternatively, carefully mapping and extrapolating specific psychiatric symptoms onto smartphone sensor metrics in the first instance would also provide a stronger frame of reference going forward.[3] Regardless, data derived from sensor-based metrics has yet to demonstrate acceptable reliability when predicting mood in any clinical context and issues pertaining to preregistration, analytical standardisation, replication and data transparency remain widespread.

While these errors are less likely in research areas where there has been considerable progress (e.g., medical diagnoses from scans), predicting social outcomes (e.g., people at risk) remains challenging across psychological medicine. Indeed, traditional regression modelling with a handful of variables can often outperform more computationally intensive methods (Dressel and Farid, 2018). Inaccurate predictions are of even greater concern, as they could have serious implications for patients, health practitioners and associated services. These practical limitations also sit alongside controversial data-sharing issues exposed as part of other systems and research that used data without patients' consent. For example, Google recently used data from around 1.6 million patients, without asking permission (Iacobucci, 2017).

Smartphone sensor-based metrics alone are therefore not yet suitable for interventions that aim to help assist with well-being and any automated systems used to flag low mood struggle when operating at scale. One recent example concerns a Twitter plug-in developed by the Samaritans called *Radar*. This attempted to identify users who might be 'struggling to cope'. However, after a series of concerns were raised relating to privacy and accuracy, it was quickly withdrawn.[4] Interventions that aim to improve well-being, diagnose or treat those with a mental health concern remain at a comparatively early stage when contrasted with physical health-based interventions. The majority of apps simply change based on a limited range of participant responses or instead rely entirely on preprogrammed routines.

2.3.1   *Well-being Interventions and Psychological Harm*

Like interventions that target physical activity, smartphones and wearable devices make new kinds of mental health interventions possible because

---

[3] See Chapter 4 for a related discussion concerning personality prediction from smartphone metrics.
[4] www.samaritans.org/about-samaritans/research-policy/internet-suicide/samaritans-radar/

they can take place in the context of other everyday activities, where current health-care systems may struggle to support large numbers of individuals. As with issues pertaining to physical health, mental health problems continue to place a high burden on society and interest governments that want to ensure the working population remains productive (Wykes, 2019).

Web-based systems can already deliver cognitive behavioural therapy or e-resources to assist with self-management (Gravenhorst et al., 2015; Karasouli and Adams, 2014). The threshold for engagement is often lower than attending conventional therapy and can reach those who may not even have access in the first instance. Smartphones also allow for the delivery of these interventions to take place remotely, but still employ some form of symptom or behavioural monitoring and request input from a participant. This might include a form of gamification or reminders or simply provide guidance. As with physical activity, many standalone apps address issues associated with depression, anxiety, substance abuse, self-harming thoughts, sleep problems and smoking cessation (Torous et al., 2020). These can leverage other data from the device that web browsers might not have access to and react accordingly to participant responses.

In recent years, researchers have started to focus on EMIs as a way to deliver momentary health treatments, which can be highly personalised (Schueller, Aguilera and Mohr, 2017). Complex EMIs can have multiple intervention options and decision points. The idea of a system that evolves over time, continuously improving based on a patient's pattern of responses, is perhaps more prevalent within well-being interventions than those that aim to improve physical health. Examples include apps that prompt specific relaxation exercises, provide specific information in the form of text and videos, or reflect on existing stressors throughout the day (Firth et al., 2017a, 2017b).

In terms of their effectiveness, the evidence for such interventions is arguably weaker when contrasted with physical activity interventions. However, well-being interventions share similar patterns regarding success and failure. Early meta-analyses suggested that smartphone apps could reduce anxiety and depression in the short term based on a handful of randomised controlled trials (RCTs) (Firth et al., 2017a; Firth et al., 2017b). The specific type of intervention (e.g., cognitive behavioral therapy or mindfulness training) does not appear to impact on study effect sizes for depression (Firth et al., 2017b), and caution has been urged to clinicians because there is insufficient support for any specific app (Lui, Marcus and Barry, 2017).

   As with interventions that aim to encourage physical activity, long-term usage is low and drop-out rates are considerable across the board but improve for apps that target depressive symptoms when human feedback and mood monitoring metrics are available (Baumel et al., 2019; Torous et al., 2020). Another meta-analysis observed that the effects for most areas of mental health domains were smaller when compared to digital mental health interventions that were delivered using the internet. Transferring web-based systems to smartphones is unlikely to be effective (Weisel et al., 2019). This may simply reflect the infancy of existing work. It is also worth noting that very few standalone or self-help treatments work in any medical disorder. Many participants will be reluctant to engage with new material, and the majority of people use only a handful of popular apps regularly. Incentives to engage with new apps may still be required in the first instance. Several technical barriers remain including issues associated with operating systems, battery drain or security. These apps are therefore likely to be effective when used to augment and extend treatment with support from a clinician, peer or other social networks. However, it remains unclear exactly how these interventions are driving any effect (good or bad).

   Insignificant findings highlight the need for discussing the potential harm of currently available apps, which might keep users away from evidence-based interventions while bearing a substantial risk of being ineffective (Weisel et al., 2019). The issue of harm from a health perspective has become more prevalent in the existing literature base, and it is conceivable that people may become over-reliant on automated systems that provide a false sense of security or fuel a self-driven misdiagnosis (Mertz, 2016; Piwek et al., 2016b). Similarly, while self-help treatment delivered via an app may allow patients to become responsible for their own health, service users often do not want to lose human contact (Wykes, 2019). Excessive self-monitoring could also lead to discomfort and a sense of intrusiveness amongst patients. For instance, the impact of activity tracker interventions on quality of life and mental health remains unknown for many populations (Oliveira et al., 2019). Other concerns are becoming more frequent, with Etkin (2016) observing that while counting steps led participants to move more, it decreased people's enjoyment of walking. In other words, instead of supporting people by construing exercise as an enjoyable and meaningful activity leading to prolonged engagement, apps may establish new mechanisms which guarantee a short-term increase in activity at the risk of negative long-term effects. Perhaps in response, Schueller and colleagues (2017) argue convincingly that it is important to distinguish between proximal and distal outcomes. Specifically, did an intervention make you feel better now or has it made you more well over time? Proximal outcomes can be reported immediately: 'Did completing this task improve your mood?' Distal outcomes may be recorded over longer periods of time. These are also likely to evolve more slowly, whereas proximal outcomes may change more rapidly, in response to a specific intervention.

Other work has considered specific populations that are more likely to be at risk of harm. While some research has shown a positive impact on those with serious mental illness over a six-month period (Naslund et al., 2016), others have suggested that the potential to cause additional stress still remains. For example, Simpson and Mazzeo (2017) observed an association between the use of calorie counting, fitness trackers and eating disorder symptomology. This supports earlier research where individuals who report using calorie counters manifest higher levels of eating concern and dietary restraint (Jacobi et al., 2004). Similar issues have been reported with sleep trackers, where false positives lead patients into seeking treatment for sleep disorders that do not exist (Baron et al., 2017). The quantified self-literature, which refers to the cultural phenomenon of self-tracking with technology, also points out that an unrealistic quest for perfection in movement or sleep can cause more harm than good, particularly when individuals start to place so much faith in data that they believe is more consistent with their experience than other more validated techniques (van Berkel et al., 2015). For example, mental health apps that specifically aim to prevent suicide or improve depressive symptoms often fail to include or misreport helpline phone numbers and lack evidence-based prevention strategies (Martinengo et al., 2019). Similarly, many apps that aim to assist with self-management lack features that would enhance medication adherence (Huang et al., 2019). Leaving any regulation solely with app stores and industry is unlikely to be an effective strategy. Beyond poor designs that contain excessive advertising, many apps may cause harm by suggesting benefit because they drive an expectation of success. Of course, even the most successful therapy will include individuals who do not achieve a benefit, and this can lead to a sense of failure (Wykes et al., 2019). This individual variation is something that, as with physical activity interventions, is often not captured in evaluations that rely on traditional RCT designs.

2.4   Individualised Interventions: The Future of RCTs

A common theme is that smartphone and digital interventions may struggle to fit around RCTs, which have extended outwards from being a key way we assess pharmacological interventions to the primary method for evaluating all health-related interventions (Blandford et al., 2018). While these tell us if something was effective over time, they often provide no information on why and how much input was required to achieve a desired effect. There are also many other questions that remain important when it comes to understanding interactive interventions of this nature, including usability (Blandford et al., 2018).

Individual variance is increasingly difficult to ignore. For example, Conroy and colleagues (2019) recently used three different types of message to encourage physical activity. These targeted social-cognitive processes associated with increasing physical activity, social-cognitive processes associated with reducing sedentary behaviour, or general facts unrelated to either physical activity or sedentary behaviour. Their results revealed heterogeneous responses to different message types that varied between people and between weekdays and weekends. Powerful research designs in the future could manipulate the specific techniques deployed as part of an intervention and record a participant's interaction with a device to understand which specific methods are more effective.

A number of authors have started to consider these developments in the context of the behavioural intervention technology (BIT) model (Mohr et al., 2014) to better understand how EMIs affect specific outcomes. This model makes a distinction between BIT 'treatments' and BIT 'interventions'. An intervention refers to a specific single interaction between a user and an element of the technology that might be a push notification or single text message. A BIT treatment, on the other hand, is the sum of a number of interactions over time. This could also assist with further unpacking Schueller and colleagues' (2017) distinction between proximal and distal outcomes. For example, an intervention might involve an application that provides instructions for deep breathing to reduce stress and aid relaxation. The intervention begins with a 50 per cent chance of being presented to the user over a four-hour period. However, if this intervention is successful, the odds will be increased in favour of the intervention being presented. The impact may be influenced by time of day, recent events, location or other variables, which could include physiological data from an attached smartwatch. As the intervention progresses, delivery will be customised to maximise its effectiveness. Another related solution involves the use of microrandomised trials (MRTs) proposed by Klasnja et al. (2015). These involve a sequential factorial design that randomly assigns an intervention component to each individual at relevant time points. In an MRT, each individual is randomised multiple times, and this can further help separate immediate (proximal outcomes) and long-term (distal outcomes) effects of a particular intervention component. This can, in turn, determine which variables are more important for each individual and when they should be manipulated to maximise short and long term effects. Similar discussions have considered the notion of *N*-of-1 designs within health psychology (Kwasnicka et al., 2019).

These approaches present new challenges for teasing out results from large-scale evaluations because not every user will receive the same intervention. Like the issues around physical activity, when these are evaluated at a group level, the sum of interventions, tailored variables, decision variables and decision rules may evolve so much over the course of a trial that traditional RCTs may be a poor fit for EMI development. Where digital interventions include learning models and no standard treatment approach, one way forward is to consider knowledge at an individual level first and then move to generalise at a population level. This is in stark contrast to RCTs that make inferences based on means (i.e., group-level analyses first) before conducting within-person or moderator analyses that then lead to recommendations for practitioners or policy makers.

Many questions remain. Will these methods be taken seriously by the medical community? How would results be utilised in practice? The medical community argues that future evidence should come in the form of RCTs (Bakker et al., 2016; Vaidyam et al., 2019; Versluis et al., 2016). However, the reporting of specifics remains a problem for existing RCTs, which often lack information regarding long-term patient outcomes and information required for replication (Oikonomidi et al., 2019). This could become even more problematic for MRTs. Similarly, when moving away from RCTs, existing behaviour change theories do not account for interactive apps that are personalised to an individual (Ajzen, 1991; Kwasnicka et al., 2019; Leventhal et al., 1992).

Some level of decoupling and theoretical remapping may be essential if the discipline is to move closer to the precision required for digital interventions to be effective. Reverting back to smaller data sets has been proposed as a way forward that could be combined with large-scale approaches (Hekler et al., 2019). Specifically, collecting qualitative and quantitative data from fewer individuals can help researchers manage complex, multi-causal phenomena before extending outwards to large-scale approaches. In addition, innovative methods of evaluation can sit alongside existing RCT designs that are likely to remain the gold standard when it comes to demonstrating the effectiveness of any intervention. However, these do not need to be viewed in direct opposition to or in conflict with traditional approaches to treatment evaluation (Cresswell, Blandford and Sheikh, 2017).

2.5   Care Delivery: A Complete Systems Approach

Mobile technology has already started to revolutionise health, at least from an everyday perspective, as patients and practitioners use a variety of digital devices (e.g., thermometers and glucose monitors) to identify and discuss symptoms. Currently, smartphone technology allows people often to (at least think they) know much more about their health than previous generations. For example, a third of general practitioners in the United Kingdom report that patients arrive with suggestions for treatment based on online search results. Smartphones and wearable devices have already become the next 'Dr Google'. By 2025, a majority of the projected eight billion people in the world will carry a smartphone or related device (Portio Research, 2011).

The predictive analytics and interventions discussed in this chapter are perhaps more likely to become part of a larger set of patient monitoring systems across a digitised health landscape. These may need to include other linked devices or services that monitor behaviour directly or help support and motivate individuals and groups (Muse et al., 2017). mHealth is broadly defined as the range of medical and public health practices supported by mobile devices or services (Tomlinson et al., 2013), and smartphones can support many related domains in this respect.[5]

New platforms are now starting to track health in the long term, record engagement with health-care providers and provide access to test results (e.g., *Evergreen*).[6] Primary care in the United Kingdom has often been at the forefront of adopting new technology in the National Health Service. For example, the Royal College of GPs Technology Manifesto aims to establish how new technology can improve primary care systems.[7]

Such developments may be especially valuable when resources are stretched, which can affect patients and practitioners. At a population level, these can then allow for the ethical surveillance of disease outbreaks.

---

[5] See Chapter 5 for a related discussion on how games might track cognitive function to model health over time or act as diagnostic tools.
[6] www.evergreen-life.co.uk/   [7] www.rcgp.org.uk/policy/rcgp-policy-areas/technology.aspx

For example, Mtema and colleagues (2016) designed a mobile-phone-based surveillance system in Tanzania for frontline health workers to report patients presenting with clinical signs of rabies and for livestock field officers to report mass dog vaccination campaigns and suspected animal cases. This has since been extended to smartphones as well as Java-enabled phones. However, secure systems could be developed that empower patients themselves to track and share relevant information. In times of a crisis (e.g., during a pandemic), smartphones would therefore increase their value for all of humanity if they became part of worldwide health-care provision.

Systems that rely on any form of artificial intelligence are likely to remain helpful tools rather than replace core parts of health-care provision. Relatedly, complete systems that include digital interventions will require input from those with an operational understanding of health systems and patient needs. An over-reliance on automated systems developed in isolation can lead to unwanted biases (Obermeyer et al., 2019). A new goal might be to move towards sustainable integration within existing health-care systems. This will involve patient and public involvement (PPI), whereby research is conducted with or by members of the public rather than for them, which can help alleviate concerns relating to usability and practicalities when using apps in the future (Ryan, 2019). This equally applies to the development of advanced machine-learning techniques that make it difficult to describe to a clinician or researcher exactly how a prediction occurs (Kelly et al., 2019).

Smartphones and related devices can help encourage engagement with health-care services in the first instance (Guy et al., 2012). Therefore, systems that are developed collaboratively will be trusted, support existing expectations and ensure that the values of health-care professionals are incorporated at each stage (Mistry, 2019). While new frameworks have been proposed to standardise the evaluation of health apps (Henson et al., 2019), a form of self-certification involving patient and clinician use that feeds back into app development may help improve designs in the future (Rodriguez-Villa and Torous, 2019). This integration and standardisation may also be key to tackling the plethora of ethical challenges surrounding digital health (Nebeker, Torous and Ellis, 2019) and delivering better interventions, which are typically most effective when paired with follow-up (Tomlinson et al., 2013). The field can then move further away from hype and closer towards a realistic model in the future (Car et al., 2019).

Conversely, many technological approaches may not help patients who are most at risk of non-adherence (Gross et al., 2019) and some areas of health are, for the present time, going to remain in the analogue domain, and it is important to appreciate such limitations. For example, video consultations can be provided via smartphones, but these may only be suitable for problems that do not require physical examination (Hammersley et al., 2019). Despite video-conferencing technology being around for some time, this has not entered the mainstream (at least not in the United Kingdom) with telephone consultations remaining more common. A recent comparison observed that the content and length of video consultations were similar to those conducted via telephone, and both were less information rich than traditional face-to-face consultations. While patients really liked video consultations, technical problems were common and infrastructure issues would need to be addressed before this could become a mainstream approach (Hammersley et al., 2019). However, the ability to capture patient behaviour that includes interactions with clinicians across a variety of contexts provides many new exciting avenues for future research.

2.6   Conclusion

Smartphones and related devices are starting to decode complex patterns of behaviour, feelings and context, but they can also help tailor interventions that are, in theory, always available. Exercise, for example, could be tailored based on a person's mood, the weather outside and previous activity levels. Many of these more complex interventions are already being tested, but we are probably only at the beginning as health psychology starts to apply AA methods with increasing regularity.

While prescribing smartphone apps is perhaps some way off (Segui et al., 2018), it is difficult to see why smartphones as a method will not be the preferred option for future research within health psychology because they remain readily available and are used frequently by the majority of the general population (Wilcockson, Ellis and Shaw, 2018). There is no doubt that basic psychological research has much to gain from the ability to track and monitor a variety of health metrics via smartphones. Applied research agendas are less concrete on how they might develop. Smartphone technology has certainly extended the horizon for monitoring and tailoring treatment. At the same time, lines between consumer technology and medical devices begin to blur. It is now possible for smartphones and wearable devices to monitor a range of medical risk factors (Figure 2.1). Potentially, these systems could give patients direct access to personal analytics that can contribute to long-term health, facilitate preventative care and aid in the management of ongoing illness (Piwek et al., 2016b).[8] They can also act as a hub for care provision for patients, practitioners and health-care systems.

Some will continue to point towards a potential utopia that can transform all aspects of health, providing digital and social inclusion. Conversely, the digital landscape may become a dystopia that is characterised by division and exclusion. The World Health Organization has acknowledged that the use of digital technologies provides new opportunities to improve people's health, but there are significant challenges ahead. This will include demonstrating their ability to be integrated into existing health systems and deliver long-term improvements that go beyond traditional methods. The majority of commercial apps, for example, do not provide evidence to support their claims or explain the chances of false positives (Larsen et al., 2019; Leigh and Flatt, 2015; Ryan, 2019). Ensuring that patients can socially engage with clinicians, support networks or feedback systems appears to be one of the few consistent markers of success at least in terms of apps that aim to help with depression and anxiety; however, equivalent effects might also be achieved with various other communication avenues tied to a smartphone (e.g., making a phone call or sending a text message). Another unifying feature, therefore, is the lack of investment concerning formative research and evaluation (or agreement) regarding specific apps' efficiency (Jewkes and Dartnall, 2019; Oikonomidi et al., 2019).

Establishing how metrics derived from smartphone sensing (e.g., physical activity and sociability) map onto other health outcomes (e.g., doctors' appointments, health screening) will help drive further integration. Low levels of sociability, for example, are often associated with a lack of physical activity and irregular sleep. Understanding how these behaviours individually or collectively affect well-being and, in turn, reduce engagement with health-related services is a research challenge that is on paper methodologically possible (Cohen, 2004; Shankar et al., 2011). The identification of critical thresholds for these behaviours may be fundamental to developing successful personalised interventions for public health.

The growth of technology continues to outstrip the evidence base in all global settings. Similarly, many people studying the impacts of such technology are, from a research perspective, completely detached from groups that are likely to use any intervention. If basic research is not

---

[8] The fact that health-related functionality is available at such a scale is frequently overlooked by research that fixates on the negative aspects of smartphones (see Chapter 1).

completed at all and applied research fails to demonstrate how 'big data' approaches can fundamentally change health care, the limited funding available will be squandered.

Useful Resources and Further Reading

Blandford, A., Gibbs, J., Newhouse, N., Perski, O., Singh, A., & Murray, E. (2018). Seven lessons for interdisciplinary research on interactive digital health interventions. *Digital Health*, *4*, 2055207618770325.
Reveals the parallels between developing and testing digital health interventions across different disciplines. Also provides guidance for future research.
Piwek, L., Ellis, D. A., Andrews, S., & Joinson, A. (2016). The rise of consumer health wearables: Promises and barriers. *PLOS MEDICINE*, *13*(2), e1001953.
A short article that considers whether wearable technology can become a valuable asset for health care. Despite considerable research in this area, many of the arguments remain equally as valid today.

CHAPTER 3

Social Interaction and Interpersonal Relationships

Long before mobile technology facilitated remote communication, psychological science concluded that people have an intimate desire to connect with others. This need to affiliate drives people to form positive and lasting personal relationships in online and offline domains (Hogg and Vaughan, 2005; Nadkarni and Hofmann, 2012). Several avenues of research have further confirmed that sociability and the subsequent generation of interpersonal relationships remain inherently linked to emotional well-being (Cheek and Buss, 1981). For example, social interaction across the day, in some instances, appears to improve cognitive function more than physical activity (Bielak, Mogle and Sliwinski, 2017), although there is some debate regarding the importance of this link (Cohen, 2004). While it is generally accepted that social relationships and affiliation have a positive impact on health, the exact mechanisms are less clear (Berkman et al., 2000). Regardless, long-term social separation has a negative impact on general health and well-being, particularly when this occurs earlier in life or following the death of a close partner (Holt-Lunstad et al., 2015; Stroebe et al., 1992). Considering more immediate effects, social rejection activates portions of the brain associated with physical pain (Eisenberger, Lieberman and Williams, 2003).

Early virtual communities in the 1980s allowed people to chat with groups that had common interests (Rheingold, 1993). Graphical web browsers followed in the mid 1990s. Both developments opened up new opportunities for communication between members of a community with common interests via the internet. Today, there is little doubt that the internet has completely changed how people develop new relationships and join groups. The rapid adoption of smartphones (World Bank Group, 2015) has led to a second wave of dating apps, including Tinder and Grindr.

Smartphones therefore go beyond web-based systems because they allow for location awareness where potential new relationships are triangulated to an individual's location. However, even for those who are not physically near other people, smartphones offer a unique advantage by providing instant and constant membership with a community (Wei and Lo, 2006). Their availability also means that relationships can be started, developed and ended at any time. This has transformed social norms as more people than ever use these apps to meet new people (Smith and Anderson, 2016). A variety of instant messaging (IM) systems have, in turn, become the default method of communication. This allows for the real-time exchange of text, images and video and reportedly accounts for 75 per cent of mobile traffic (Juniper Research, 2014). This also changes society. For example, many pubs and clubs have closed in the United Kingdom as young people are already well connected before leaving the home (Connolly, 2015).

Following individual and societal changes, many psychologists have started to question whether smartphones impede, enhance or have no effect on social interactions and relationship formation. Similar to issues around general smartphone usage, many investigations tend to focus on the idea that smartphones are subtracting components of what it means to be a socially productive human being. This has to be squared against the fact that smartphones were designed to facilitate social interaction and have become a facilitator and generator of social relationships. It would also appear at the outset that smartphones provide many opportunities to reduce social isolation, especially for those who are unable or less willing to engage with traditional face-to-face (F2F) interactions. Irrespective of the communication platform, digital traces can provide a record of how new relationships begin and develop over time.

Therefore, this chapter first considers how smartphones are changing the way we communicate and form new relationships. A second strand will focus on how new methodologies are improving our current understanding of sociability in the digital age, which can also reveal social processes associated with F2F and computer-mediated communication. This often considers a participant's own experience or data derived directly from apps themselves (Davidson, Joinson and Jones, 2018). While clear differences exist between computer-mediated systems and F2F interaction (Tidwell and Walther, 2002), people are often able to regulate these two forms of communication that dominate occupational and personal relationships.

3.1   Do Smartphones Impede Social Interaction?

As technology continues to dramatically reshape the landscape of social behaviours and the nature of social interactions, psychological science has a duty to evaluate or anticipate changes (Davidson and Ellis, 2019).

Smartphones specifically are certainly providing new contexts (Hunter et al., 2018), but whether they are changing social processes is another question entirely. Psychological research typically considers how smartphones disrupt F2F communication. For example, Kushlev et al. (2019b) asked pairs of college students to arrive at a small waiting room with or without their smartphones. Students were given no other instructions but were unknowingly filmed. Researchers then coded videos and measured how often participants smiled. The results demonstrated that people with smartphones smiled less than those without them. Similar results were previously reported by the same authors suggesting that phone use makes social interactions less enjoyable (Dwyer, Kushlev and Dunn, 2018). The mere presence of devices, at least amongst strangers, also appears to be more impactful when individuals are discussing topics of personal importance (Przybylski and Weinstein, 2013). Digging deeper, several studies have suggested that phones interfere with conversation and reduce the quality of social interactions (Rotondi, Stanca and Tomasuolo, 2017). Other research has demonstrated that phone use is specifically associated with reduced interaction quality with friends (Misra et al., 2016) and lower relationship satisfaction with a romantic partner (Roberts and David, 2016). For example, a stranger who checks their phone during a short conversation is viewed more negatively as they were rated as less polite and less attentive. The authors argue that this is due to the violation of conversational norms (Abeele, Antheunis and Schouten, 2016).

Researchers have started to provide their own definitions to describe new behaviours that may be considered socially undesirable, but which are slowly becoming socially acceptable. Phubbing, for instance, is the act of snubbing others in social situations and focusing on a smartphone instead (Haigh, 2015). Drawing from a survey among 145 adults, Roberts and David (2016) observed that individuals who are phubbed feel socially excluded. Of course, while the initial connotations are negative, such behaviour may simply reflect aspects of natural social interaction or relationship satisfaction (Chotpitayasunondh and Douglas, 2016; Roberts and David, 2016).

Similar concerns have been raised concerning the negative impact of smartphones on caregivers. One short observational study found that phone use affected the responsiveness of parents to their children (Abels et al., 2018). The authors here argue that this could have implications for child development. Another study asked parents to use their phones as much or as little as possible while visiting a museum with their children (Kushlev and Dunn, 2019). Frequent phone use in this environment led parents to feel more distracted, which impaired feelings of social connection when spending time with their children. A second diary study found that smartphones can distract parents when spending time with their children. The same authors go as far to suggest that internet technologies may have some negative impact on the fabric of social life. In recent years, a theoretical mechanism has been proposed to explain these potential negative effects on well-being during F2F social interactions. The pathways to harm in this instance focus on how attention is drawn away from friends and family in F2F contexts and on how smartphones may supplant such interactions altogether (Kushlev et al., 2019a). For example, participants who report a mix of any online communication and F2F socialising in the same episode have also reported feeling less connected than when only engaging with F2F interaction (Kushlev and Heintzelman, 2018).

As outlined previously, the above has to be placed in the context of why communication devices are popular. Smartphones allow people to network and organise social and occupational identities across multiple apps with different motivators. Smartphones may, in turn, provide new social avenues that improve well-being and aid relaxation. For example, Hunter and colleagues propose that smartphones can help reduce the negative psychological and physiological impacts following social exclusion (Hunter et al., 2018).

In one experiment, participants were randomised to (1) having their phone present with use encouraged, (2) phone present with use restricted or (3) having no access to their phone. During the study, saliva samples of participants and self-report data were collected throughout to assess salivary alpha amylase (sAA), cortisol and feelings of exclusion. Salivary alpha amylase can increase in response to psychological stress through interactions with the autonomic nervous system, and it has been found to be a useful marker of activity in the autonomic nervous system. Similarly, more cortisol is produced when the body responds to stress. In this study, Hunter et al. (2018) observed that those in the restricted-phone condition showed a decrease in sAA after exclusion, while people in the no-phone condition showed a gradual increase. Phone users exhibited little change. They suggest that smartphones can act as a 'digital security blanket' (Hunter et al., 2018). When an environment is unpleasant, smartphone use may reduce the need to engage with unfriendly people. Alternatively, a smartphone may provide benefits when facing social exclusion in an offline context.

3.1.1   Limitations and Future Research

Several key caveats to the research documented previously are worthy of further discussion. First, there are many alternative explanations as to why smartphones might improve or harm social interaction. As with phubbing, their use may simply indicate boredom with an existing connection or being lured away with the possibility of new connections that are more interesting (Al-Saggaf, MacCulloch and Wiener, 2019; Chen and Li, 2017). Similarly, while one might argue that people find social interactions less enjoyable and meaningful when using a smartphone, these effects are likely to replicate with any other solitary distraction or activity (e.g., a good book). Experimental studies fail to include any control to allow for direct comparisons. In other words, how unique these findings are to smartphone technology remains unknown. While smartphones are a unique distractor in that they provide multiple diversions (e.g., Dwyer, Kushlev and Dunn, 2018), current evidence does not exclude the notion that they aid the natural ebb and flow of everyday conversation.

Second, while much of the literature focuses on the notion that smart-phones are removing F2F interaction at the expense of online activities, existing studies do not measure what people were using their smartphone for while phubbing or ignoring a new social situation completely. The net gains or harms will depend on how people use their device. For example, using Facebook to actively engage with friends is different when compared to scrolling passively through others posts (Verduyn et al., 2017). Similarly, estimated time spent using image-based platforms like Instagram and Snapchat (but not text-based platforms like Twitter) is associated with decreased loneliness (Pittman and Reich, 2016). On the other hand, those who broadcast content report increased loneliness (Yang, 2016). It remains probable that smartphones encourage more meaningful social interactions by providing a way to interact with people who share similar interests and, in turn, increase social capital (Piwek and Joinson, 2016). In addition, many other types of use (e.g., playing games like Pokémon Go) will generate new social interactions in less direct ways. Future research will need to provide a more refined level of detail given the variety of platforms that can provide social interaction.

Third, the context of any social interaction, rather than being better or worse, may simply provide a different experience. For example, rather than social interaction declining, online interaction may simply be a form of rehearsal (Ditchfield, 2019). Such differences appear even at the very early stages of a new social interaction as illustrated by Wall et al. (2013), who tested if 'rich' contexts led to more accurate personality judgments than information from 'lean' contexts. In a short experiment, pairs of strangers made judgments about one another's personalities after interacting in one of three increasingly rich contexts: internet 'chat', telephone or F2F.

Accuracy was assessed by correlating participants' judgments with a measure of targets' personalities that averaged self and informant ratings. While visible traits of extraversion and conscientiousness were judged more accurately than the less visible traits of neuroticism and openness, judgment accuracy also depended on context. Judgments of extraversion and neuroticism improved as context richness increased (i.e., from internet 'chat' to face-to-face), whereas judgments of conscientiousness and openness improved as context richness decreased (i.e., from face-to-face to internet 'chat'). These findings suggest that context richness shapes not only the availability of personality cues but also the relevance of cues in any given context (Figure 3.1).

Finally, research concerning how smartphones allow people to manage their social availability appears to be largely absent. For example, privacy regulation argues that a person's affiliative behaviour is an outcome of their desire to be more or less accessible and open to others (Altman, 1975, 1993). Thus, the need to affiliate is not based around the need to constantly interact with others. Privacy regulation theory therefore aims to account for changes in affiliative behaviour and the regulation of physical distance between people. However, like many other habitual behaviours (e.g., smartphone usage), time spent actively socialising with other people (e.g., talking to others) is very stable over several weeks (Mehl and Pennebaker, 2003). Different social behaviours like text messaging and F2F conversation appear to be correlated to some extent when measured objectively. People who spent a lot of time communicating via text also spent more time talking to others and making more phone calls (Harari et al., 2019).

Explanations for such consistency consider the social affiliation model (O'Connor and Rosenblood, 1996). This focuses on homeostasis. Just as people regulate a variety of behaviours (e.g., sleep), we also control the level of contact with others, keeping it both stable and close to a desired level. In a study methodology that was many years ahead of its time, O'Connor and Rosenblood provided portable beepers to students for a period of four days. These beepers would sound at intermittent intervals, but roughly every hour. At this point, participants were asked to write down their *actual level* of contact: for example, (a) completely alone, (b) in the company of others but without social interaction or (c) in the company of others and engaging with social interaction. Participants were also asked if they wanted to be alone or not, which was a measure of *desired level* of contact. Most participants reported interacting with others at a desired rate across the four-day period and had therefore been successful in regulating their social behaviour. Today, option (a) might be rarely selected because

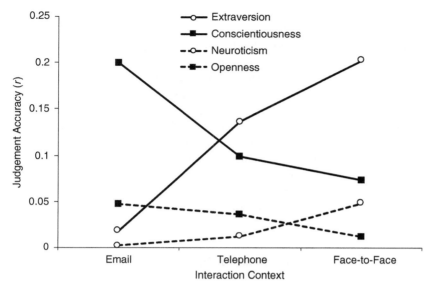

Figure 3.1 Interactant judgment accuracy as a function of interaction context
and personality trait following a short social interaction (Wall et al., 2013)
Note: Overall, the main implication of these findings is that information-rich
contexts are not always preferential when judging personality. It appears that cues
relevant to judging traits such as conscientiousness and openness may become
'washed out' by the paralinguistic and non-verbal cues that form a part of information-rich contexts. This may be explained using the realistic accuracy model (RAM)
of personality judgment (Funder, 1999, 2012). According to RAM, the accuracy of
personality judgments is determined by the degree to which cues are available to the
judge, providing that such cues are both relevant to the judgment being made and
detected and used appropriately by the judge. When relevance, detection and
utilisation are held constant, RAM predicts that greater availability of information
will lead to more accurate personality judgments. However, as RAM would predict,
and our data suggests, it is possible for these four stages to interact. This provides
a starting point for future research that could longitudinally investigate how relationships develop across online and offline contexts.
Wall, H. J., Taylor, P. J., Dixon, J., Conchie, S. M., & Ellis, D. A. (2013). Rich
contexts do not always enrich the accuracy of personality judgments. *Journal of
Experimental Social Psychology, 49*(6), 1190–1195.

one might question if anyone with a smartphone is genuinely ever completely alone! However, it is possible to regulate social interactions by
modifying smartphone apps, notifications and subsequent engagement.
Answering this specific question in relation to smartphone use and social
interaction would involve the use of objective measures in combination
with self-report methods used by O'Connor and Rosenblood (1996). It

could also involve the innovative use of sensors discussed later in this chapter. There remains huge potential to better understand how people regulate such interactions in the digital age.

People enjoy the personal connections smartphones deliver and will continue to go to great lengths to connect with others (Emanuel et al., 2015). Current work appears to ignore many alternative explanations and previous evidence that suggests people are perfectly able to regulate other social behaviours. Similar to issues surrounding overall usage discussed in Chapter 1, these studies tell us very little about how smartphones are triangulating, displacing or encouraging F2F social interaction at the level of individual relationships. However, another avenue of research has started to consider if long-term relationships that develop from early online interactions are more or less successful than traditional F2F meetings.

3.2   Long-Term Relationships: Same But Different

3.2.1   Same

> We theorize that social media specifically – and time spent online generally – is not 'bad' per se for forming social connections. Rather, it is simply not well-suited to forming deep and meaningful connections.
>
> (Sbarra et al., 2019, p. 604)

Sbarra et al. (2019) have made the case for an 'evolutionary mismatch' when it comes to smartphones and close relationships. These mismatches are defined as situations when human adaptations that emerged to foster reproductive and inclusive fitness in ancestral environments become maladaptive in a new context. For example, cravings to eat sweet-tasting food that was not readily available in an ancestral environment misfires in a contemporary environment where sugar-enhanced foods are readily available (Brownell and Horgen, 2004). This has helped generate a global obesity epidemic. When it comes to smartphones and close relationships, they argue that smartphones disrupt a variety of processes linked with human bonding. This includes an increase in distractions associated with technology, which interferes with F2F communication and a reduction of intimacy.[1] However, many of the concerns outlined

---

[1] The evolutionary mismatch hypothesis assumes that smartphones disrupt cognitive functioning and relationship processes, which has a negative impact on well-being (see Chapters 1 and 5).

by the evolutionary mismatch hypothesis are based on very weak empirical evidence. Indeed, one could argue the very opposite. Specifically, relationship formation via smartphones has many evolutionary advantages as the affordances provided by the technology allow for the rapid formation of close, intimate relationships that can quickly move offline (Davidson et al., 2018). These advantages also extend to group co-operation on a larger scale with virtual communities often founded on common interests or goals. Recent examples include the open science movement. Despite efforts of some states to control technology, collective group action, for example, has also become possible where this would have previously been dangerous in F2F contexts (Liu, 2017). Similarly, as the number of people connected to online dating platforms has increased, the number of potential partners has also increased accordingly.

Epidemiological evidence supports the notion that being in a positive long-term relationship (including marriage) is associated with well-being and has a protective effect (DeMaris, 2018). However, the variety of partner options may lead to a lack of commitment (Paul, 2014) or even an increase in objectification (Davidson et al., 2018). If developing new connections via smartphones makes for weaker relationships because they have altered the romantic acquaintance processes, then this might provide sensible evidence for an evolutionary mismatch.

Using data from How Couples Meet and Stay Together (HCMST) surveys, Rosenfeld, Thomas and Hausen (2019) demonstrated that meeting partners online has now displaced all other ways of meeting. Meeting through friends has been declining since 1995. The rise of the internet fuelled the first leap of this movement in the early 2000s. Smartphones have driven a second wave in the previous decade. Separate analyses from the same authors show that meeting through phone apps specifically was responsible for at least half of the growth in meeting online from 2010 to 2017.

The ease at which new relationships can be formed may therefore lead to a decrease in marriage rates and an increase in divorce (Paul, 2014). However, this relationship only holds for rural areas. In large metropolitan areas, internet access correlates with increases in the married population and decreases in those who are divorced or separated populations. This rise in the married population in urban areas is derived from both an increase in initial uptake of marriage and an increase in re-matching of divorcees in secondary marriage markets (Murray, 2019). Of course, the causal effect here is challenging in that relationship dissatisfaction may simply motivate the use of new digital services that provide opportunities to leave. However, research with longitudinal follow-ups after HCMST 2009 demonstrated that neither breakup rates nor relationship quality was influenced by how couples actually met (Rosenfeld, 2017; Rosenfeld and Thomas, 2012). Once couples are in a relationship, how they met does not determine relationship quality or longevity. Longitudinal evidence specifically demonstrates that when relationships begin online they are no more or less likely to fail. Over and above this, there is no evidence that loneliness is increasing worldwide (Hawkley et al., 2019; Trzesniewski and Donnellan, 2010).[2]

This evidence appears to contradict the notion of an evolutionary mismatch alluded to previously. Indeed, beyond the number of potential partners, contact theory would support the notion that the processes involved with multifaceted cross-group interaction will provide many benefits that include improving attitudes towards outgroups. Such interactions may also assist with problem-solving, increasing cognitive flexibility and fostering creativity (Hodson et al., 2018). Even without social interaction, experiential diversity is associated with improved cognitive and affective functioning (Heller et al., 2020; Van Praag, Kempermann and Gage, 2000). Researchers who suggest the opposite for smartphone interactions and subsequent relationships may wish to draw on guidance from related areas of psychology regarding what a suitable programme of research might look like (Kazdin, 2007). Specifically, there must first be a plausible and coherent explanation for why and how a causal pathway operates in the first instance before considering in detail how variables should be operationalised. Only then can empirical evidence, which may include suitable observational data, confirm causal relationships between smartphone use and social ties (Rohrer, 2018).

3.2.2   *Different*

While long-term outcomes for relationships appear to be similar, research that considers the key differences between social processes in different contexts suggests a more productive pathway forward. However, this also struggles to keep pace with technological developments. Historical research that sought to explain communication technology's impact on social relations observed that it is more likely to modify the efficiency of interactions rather than change the social circle (Katz, 1997). For example, the arrival of landline telephones made it easier for people to stay in touch with relatives who were further away, but it did not change who interacted

---

[2] https://ourworldindata.org/loneliness-epidemic

with whom. Most telephone calls were made to people one already knew (Fischer, 1994). In contrast and unlike previous technologies that reinforced F2F social networks, which were theorised as being optimal for mate selection, digital dating may have displaced friends and family from their former roles as key intermediaries (Finkel et al., 2012).

Today, the speed of intimacy can be rapid in an online context where conversations might continue long after a single date or F2F interaction. Finkel et al. (2012) focused on two key differences: the compatibility matching process and the romantic acquaintance process. Compatibility matching was often completed by friends who would associate with specific individuals over time. In an online context, this is entirely at the mercy of those online who interact with a specific service or the matching algorithm. Similarly, the romantic acquaintance process is based on more than F2F first impressions, but instead can rely on the disclosure of other data (e.g., a biography and demographic details).

Computer-mediated communication was previously characterised as leading to higher levels of self-disclosure compared to F2F dyads. Indeed, early incarnations of internet communication led to visual anonymity. For example, those with lower self-esteem are more likely to use a computer-mediated form of communication compared to those with higher self-esteem who will select face-to-face as a preferred option. Joinson (2004) also provided participants with rates of rejection for a specific scenario (e.g., asking for a pay rise). A greater chance of rejection also led to email being preferred to F2F communication. The choice of social interaction may therefore be motivated by a desire to self-protect, indicating that shy people in particular may benefit from computer-based communication more generally (Scharlott and Christ, 1995).

Biographies on dating profiles, specifically, allow people to control their self-presentation. However, smartphone apps that facilitate the development of new relationships do not align with early versions of internet dating. These are now more socially gregarious experiences. People have, for instance, always chosen photos in which they appear most attractive (Mikkola et al., 2008); however, 33 per cent of dating profile photographs were inaccurate from an independent judge's perspective. Photographs posted by women were likely to be less accurate than men's (e.g., the photograph is old or digitally manipulated) (Hancock, Toma and Ellison, 2007). These deceptions, however, may have wavered in recent years as smartphone apps aim to kick-start F2F interactions quickly. Tyson et al. (2016) observed that due to women being more concerned about deception online, the more profile photos the male's profile has, the more comfortable she will be pursuing them as a potential partner. Similarly, Ramirez et al. (2014) and Ramirez and Zhang (2007) suggest that online daters could benefit from meeting sooner rather than later.

The choice of communication channel can be varied further based on an individual or group's preference, including interpersonal risk (Piwek and Joinson, 2016). For example, recent forms of communication (e.g., Snapchat) involve the sharing of content that is then only available for a short period of time. In addition, and unlike other services, Snapchat will only work via a smartphone. As a result, some have suggested that Snapchat can lower individual inhibitions because messages, photos and videos are less permanent (Roesner, Gill and Kohno, 2014). However, these decisions can also be dependent on a variety of other motivators depending on the current state of the relationship (Li-Barber, 2012). For example, breaking up or ending a relationship can be challenging in some scenarios because online profiles may or may not map onto the lived experience of a relationship (Hogan, 2018). Avoidance is commonly reported in the early stage of any online breakup (Hogan, 2018), but many options are available, from blocking, to changing statuses, to 'ghosting' (offering no response). These continue to shift social norms on what becomes appropriate (Gershon, 2010).

In a variety of ways, digital communication has come full circle following the increase in smartphone adoption. It has transformed from a niche set of virtual communities to a variety of fully featured systems that encapsulate the majority of occupational and social organisations. Catfishing is still possible, but smartphones now provide a socially acceptable way to meet people and build new relationships. It is also worth noting that many traditional theories concerning first impressions, relationship formation and development map onto how people experience new digital platforms (Baxter, 1982). This therefore provides new avenues for research as they apply to understanding social processes in the twenty-first century. In response, more work is starting to focus on describing patterns of social behaviour. Such research is valuable for psychological science as a whole, but remains essential for those who want to better understand the impact of technology on social interaction and relationship development.

3.3   Automatic Tracking of Social Behaviour

Smartphones have become personalised social hubs and a growing body of work has started to consider a participant's own experience or data derived directly from apps themselves (Davidson et al., 2018). Several new advances are also helping researchers track social behaviour beyond the device itself, and it is now possible to explore real-world social interaction using a variety of on-board smartphone sensors, which can also reveal group dynamics (Piwek, Ellis and Andrews, 2016). This has sometimes been referred to as Social fMRI,[3] whereby researchers have been able to quantify social mechanisms in the real world (Aharony et al., 2011). Beyond the laboratory, we know less about differences in socialising behaviour, which is now multifaceted and no longer limited to phone calls and F2F communication. It also speaks to concerns regarding the time spent socialising online versus face-to-face, which aligns with calls to advance descriptive research concerning everyday behaviours (Baumeister, Vohs and Funder, 2007).

3.3.1   *Digital Dating Metrics*

Data from smartphone apps and other digital services often confirms identical patterns to what also drives relationship formation in F2F contexts. For example, large studies of online dating confirm that older men prefer younger women, and women prefer older men. It has also been observed that the most desirable men for women are 'white, athletic or thin, tall, well educated, drinkers, and nonsmokers' (Kreager et al., 2014, p. 396). Several researchers have also observed that physical appearance exceeds many other attributes when it comes to predicting overall profile attractiveness and deciding who to contact (Fiore et al., 2008; Whitty, 2011). At the first F2F meeting, Whitty (2007) reports that online daters are most concerned with what their date looks like and how they behave. As one might expect, daters interpret the absence of photos negatively and Tyson and colleagues (2016), specifically on Tinder, found that the number of matches on a female profile increases by 37 per cent when you increase the number of profile photos from one to three, and this effect is even higher on men's profiles. However, while people believe they will like partners more when they know them better and have more information about them, this is not always consistent when additional information is actually provided (Norton, Frost and Ariely, 2007). For example, men prefer short biographies whereas women preferred longer profiles for men (Davidson et al., 2018). In addition, if men have a postgraduate degree, this is seen as a desirable attribute; however, women with postgraduate degrees

---

[3] Social Functional Mechanism design and Relationship Imaging (Social fMRI). Like traditional fMRI, which allows researchers to view functional activity of the brain, Social fMRI allows behavioural scientists to see what was previously invisible.

are not seen as attractive by men with similar education levels (Kreager et al., 2014).

Many researchers have tested the 'similarity-attraction' hypothesis, suggesting that people are most attracted to individuals who are similar to themselves. Actual and perceived similarity have repeatedly been found to have a positive impact on attraction (Montoya, Horton and Kirchner, 2008). Fiore and Donath (2005) performed an analysis involving 65,000 users and showed that users sought people like themselves much more often than chance would predict, which provides corroboration of the similarity-attraction principle. Opposites do not attract in the short term. However, Wetzel and Insko (1982) previously introduced a distinction between one's ideal self and one's actual self. They demonstrated that when these components are separated, similarity to the ideal self can be seen to exert a major influence on attraction, but similarity to the actual self was an inconsistent influence. Theoretically, attraction is driven by similarity to the ideal self because this is the valued or desired state of affairs (Herbst et al., 2003). For example, online daters regarded as desirable message other desirable users, which implies some support for homophily (Kreager et al., 2014). Aligning with the actual/ideal self, this also supports the notion of online daters seeking to find partners more desirable than themselves.

When it comes to starting the conversation, initial contacts came from men in comparison to women (Fiore et al., 2010). Schöndienst and Dang-Xuan (2011) studied the linguistic content of 167,276 initial contact messages. Their findings suggest that the most successful initial contacts are those which contain a significant amount of self-disclosure and avoid showing negative attributes (e.g., depressive symptoms) and instead focus attention on the recipient. Men are, in fact, more likely to respond to initial messages that contain words referring to sexual processes. However, this would jeopardise the likelihood of a women replying if this is referred to in any response they send (Schöndienst and Dang-Xuan, 2011).

Where it has been difficult to source information directly from apps, researchers have had to rely on innovative ways to retrieve data based on the last previous communication (e.g., Snapchat). For example, Piwek and Joinson (2016) used a memory sampling method to understand the very last image or video each participant sent or received. They observed that users mainly share 'selfies', or embed text and 'doodles' with photos. Snapchat was used mostly at home and primarily for communication with close friends and family as an 'easier and funnier' alternative to other messaging services. These communication methods may be specific to the platform as Snapchat is used as a playful way to enhance bonding amongst people who have existing F2F connections (Piwek and Joinson, 2016).

3.3.2   *Sensing Social Behaviours*

Even before smartphones, call records from mobile operators have been used to understand local and global structures of large communication networks. Onnela et al. (2007) explored eighteen weeks of call records from over 17 million users. The length and repetitive nature of calls provided clues about the social importance of a contact. A single call was less meaningful, whereas multiple calls to the same number of a long duration provided a marker for a friend, family or occupational relationships. Call data has also been used specifically by psychologists to explore how women selectively avoid male kin (fathers) during periods of peak fertility. Lieberman, Pillsworth and Haselton (2011) linked call records with fertility cycles. Their results might be interpreted as showing that women simply prefer contact with their mothers rather than actively avoid fathers; however, the authors caution against such an interpretation as while women who reported being close to their mother increased their number and duration of calls, closeness was not associated with the reduction of calling behaviour to fathers. In addition, no correlations were observed to suggest that talking more frequently with mothers during periods of peak fertility left less time to talk to fathers. In recent years this line of research has combined cellular tower location data with call and text-messaging logs. Eagle, de Montjoye and Bettencourt (2009) examined four years of mobile data from 1.4 million individuals to demonstrate that urban and rural communities differ not only in their personal network topologies but also in terms of how they travel.

Other research has focused on F2F interaction in isolation using smartphone sensors to infer proximity. For example, a variety of designs have combined longitudinal data that includes call logs, Bluetooth devices in proximity, cell-tower IDs, application usage and phone status. Some have demonstrated that it is possible to accurately infer 95 per cent of friendships based on the location and physical proximity patterns between two dyads (Eagle, Pentland and Lazer, 2009). Predictive analytic work from Do and Gatica-Perez (2014) used similar data to predict the next location and which application he/she would use. Specific app usage (including social apps) is highly dependent on contextual variables like time of day, and day of the week (Shepard et al., 2011).

More recent work has focused on the habitual nature of everyday life, which in many ways mirrors the similarities of technology usage itself (Wilcockson, Ellis and Shaw, 2018). While many people seek spontaneity throughout life, our daily mobility (and social interactions as a consequence) is remarkably consistent (González, Hidalgo and Barabási, 2008). De Montjoye et al. (2013) examined 15 months of location data from 1.5 million individuals. They observed that human mobility traces are unique but consistent. When the location of an individual is provided at hourly intervals, only four spatiotemporal points were enough to uniquely identify 95 per cent of individuals in the data set. Osmani et al. (2014) focused on proximity detection using a system that recorded overlaps of data using Bluetooth and Wi-Fi hotspots. These methods can reveal temporal patterns that occur across online and offline social networks. Similar research has also been used to examine crowd density estimation at sporting events and passenger journeys in public transport and to infer relationships (Stopczynski et al., 2014). However, one limitation of this approach concerns under- or over-estimating the number of people around the user. Specifically, it can be difficult to identify people from devices. People who carry both a phone and laptop that transmit these signals will result in over-estimates of the number of co-present people (Harari et al., 2017a). These methods also cannot confirm whether any form of social interaction actually occurred.

Data-intensive approaches with fewer participants living in small communities have collated multiple streams of personal data, including financial transactions, location, movement, proximity and communication activities alongside the daily recording of mood. This has started to challenge existing theory concerning positive associations between social interaction patterns and wealth (Eagle, Macy and Claxton, 2010). Researchers tend to agree that diverse social relationships provide more information and benefits that are maintained long term (Page, 2008). For example, Granovetter's weak tie theory (1973) and Burt's theory of structural holes (2003) would support this proposition. Aharony et al. (2011) examined, at an individual level, relationships between one's financial status (household income) and their interaction diversity by taking survey data and phone sensor data into consideration. There were considerable income changes among participants, and if socially successful individuals are deprived of their incomes, they should continue to keep their diverse interaction behaviour. However, social diversity patterns only correlated with current income, thus their findings suggest the opposite – individuals lose their social diversity when their financial status gets worse and gain social diversity when it improves.

They hypothesise that a good financial status ensures people feel secure in exploring new social potential (Aharony et al., 2011). Other findings from the same team demonstrated that people who spend more time with each other in F2F contexts share common apps. However, this effect was not driven by self-perceived friendship ties (Aharony et al., 2011). While much of the research aims to carefully map the interconnections of people and society, it remains exploratory and there is still a need for further experimentation. However, many of these results demonstrate how these designs could provide new perspectives to long-term debates in social psychology.

The quantities of data collected in these designs create a challenging environment for psychologists, and it is only in the last few years that social scientists have started to devise similar studies that also aim to improve our understanding of everyday social behaviour. One study by Harari et al. (2017b) explored a variety of student behaviours over a 10-week academic term. This relied on a smartphone sensing application to objectively measure students' naturally occurring activity and sociability behaviours. Specifically, the StudentLife application captured activity from the accelerometer and duration of ambient conversation from the microphone sensor (Wang et al., 2014). The content of conversations was never recorded, and similar to other designs the data relied on classifiers derived from previous work to determine if someone was around conversation or not. They were also able to explore between-person variability, stability from day to day and relationships between different socialising tendencies. This allowed the researchers to provide a descriptive account of young adults' tendency to engage in different forms of communication throughout the day. The results demonstrated that in a small cohort of students, activity and social durations decreased across the first half of the term but sociability increased in the second half. However, generally speaking, behaviours were very stable, suggesting that, like smartphone usage, less data than one might expect is required to better understand everyday social experiences. This also produced some surprising results that are worthy of further investigation. For example, conversation behaviours were not associated with loneliness, but with a variety of other well-being outcomes including lower levels of perceived stress (Wang et al., 2014).

Finally, another study by Harari et al. (2019) considered social behaviours across four communication channels: conversations, phone calls, text messages, and the use of messaging and app usage behaviours. In young adults, daily social behaviours appear to be very different between individuals but consistent over time. However, this study drew inferences from multiple samples and this stability did vary somewhat, with app use and texting behaviours appearing more consistent than calling. Sample characteristics may have had an impact. Different social behaviours generally overlapped – conversation, calling and texting were positively related to each other, but these either showed no relationship or a negative association with other metrics (e.g., messaging app use was negatively correlated). Comparing levels of conversation to other studies, these were generally lower, but this could be due to the way in which ambient audio is recorded and classified by the smartphone. Wearable recorders used in previous research will inevitably be more accurate because they are not likely to be stored in a bag or pocket (Mehl and Pennebaker, 2003). On the other hand, results may over-estimate app conversation because using Facebook does not guarantee an individual is engaged with active conversation.

This work is technically impressive and gets much closer to answering questions concerning how F2F interaction may be supplanted or encouraged by the use of smartphones. Building on this research, it should be possible to understand the psychological significance of these different behaviours individually and collectively. This would provide a much stronger foundation for future theorising, particularly if multiple devices could be tracked in combination with wearable audio recorders. However, the authors acknowledge that there are qualitative gaps. These unknowns are important and might include information on who people are talking to (e.g., friend vs stranger), the content and location. Specifically, linguistic markers are important throughout the development of relationships both offline and online. High language-style matching is an indicator of interpersonal and group mimicry and has been shown to influence psychological factors and behavioural outcomes. Based on the text people write or how they speak, higher levels of matching are important for positive online and offline relationship development (Ireland et al., 2011; Shaw et al., 2019). Combining quantitative with qualitative elements would get researchers closer to understanding how long-term relationships are developing. From a social processes point of view, this is the next big challenge where the field moves from descriptive metrics to theorising around how relationships and groups form, develop and succeed or fail.

3.4   Shape Shifting between Contexts

Previous discussions demonstrate that almost all relationship formation and development occur as a result of rapid switching between F2F communication and computer-mediated interfaces (e.g., online chat systems, social networking sites). This is especially prominent when developing new relationships. Whitty (2007) found that over half (approximately 57 per cent) of online dating site users who had arranged to meet face-to-face with a prospective partner had done so within one or two weeks of their initial contact with one another.

While similar methodologies can aid the analysis of both interactions, current research fails to show the dynamics of impression formation and relationship development across contexts within participants. How these patterns of behaviour affect group cohesion is also of vital importance for social science if we are to understand how individuals communicate and collaborate in the twenty-first century. This can include a variety of groups with very different aims. For example, Wikipedia is the result of a collective who have never met. Yet this interaction can also work against society – exemplified by groups such as Anonymous (internet hackers), who are able to function as a very effective, co-ordinated team. It is not clear whether that close network would continue if they ever met each other in person. However, this move towards digital communications has not removed the value that individuals and organisations place on F2F communication, and apps like Tinder are primarily aimed at ultimately leading to a F2F interaction.

This within-person interaction between online and offline communication is the next big methodological challenge. Early impression formation can be inferred from experimental approaches. For example, personality judgments change and become more accurate when moving from photographs to short social interactions as people attempt to reduce their uncertainty about others (Satchell, 2019; Sunnafrank, 1986). Longer term and in offline contexts, however, other processes including the effects of actual and perceived similarity appear to change depending on the stage of a relationship. Actual similarity can make a potential partner more attractive before a first meeting, but has less of an impact on attraction as relationships develop. The mere perception of being similar to a partner (even when false), however, appears to be important for attraction throughout relationship development (Montoya, Horton and Kirchner, 2008). The flow of information about a potential friend or partner can, in turn, impact how a relationship develops over time. More information will not always lead to more liking and can have a negative impact if this leads to increased levels of dissimilarity over time. On the other hand, if initial perceptions are confirmed then a relationship is more likely to blossom (Norton, Frost and Ariely, 2007). Therefore, people who remain attractive or liked in the long run are those who are perceived as similar with some actual affinities, but remain a bit ambiguous. This reveals the importance of perceptions rather than actual similarity. However, these results may not replicate as the smartphone has enabled people and groups to instantly jump between online and offline contexts. This applies to both new and existing relationships.

Future research will therefore require more advanced methods to capture F2F and computer-mediated communication over time. These could start to test or extend integrative models that have attempted to explain distinct relationship stages based around familiarity and attraction that occur in different contexts (Finkel et al., 2015). With a handful of exceptions (e.g., Davidson et al., 2019), very few studies have considered how behavioural roles evolve over time in a single online context and even less research has investigated switching between different social communication apps. It remains unclear, for example, what motivates people to move from Tinder to WhatsApp to face-to-face as a specific relationship progresses. No research has yet documented this switching experimentally.

Despite its importance, current models concerning the switch between CMC and F2F at an individual level have only considered this transition in a single direction using survey-based designs (e.g., McEwan and Zanolla, 2013). New lines of research could begin by considering the implicit formation of impressions and subsequent behaviour in dyadic interactions between two strangers. For example, participants might complete a standard personality measure before they meet in an online chat room (CMC) or in person (F2F) and, consistent with previous studies, engage in short discussions with their designated partner 'about anything they want' (Letzring, Wells and Funder, 2006; Markey and Wells, 2002). The order of interaction (CMC/F2F) will be reversed for half of these pairs. Finally, participants will rate the person they have just met on several dimensions after each interaction. Essentially, this combines elements of speed dating across online and F2F contexts.

During F2F interactions, participants could wear a Sociometric Sensor (Choudhury and Pentland, 2002) to measure a variety of individual and interpersonal behaviours during a social interaction, such as degree and direction of movement, proximity between agents and identity-tagged speech recordings. Previous research has used such data to accurately predict the outcomes of speed dating and job interviews. Alternatively, conversations could be recorded using a wearable audio recorder. A variety of textual and behavioural analyses could consider how impression formation at each time point changes (Tausczik and Pennebaker, 2010). Beyond experimentation, longitudinal methods could capture, for example, students as they develop new relationships at the start of term using apps, smartphone sensing methods and wearable devices, including radio frequency identification (RFID) tags or electronically activated recorders (EAR) (Elmer et al., 2019; Sun and Vazire, 2019). Combined, these would detect F2F interactions between the same individuals. Early descriptive work using EAR recorders already appears promising as researchers have quantified the temporal stability of language from individuals throughout the day (Lazarević et al., 2020). Additional analyses could also leverage existing university or organisational data that is routinely collected via apps. For example, enrolment and attendance networks could be combined with experimental or other longitudinal approaches to better understand the development of relationships over time.

3.5   Conclusion

Smartphones have augmented how we make, develop, maintain and end relationships. The mechanisms and empirical evidence to support the notion that smartphones are causing social harm, however, remains unconvincing and somewhat ignorant of those who have started to explore such interactions at an even greater level of detail. Theoretical development that is better aligned with epidemiological or other data intensive methods is therefore more welcome when compared with researcher-defined concepts that appear to be based on personal experience. Phubbing, specifically, is interpreted as rude by researchers themselves. However, what researchers in many areas fail to keep in mind is that their experience of technology will *not* be the same as others, especially their participants (Selwyn, 2011). This often leads to incorrect assumptions about new behaviours that have already become perfectly acceptable within a specific group that researchers are not exposed to (e.g., students outside the lecture theatre). This runs the risk of sending psychological science back into the realms of introspection.

It is difficult to square these concerns against smartphones acting as a social enabler. Current theorising also tends to ignore similarities between how people make decisions and build romantic relationships within and between different contexts. In the previous decade, smartphone apps that aim to generate new social connections encourage more F2F contact with a variety of purposes in mind. These have cultivated a huge market for individuals who wish to develop successful traditional (e.g., Tinder) or specific relationships (e.g., Feeld). Many of these relationships would be more difficult to develop and maintain without modern technology. On the other hand, relationships (and love) are messy and technology can be used to 'opt out' of traditional avenues altogether (Davidson et al., 2018).

Associated streams of user-generated data from those who do engage are now helping psychologists to study relationship formation and development; however, three overbearing questions remain. First, are smartphones specifically damaging F2F interactions, or are they providing a new way to escape boredom and extend social networks beyond our locality? Future experiments could, for example, reveal the mechanisms that underpin how smartphones can improve or damage social interaction and subsequent relationship formation. This is no easy task. For example, while well established, even understanding the psychological and behavioural mechanisms that connect close relationships with health remains equally challenging (Farrell and Stanton, 2019). Second, how do people regulate their affiliation in the digital age? This will involve gaining a better understanding of how people control and balance digital and offline interactions. Such a question is particularly pertinent as occupational and personal interactions occur within the same device (Allen and Shockley, 2009; Derks et al., 2016; Mazmanian, Orlikowski and Yates, 2013). Third, how do relationships and communication patterns develop across contexts within groups and individuals? This was previously technically challenging, but is now possible by utilising smartphone and wearable technology.

Perhaps in response, and given that social psychology has a rich history when it comes to exploring intergroup behaviour, research that specifically considers in-group and out-group interactions (e.g., contact theory) is slowly starting to make use of new technology (McKeown and Dixon, 2017). For example, the Contact Logger app allows participants to record interpersonal and intergroup encounters over time alongside location (Keil, Koschate-Reis and Levine, 2020). While smartphone technology has been used less to study small group processes, combining such an approach with other smartphone methods that can quantify dyadic or group contacts in offline and online environments could transform the field. Specifically, understanding the conditions that support positive intergroup contact could improve intergroup interactions and reduce prejudice (Pettigrew and Tropp, 2006).

In summary, while the latest wave of research to date is descriptive, it provides many new methodological avenues to explore, but our understanding is often playing catch-up given the sheer variety of social communication platforms that are now available to the average smartphone user. However, we should persevere with these approaches. There has been a major societal shift towards communications that are not conducted face-to-face but are instead mediated by interfaces such as mobile phones and social networking websites. This is unlikely to change.

Useful Resources and Further Reading

Davidson, B. I., Joinson, A., & Jones, S. (2018). Technologically enhanced dating: Augmented human relationships, robots, and fantasy. In Z. Papacharissi (Ed.), *A Networked Self and Love* (pp.145–171). Routledge.
Considers how traditional theories of attraction and interpersonal relationships have been tested using digital data. Some of this is derived from mobile applications used for interpersonal communication (e.g., Tinder).
Wall, H. J., Taylor, P. J., Dixon, J., Conchie, S. M., & Ellis, D. A. (2013). Rich contexts do not always enrich the accuracy of personality judgments. *Journal of Experimental Social Psychology, 49*(6), 1190–1195.
Serves as a reminder that different technological contexts can add or subtract from first impressions generated during a short social interaction.

CHAPTER 4

Personality and Individual Differences

Smartphones have often been described in both popular culture and the academic literature as an extension of the self (Meadow, Altrichter and Green, 2014). Even device ownership alone can become psychologically interesting (Andrews et al., 2015; Shaw et al., 2016). Behavioural residues of personality, however, already exist in abundance. Information about individuals can be gleaned from spending records to the layout of a room (Gladstone, Matz and Lemaire, 2019; Gosling et al., 2002; Vazire and Gosling, 2004). Yet the study of personality and individual differences has been driven largely by self-report assessments, which aim to predict behaviour or life outcomes in the absence of any real-world measure. Going beyond this, digital devices and services can facilitate the measurement of multiple behaviours that can predict and understand personality (Piwek et al., 2016b). Data from smartphone apps and sensors can, for example, provide a wealth of information about their owner and surrounding environment. Indeed, the notion that we might curate accurate profiles of individuals from real-world behaviour can actually be traced to the 1950s (Cattell, 1958). This is particularly pertinent when it comes to understanding personality traits (e.g., levels of extraversion – a measure of sociability) that are automatically deployed in new situations seamlessly and non-consciously (Roberts and Hill, 2017).

Only in recent years has the field started to recognise opportunities in this area, and a growing number of studies have correlated data from digital services with traditional psychometric tests. Accordingly, the theoretical and methodological assumptions used to develop pen-and-paper psychometric tests appear dated when compared with computational developments that utilise digital traces. There also remains an inherent assumption that digital traces should be validated against these traditional psychometric tests and not with subsequent behaviour. Therefore, any computer or algorithmic-based judgment developed in this fashion will only ever be as accurate as the original measures that they are expected to emulate. Slow progress can also, in part, be attributed to the lack of user-friendly tools (e.g., analytical routines and software) that are specifically tailored for the field.

> Deeper insights in this domain will not occur if psychologists continue to rely only on self-report instruments to measure personality. (Kagan, 2001, p. 84)

Therefore, this chapter considers the notion of the self as it applies to smartphone ownership before discussing how, as a technological tool, the smartphone is starting to challenge and may even revolutionise how we conceptualise a variety of individual differences, including personality.

4.1   Personal Microbe: Biological Traces

Personal traces from a smartphone actually begin at the point of any physical contact. While smartphones are exposed to changing environments, they are also frequently touched by the same person throughout the day (Andrews et al., 2015). Several studies have considered the large levels of sometimes harmful bacteria found on mobile phones that also appear on an owner's hands or other body parts (Brady et al., 2009, 2011; Pal et al., 2013). Early research considered pathogenic bacteria in health-care settings, rather than how unique patterns might provide a link back to the original owner. In this latter context, Meadow et al. (2014) define the personal microbe as a 'collection of microorganisms associated with the personal effects of an individual'. This varies significantly from person to person; for example, microbes found on the skin are highly variable. The frequency with which people touch their smartphone also ensures that the bacteria left on a smartphone is indicative of human contact. It is possible, for example, to compare the bacterial properties of an individual's thumb and index finger with the screen of their device. Meadow et al. (2014) observed that men and women differ in their microbial connections to their phones, with women having a stronger microbiological connection to their phones than men. Overall however, microbial communities sampled from the device over-lapped more with an owner's skin microbiome when compared to bacterial taxa shared across other participant's phones although the observed effect was small. Extending this to physical biometrics, thumb length can also be inferred from how individuals interact with a device. Specifically, people with longer thumbs have quicker and shorter swipe gestures than people with shorter thumbs (Bevan and Fraser, 2016).

Of course, fingers are only one source of physical or microbiological data that can be detected by a smartphone, but related traces like these may also be useful when characterising exposure to other biological threats (e.g., air pollution). However, repetitive interactions like these have led an increasing number of researchers to consider how these devices extend a person's identity.

4.2   The Extended Self: Psychological Traces

Extended self theory argues that the greater power and control a person exerts over an object, the more it becomes part of his or her self-identity (Belk, 1988). In addition to spending long periods of time using these devices, individuals also have a large amount of control over their smartphones, which are highly customisable. Each owner has a relatively unique library of downloaded apps, contacts, music and photographs. This personalisation has already allowed for psychological inferences to be made about the end user (Chittaranjan, Blom and Gatica-Perez, 2011). Elements of smartphone use and ownership can therefore be considered within the context of an extended self, which has been updated to account for changes caused by digital environments (Belk, 2013). For example, music and videos have become dematerialised as they no longer exist as a physical row of CDs and DVDs but can now be accessed anywhere in the world digitally via the cloud. However, the smartphone as an object in itself provides the gateway to engaging with and sharing this digital content. Belk's original theory concerning possessions therefore remains highly pertinent when considering how digital services and devices may extend the self.

The smartphone operating system provides a useful starting point in how the smartphone extends the self further (Andrews et al., 2015). Previous empirical evidence supports the notion that when a person wears an item of clothing, they embody its symbolic meaning (Belk, 2013). Specifically, people who wear a watch identified themselves as more conscientious than those who do not and exhibited behaviours that were consistent with this personality trait (Ellis and Jenkins, 2015). When applied to smartphone ownership, one might expect that a person will 'embody' the semantics attached to each smartphone brand (Adam and Galinsky, 2012).[1]

---

[1] A recent, pre-registered replication by Burns et al. (2019) found no effects of clothing on selective attention as observed by Adam and Galinsky (2012). Effects may still appear in some domains and not others, but this will involve establishing a theoretical basis. See Adam and Galinsky's (2019) reply for a complete discussion regarding these developments.

Two systems continue to dominate the marketplace, with iPhone and Android smartphones accounting for more than 90 per cent of all smartphones sold worldwide (IDC, 2016). Both engage in extensive but very different advertising campaigns (Mickalowski, Mickelson and Keltgen, 2008). As a result, considerable discourse surrounds these two operating systems. Previous speculation suggested that iPhone users are better educated, more affluent and more likely to be 'addicted' to their smartphones than those who choose Android devices (Forbes, 2014). However, until recently no empirical investigation had systematically considered the existence or accuracy of these claims. This is surprising because the current 50/50 market split provides an interesting divide, in which to test how existing theoretical constructs that pertain to the self may also help explain how individuals align themselves with a specific smartphone operating system.

In 2016, we considered how theories relating to the extended self can also be applied to help explain differences between individuals who use Android or iPhone devices (Shaw et al., 2016). Our predictions were based around the notion of brand personality (Aaker, 1997). Researchers in this domain have focused on how a purchase choice allows an individual to express the self (Belk, 1988). Specifically, the more congruity that exists between the human characteristics that describe an individual's genuine or perfect self and those that portray a brand, the greater the preference for that brand (Malhotra, 1988). This idea has subsequently been developed further into a theoretical framework where multiple personality dimensions can be isolated for each brand. Demographic characteristics such as gender, class and age are also likely to influence brand preference (Aaker, 1997). Like personality, demographic characteristics may also be inferred from brand imagery or other brand associations. For example, Apple is frequently viewed as young and IBM is considered to be an older alternative.

As predicted, iPhone users were younger and more open in comparison to those who use Android devices. Conversely, Android users consistently appear to demonstrate higher levels of honesty–humility. Higher levels of honesty–humility are associated with people who avoid manipulating others for personal gain, feel little temptation to break rules, are uninterested in lavish wealth and luxuries, and feel no special entitlement to elevated social status (Ashton, Lee and De Vries, 2014). iPhone users were also more likely to view their smartphone as a status object and less concerned about owning devices favoured by the majority of the population. Interestingly, gender was the strongest predictor concerning smartphone ownership, as women were twice as likely to own iPhones than men.

Recent research has demonstrated that men and women use their phones in different ways. For example, women make more phone calls, take more pictures, and send and receive more texts (Joiner, Stewart and Beaney, 2015). On the contrary, men use their phones more for entertainment purposes as they play more games and watch more videos (Joiner et al., 2015). However, this alone is unlikely to explain why women are more likely to choose an iPhone in comparison to men.

This confirms that the personalisation of a technological experience begins at the point of choosing between the iPhone or Android operating system and, as personal devices, smartphones can be considered as an item that extends the self (Belk, 1988). Similar findings have been observed (e.g., Tuzcuiglu et al., 2018) with other research reporting smaller but consistent effects (e.g., Götz, Stieger and Reips, 2017). However, collectively these findings say very little about the direction of any effect. The decision to own a specific type of smartphone may be driven by some of the traits identified here in the first instance. Alternatively, a purchase may simply be motivated by a desire to become closer to their actual or ideal self by adopting a specific brand (Sundar and Noseworthy, 2016). Some participants in these samples may not have chosen the smartphone that they currently own and could have received it as a gift. Younger participants may have had a parent or guardian purchase the phone on their behalf, for example. Of course, these participants may still 'embody' the semantics attached with each smartphone brand, but future research would need to consider cause and effect.

However, while iPhone and Android devices have separate operating systems containing some unique features, the apps and functionality available have become remarkably similar. Other research has now started to consider if people use iPhones and Android phones in unique ways – for example, if the type of apps downloaded (e.g., social and gaming) may differ between devices. Hu, Bezemer and Hassan (2018) explored differences between star ratings for apps that are available in both Apple and Android stores. They observed large differences between scores which they attribute to quality assurance issues for developers across different platforms. Specifically, almost twice as many cross-platform apps have a higher average star rating in Android than in iOS. However, an alternative explanation might consider how these results chime with our findings, whereby iPhone users are more concerned about their device and are likely to feel disappointed when products fail to meet expectations.

If the self is therefore expressed differently through the type of device owned, these results also raise additional issues as they pertain to psychological research methods. Data gathered within computational social science or PsychoInformatics is often from smartphone sensors and apps using a single smartphone operating system only. However, as individual differences occur between users of different smartphone operating systems, the 'type' of people who use these devices may have driven findings from previous research. As a result, some conclusions may not generalise beyond that group of smartphone users. Consequently, any research that uses smartphones as a data collection tool in psychology should be aware of these individual differences and aim to collect data using both iPhone and Android smartphone apps where possible.[2] However, more research and discussion are required in terms of how researchers might also need to control for other physical biometrics from participants themselves (Bevan and Fraser, 2016).

On the other hand, while owning a specific brand of smartphone can tell us about the owner, the absence of a device or lack of use can also be informative. Researchers have speculated that this is likely to be of growing importance when the vast majority of the population now own a smartphone. In a similar design to Shaw et al. (2016), Pedrero-Pérez et al. (2019) compared people who do and do not use their smartphone regularly. They found non-users more likely to be male, be older, have a lower educational level and belong to an underprivileged social class. In addition, the non-users showed worse mental health indicators and a lower perceived quality of life relating to their health. This lack of use is likely to act as a proxy for other health-related factors, but it adds weight to an argument outlined in Chapter 1 that those who are offline or digitally inactive may well be engaging with a form of social withdrawal. Alternatively, avoiding a technology may be deliberate and have specific underlying reasons tied to an individual or location where reduced usage is preferable (Kneidinger-Müller, 2019). It is worth noting that this study considered lack of use, rather than lack of ownership, but the results are likely to align with other factors that govern the digital divide.

In summary, research that has focused on how devices may extend the self has made some progress and has a renewed focus as digital services provide a route to ownership that does not involve physical goods (Belk, 2013). This framework also provides an avenue to perhaps explore social identity theory in the context of smartphones specifically in the future

---

[2] An in-depth textual analysis of Trump's tweets in 2016 confirmed that he uses an Android device, while other members of his team use iPhones. http://varianceexplained.org/r/trump-tweets/. This was replicated in 2017 http://varianceexplained.org/r/trump-followup/.

(Davis, Love and Fares, 2019). However, within psychological science and related fields, including computer science, this work has been dwarfed by research that is using complex streams of smartphone data to predict a variety of other individual differences.

4.3   Personality

Personality researchers have started to consider how smartphones and associated digital services can predict and enhance our understanding of personality assessment (Hinds and Joinson, 2019). These lines of enquiry have become increasingly popular in the previous decade and stretch far beyond psychology. While this has raised the profile of the field, research is scattered across disciplines that appear to be largely unaware of each other's existence (Montag and Elhai, 2019). Those working in computer science, for example, publish conference proceedings in the Institute of Electrical and Electronics Engineers (IEEE) journals that may be missed by personality psychologists. Despite challenges, individual differences research has previously devoted many resources to developing new methods that can identify and assess personality constructs (Clegg, 2018).

4.3.1   A Brief History

The major dimensions of personality appear to have emerged in the last few decades (Matthews, Deary and Whiteman, 2009). By about 1990, psychologists were converging on a consensus that there might be only five principal personality traits, generally referred to as the Big Five, or the Five-Factor model (Gosling, Rentfrow and Swann, 2003). A brief sketch of each of the traits in the Five-Factor model is documented in Table 4.1. The names used here are the most common, but slight variations are used in different measures.

These dimensions are proposed to represent the basic structure and underlying variations in human behaviour and associated thoughts, attitudes and feelings. Each of these traits also has a normal distribution in the normal population and allows individuals to be compared and contrasted. Beyond five-factor models, other frameworks also appear promising and have continued to grow in popularity. Specifically, the HEXACO model of personality is based on lexical research concerning personality where factor analyses were conducted on self and peer ratings of the familiar personality-descriptive adjectives of several languages (Ashton and Lee, 2009). This led to the identification of six dimensions rather than five, which can capture

Table 4.1 *Key traits of the Big Five model of personality.*

Trait	Facets
Neuroticism	Anxiety, anger, hostility, depression, self-consciousness, impulsiveness, vulnerability
Extraversion	Warmth, gregariousness, assertiveness, activity, excitement, seeking, positive emotions
Openness to Experience	Fantasy, aesthetics, feelings, actions, ideas, values
Agreeableness	Trust, straightforwardness, altruism, compliance, modesty, tender-mindedness
Conscientiousness	Competence, order, dutifulness, achievement, striving, self-discipline, deliberation

other key aspects of personality variance that are not represented within five-dimensional models (Lee and Ashton, 2012). Correlations between HEXACO factors and the Big Five are consistent with theoretical expectations; however, emotionality replaces emotional stability with high scores indicating an increased fear of physical dangers and higher levels of day-to-day anxiety. Conversely, low scorers are less concerned with physical harm and little need to share their concerns with others. In addition, honesty-humility measures levels of sincerity and modesty, with low scores indicating pretentiousness and deceit. Other models continue to be developed that include more or less factors (e.g., Soto and John, 2017). Regardless as to which model is adopted, the conceptualisation is often comparable with the Big Five.

Personality judgments and its assessment have, in turn, had an enormous impact on psychological science, partly because they are related to important behaviours and life outcomes, including job performance and mental health (Ozer and Benet-Martinez, 2006; Paunonen and Ashton, 2001; Roberts et al., 2007). Personality is also reported to be the strongest and most consistent cross-sectional predictor of subjective well-being (Boyce, Wood and Powdthavee, 2012; Deary, Weiss and Batty, 2010; Ferrer-i-Carbonell and Frijters, 2004) and, as a result, is often measured so it can be included as a covariate to better understand the variability of interventions between individuals (Tsapeli and Musolesi, 2015). Our personality judgments also affect many aspects of daily life in terms of who we become friends with and how organisations market products (Aaker, 1997).

Finally, unlike other areas of psychological science, many findings in personality appear to be comparatively robust.[3]

4.3.2   *Personality Measurement and Prediction*

Psychologists typically rely on self-report as the gold standard when it comes to measuring personality. Scores can be cross-referenced with self–other agreement whereby an individual's own score is correlated to that of another person who knows them well. It is also possible to combine scores from multiple observers in order to improve or ensure accuracy (Funder, 1995, 2012). However, the ability of personality to predict a behaviour or life outcome is also considered to be a marker of accuracy (Hinds and Joinson, 2019). Digital traces therefore already provide some of the most exciting developments for researchers in this area. For example, simply liking a page on Facebook is predictive of an individual's personality (Kosinski, Stillwell and Graepel, 2013). However, many people do not provide data to these services and the population in general is moving towards mobile-first social networks, including Instagram, WhatsApp and Snapchat. Smartphone data can therefore provide further opportunities in conjunction with these services, or in isolation (Stachl et al., 2019a). Even a single snapshot of installed apps or total time spent on the device can reveal key information (Xu et al., 2016). Seneviratne et al. (2014) found that traits such as religion, relationship status and whether or not someone had small children could be predicted with 70–90 per cent precision. General mobile activity can also provide similar insights in terms of age, sleep patterns and personality (Christensen et al., 2016).

Combining app metrics with situational data from sensors (e.g., GPS, environmental noise), smartphones provide additional opportunities for studying personality in the wild (Piwek et al., 2016a) with the majority of attempts to date driven by computer scientists. These typically rely on the development of an algorithm that can predict self-reported personality from a digital metric. For example, Chittaranjan et al. (2013) sampled smartphone usage, call logs and Bluetooth scans. As one might expect, extraverts were likely to make and receive more calls, and spend more time with other people. Conscientiousness was associated with more frequent use of the mail app and reduced time using YouTube. Other research also remains aligned with what existing personality frameworks might predict. For example, decades of psychological research have observed associations

---

[3] https://pigee.wordpress.com/2019/11/12/robust-findings-in-personality-psychology/

between factors of personality that are aligned with physical activity and health (Kern and Friedman, 2008; Roberts, Walton and Bogg, 2005; Tolea et al., 2012). Gao and colleagues (2019) specifically observed that those who were more extraverted had less regular activity patterns and a high level of entropy across mobile contacts. Related designs have used ambient voices, physical activity and phone usage in combination to make similar predictions (Wang et al., 2018). Of course, many other exploratory findings are less straightforward to align with what one might expect even if algorithms are able to correctly classify a person's personality as being in a higher or lower half of a specific trait. For example, de Montjoye et al. (2013) observed that distance travelled was a marker of neuroticism.

Psychological science has been slow to acknowledge this potential, and most work to date has only got as far as correlating self-reported usage of specific apps with traditional personality assessments (Ellis, 2019). These are unlikely to be reliable. Research that does use digital metrics is also far from conclusive at this stage. Previous work by Mønsted, Mollgaard and Mathiesen (2018) relied on communication behaviour but had limited success when predicting personality. However, Stachl et al. (2019a) used a wider range of behavioural indicators (including data from on-board sensors). Like Harari et al. (2019), they observed correlations between extraversion and higher rates of conversation, calling, texting and app usage behaviour. However, their machine-learning approach revealed a variety of associations between more specific smartphone metrics. For example, the use of the camera was associated with openness whereas apps associated with planning and scheduling aligned with conscientiousness (Stachl et al., 2019a).

In addition, vast quantities of textual and emoji data available to psychologists provide many more opportunities beyond the scope of this book (Boyd and Pennebaker, 2017; Kaye, Malone and Wall, 2017). In terms of language data harvested via text messages, Yakoub et al. (2015) were able to classify personality traits. However, this approach comes with huge ethical issues and is not something most participants would be comfortable to share, even if researchers can avoid looking at specific messages themselves. Of course, this still leaves a variety of public and semi-public data available from a variety of platforms that remain inherently linked with smartphones (Kosinski, Stillwell and Graepel, 2013; Quercia et al., 2011).

To summarise, the ability of an algorithm to account for variance in self-report scores relies on predictive validity alone as evidence for successful operationalisation and parameterisation (Boyd, 2020). As a result, these predictions often generate many nonsensical or misguided conclusions about the relationship between personality and behaviour.

Many studies avoid making any explicit predictions that build on previous psychological research. Without any theoretical reference, the risk of false positives also remains high given the huge volumes of data and analytical methods involved (Montag and Elhai, 2019). Even when results are sensible, there is some doubt regarding the efficacy of many effects as machine-learning techniques often provide over-optimistic results because they are unable to generalise beyond a very specific test population (DeMasi, Kording and Recht, 2017). Some machine-learning algorithms also rely on 'black-box' approaches where even researchers are unable to describe how such a prediction occurs (Bleidorn and Hopwood, 2019; Hinds and Joinson, 2019). In response, almost every author of the research discussed previously agrees that the range of conflicting results will require confirmatory research designs in the future (Burtăverde, Vlăsceanu and Avram, 2019).

4.3.3   Personality Explanation and Development

Despite questions concerning the application of various machine-learning algorithms, it is interesting to note that they are typically more accurate at predicting personality than humans (Hinds and Joinson, 2019). However, this emphasis on prediction over theoretical development may be misplaced. Most researchers would agree that while personality predicts future events, for example, it will never completely determine an outcome. Merging theoretically aligned design with modern methods may therefore help guide future research. In this way, psychology can start to consider how digital records of behaviour might further our understanding of both personality traits and processes (Bleidorn and Hopwood, 2019).

Returning to how psychology has attempted to understand such predictions from observers in the past provides some guidance in this respect. Traditional theoretical models concerning personality perception offline including the RAM allow one to understand how different cues might be associated with personalities and subsequent predictions (Funder, 1995). Specifically, self-reports and informant reports of personality typically agree with each other, but not perfectly, with both sources providing valid information (Connolly, Kavanagh and Viswesvaran, 2007). While the variable ability of observers can be problematic, the procedure continues to be used in many personality-perception studies in off-line contexts (e.g., judgments of job candidates). However, they are seldom used in studies of personality perception and digital footprints, perhaps because to date, correlations between self and other observations from different digital footprints have produced mixed results (Tskhay and Rule, 2014). For example, observers appear to be better aligned with a target's own rating of personality from Facebook profiles, but poor when making similar judgments from Instagram (Back et al., 2010; Barry et al., 2019).

An improved strategy could be applied to computer-based judgments that attempt to predict personality from a set of digital cues. Hinds and Joinson (2019) point towards the use of a lens model (Brunswik, 1956) whereby specific digital cues may map onto a specific trait (e.g., number of social apps used per day may map onto a personality rating of extraversion). They suggest that computer models could adopt the role of an observer as computer scientists often experiment with feature sets. In contrast to researchers conducting human personality-perception studies, computer scientists predetermine the cues (or features) that are collected then used by an algorithm. Once data is available, however, computer scientists then experiment with different algorithms and feature sets to evaluate how accurately they can predict personality. The advantage of this approach is that researchers can work from the bottom up and discover patterns in data that were not preconceived.

However, such an approach in isolation might struggle to overcome existing methodological and theoretical limitations. Lens-models only focus on the specific cues that are associated with judgments and person- alities. In reality, a human or computer observer may be using other cues to form judgments that are difficult to define. Using 'black box' methods outlined previously, advanced statistical models may struggle to assure researchers that cues are explicitly related to personalities or judgments. To mitigate these issues, machine-learning approaches of this nature would then need to follow a development path associated with the development of psychometric tests to ensure they are valid and reliable (Bleidorn and Hopwood, 2019).

Alternatively, general debates within the field may provide clues on how we move forward. Personality was previously assumed to be stable across different situations and several longitudinal studies have demonstrated that, for example, a person who is extraverted today is also likely be extraverted 10 years later (Edmonds et al., 2008). Conversely, other find- ings suggest that personality continues to change across the lifespan. Srivastave et al. (2003) compared Big Five scores over 130,000 individuals between the ages of 21 and 60. Neuroticism appeared to decline amongst women, but not men. Other patterns of change suggest that the Big Five are likely to be influenced by several other developmental factors not limited to adolescence, but may also include other life experiences (Bleidorn, Hopwood and Lucas, 2018; Roberts et al., 2005). This raises broad analytical implications for the measurement of personality in research, public policy and occupational settings. Personality psychology would gain a lot by further investigating how and when personality is susceptible to rapid change across shorter timescales (Roberts and Hill, 2017). On the other hand, some of this variation may be due to limitations of existing measurements or changes in context.

Indeed, most theories digging deeper into personality emphasise the notion of behavioural tendencies that are linked with motivational, emotional and cognitive domains over time and across situations (Baumert et al., 2017; Montag and Elhai, 2019). Theories such as the Cognitive-Affective Processing System (CAPS), for example, suggest people have behavioural signatures/profiles which are stable in situations that are perceived psychologically as being the same (Mischel, 2004). Mischel and Shoda (1995) proposed if–then functions to illuminate how a stable personality set – despite such behavioural inconsistencies – might present itself. They observed that behaviour becomes more consistent when situational profiles are established. For example, if I am at work then I am diligent; if I am home, then I am less diligent. This also led to the latent trait-state theory (Ziegler, Horstmann and Ziegler, 2019). Specifically, research has focused on the notion of *trait self-knowledge*. Knowledge of the self is an important topic in its own right and aligns closely with personality assessment. Blind spots are well acknowledged in how people rate both themselves and others at a trait level, which will oscillate around a variety of individual and contextual factors (Vazire and Mehl, 2008).

As a result, comparatively less is known regarding *state self-knowledge*, but this may drive trait effects. For example, if a person is unable to determine in the moment that they are being aggressive and not agreeable, then this may filter down to trait-level measurements. Sun and Vazire (2019) considered how well people know themselves from one moment to the next (*state self-knowledge*). Specifically, their main research question focused on whether people have accurate insights into their own personality states over shorter periods of time. They used an electronically activated recorder (EAR) which was controlled using an iPod Touch and recorded 30-second audio snippets of ambient sounds every 9.5 minutes from 7 a.m. to 2 a.m. These snippets were then transcribed and coded accordingly. At the same time, participants received text messages four times a day and completed short measures of the Big Five personality scales. People appeared to have self-insight into their momentary extraversion and conscientiousness, suggesting that they can accurately detect fluctuations in some aspects of their personality. However, the evidence for self-insight was weaker for agreeableness.

Combining Mischel and Shoda's (1995) theoretical approach with a tweaked version of Sun and Vazire's (2019) methodology that included GPS co-ordinates from a smartphone could help understand these personality processes further (Montag and Elhai, 2019). Specifically, situational functions could be investigated by using GPS co-ordinates or other variables, including time of the day, to understand how context impacts a person's behaviour. Do they behave in a consistent or inconsistent manner? Could this explain why personality appears to change over time? Specific GPS coordinates would log a participant's workplace and home, for example, and a researcher could explore typical conversational behaviour and record state measures as they occur at different locations. The same notion could be applied to different online contexts as people respond to state measures while using specific apps (e.g., Facebook vs LinkedIn). Montag and Elhai (2019) suggest using the same method to investigate other components of dynamic variability, including morningness and eveningness personality types (Horne and Östberg, 1976).

Relatedly, psychologists are already experimenting with dynamic digital services, environments and games. Traditional self-report alone means that the situation is to be driven by the respondent. Gamification, however, similar to the recording of location, can embed measurement within a specific context, albeit more experimentally (Canossa et al., 2015). To date, research has used narratives showing overlaps between traditional self-report and responses that guide a character through a scenario with different measurements corresponding to decisions made (McCord, Harman and Purl, 2019). It is worth noting that commercial video games (e.g., Detroit: Become Human) often provide users with a variety of difficult decisions in terms of what can happen to main characters, which are also likely to reflect a player's personality. It is conceivable that if such data was made available to researchers, then connections between decisions and personality are likely. Given the variety of online games that involve teamwork, researchers can also consider social processes and personality simultaneously. Many of these games can be presented on a smartphone platform. However, like all the approaches outlined previously, this still relies on an element of self-report to corroborate any prediction or explanation.

4.3.4   *Can Smartphones Revolutionise Psychometric Assessment?*

While the field is gradually starting to consider how big data from smartphones and other devices might help explain personality following prediction, does this notion go far enough? Existing personality data types are, by their own admission, incomplete and struggle to accommodate new innovations in research methods and theory (Boyd et al., 2020). Progress is often hampered therefore by the assumption that digital traces should be validated against traditional psychometric tests and not via subsequent behaviour or considered within themselves. As a result, any computer or algorithmic-based judgment developed using correlational approaches will only ever be as accurate as the original measures that they are expected to emulate. So, what prevents us from removing our reliance on self-report completely?

There remains a general consensus among many social scientists that, while traditional psychometric measures are far from perfect, they are the only option available. This extends to many measures used throughout social psychology and psychological assessment. While online systems have allowed sample sizes for such studies to increase considerably, the reliance on self-report has eclipsed alternative measures (Sassenberg and Ditrich, 2019). Signals derived from digital traces currently lack the benefits provided by traditional psychometric tests. This includes being straightforward to administer and score, which in turn allows for individuals to be compared and contrasted on a specific measure. Significant progress on this front has to occur before research considers in detail the relationships between sensed behaviours and consequential life outcomes (e.g., mental health, physical health, performance) (Harari et al., 2017).

Little attempt has been made to develop behavioural norms in relation to digital traces or exploring how signals from multiple sensors may be structured to increase data efficiency and subsequent analysis. This lack of standardisation prevents individuals from being compared to one another across samples. In terms of smartphone sensing specifically, research will need to identify the psychometric properties of sensor data (e.g., reliability, validity) and develop easy-to-understand behavioural classifiers. For example, while a microphone can classify whether ambient conversations are taking place around an individual, this could simply reflect someone watching TV or listening to the radio alone at home. These limitations could be overcome by cross-mapping classifiers with location or linking multiple metrics to know when an individual is near a television at home. This remains a grand challenge, however, particularly when it comes to

building open-source and easy-to-understand classifiers that make inferences about noisy data. An entire research programme in its own right, this
would require considerable investment.

In practice, this is perhaps more likely to develop incrementally over
time and some variables have reached a level of standardisation that may be
acceptable. For example, call behaviour and total screen time can now be
straightforwardly compared across studies if researchers converge and
follow identical processing pathways when using these variables.
Smartphone usage metrics including average daily use and checking behaviours have specifically reached a point where guidelines define how these
variables should be operationalised to ensure they are valid and reliable
(Wilcockson, Ellis and Shaw, 2018). However, this is less clear for dozens of
other metrics and sensor readings that record behaviours that occur infre-
quently (Montag and Elhai, 2019).

Taking a less technical and more descriptive approach may build on
these successes where each digital trace available from a smartphone or app
(e.g., accelerometer activity to quantify physical activity, GPS data to assess
location) will need to be qualitatively aligned with existing factors and
traits. As discussed previously, Hinds and Joinson (2019) point out that
many digital traces should correlate with key factors of personality. For
example, extraversion should map onto the number of calls and texts sent/
received, or locations visited where social interaction is likely to occur.
However, beyond this many aspects of personality (e.g., openness) may
either require a more complex processing path to make a signal useful or
ultimately become very difficult to determine from existing digital markers. Considered research like this would help define where existing survey
methods might be re-considered from a digital perspective or where self-
report measures are likely to remain important, even with the addition of
a digital trace. While behavioural metrics from smartphone sensors alone
may ultimately provide a more streamlined way to consider individual
differences in the future, some elements from traditional tests are likely to
remain crucial when it comes to measuring more complex emotional states.
Therefore, standard measures of personality may still have much to offer of
value and, echoing previous discussions, experience sampling methodologies are likely to increase their utility further.

Following such mapping, pre-registered analyses could then focus on
confirming expectations. Taking these behavioural metrics as a cohort, does
its factor structure appear similar to that of traditional psychometric measures
(e.g., personality)? Exploratory work with (potentially) hundreds or thousands of traits and dimensions would help identify clusters of co-occurring,

validated behaviours (e.g., Harari et al., 2019). Given the quantity of data available from smartphones, this could include language data, location, purchasing decisions, dating history and a variety of social media metrics. Such an analysis may reveal a new factor structure that is completely unlike any existing measure of personality. Machine learning, combined with highly accurate measurements, could help researchers handle this complexity and high dimensionality, thus helping inform the development and validation of new theories in personality. Such modelling, if standardised, will make it easier to compare these studies with research from other disciplines, including computer science. This would also allow insights to be translated into practical applications more reliably (Stachl et al., 2019b). Other related sources of data from connected devices could extend these lines of enquiry further. If privacy were no object, wearable cameras alone, for example, would likely generate different personality factors if thousands of people were filmed for 24 hours over a six-month period in different contexts.

Beyond concerns around privacy, these ideas might still appear computationally challenging, but may become comparatively straightforward in the near future. Such approaches may even challenge decades of existing understanding as researchers reveal how personality processes measured from behaviour fuse with personality itself (Boyd et al., 2020). Alternatively, these findings could simply reinforce and extend existing assumptions about the Big Five traits (Hinds and Joinson, 2019). Finally, research of this nature would help solidify how psychology might further refine the accuracy (or ground truth) of digital traces. This is a grand interdisciplinary challenge, but one that appears worthwhile if personality research in this domain is to become less scattered and remain productive.

4.4 Conclusion

The physicality of modern smartphones means that, at surface level, they can already provide a variety of biological and psychological clues about an owner. Beyond these comparatively recent developments, the study of individual differences, including personality, remains a cornerstone of modern psychology. The field can be proud of many great accomplishments, but it also faces some long-standing challenges which smartphones can address. Advocates of traditional personality assessment assume that a person's semantic judgments about their behaviours and beliefs are the most valid bases for inferring personality types. Much of our current understanding therefore relies on simply asking people about themselves. On the other hand, no cognitive psychologist would record participants' careful descriptions of their perceptions, memories and ways of solving problems to infer the basic cognitive competencies (Ellis, 2013). A digital-objective approach would readdress this imbalance and control for contextual cues (Lewis, 2001; Sun and Vazire, 2019). Similarly, prioritising the Big Five over other models may become a sticking point for future development as this structure is not always present in large data sets (Laajaj et al., 2019). Given their ubiquity, smartphones deployed in any capacity may assist with related challenges when it comes to capturing personality traits from culturally diverse samples.

Behavioural data from smartphones and related digital services already exists at scale and will continue to evolve. Digital footprints may even become the gold standard for personality assessment and lead to fundamental changes in how we structure and understand personality in the future. Despite this potential, personality theory emphasises more than just behaviour and it remains challenging to capture thoughts and feelings on a daily basis without explicitly asking participants or logging streams of thought via language use at regular intervals. To further complicate matters, these approaches carry major ethical challenges. Research questions have to be balanced alongside privacy concerns, involuntary assessment and informed consent (Paxton and Griffiths, 2017). This will require the development of new protocols to ensure an appropriate level of data privacy and security, which has become a critical issue when handling digital traces of behaviour that can be used to infer personality. It will be up to psychologists to mitigate these issues if the field is to prosper from these opportunities. While traditional personality research continues at great pace, the digitisation of behaviour presents new opportunities, challenges and ways in which the field could advance rapidly, with a renewed sense of purpose.

Useful Resources and Further Reading

Ellis, D. A. (2016). *Smartphone Personality Website.* Retrieved from https://psychol ogy.shinyapps.io/smartphonepersonality/
This online application visualises demographic and personality differences between iPhone and Android smartphone users as originally reported in Shaw et al. (2016).
Hinds, J. & Joinson, A. (2019). Human and computer personality prediction from digital footprints. *Current Directions in Psychological Science*, 28(2), 204–211.
Provides a succinct overview of how digital traces from a variety of sources can predict personality. This discusses trends in current research and provides recommended directions for future investigations.

Lewis, M. (2001). Issues in the study of personality development. *Psychological Inquiry*, *12*(2), 67–83.
While issues relating to the objective measurement of personality were raised in the early 2000s, others have long since considered the importance of, and attempted to measure, everyday behaviour to improve psychometric assessments (e.g., Cattell, 1958).

CHAPTER 5

Cognition

Issues that pertain to cognition and smartphones are, similar to other chapters, a tale of two halves. In one corner, research points towards the negative impacts on cognition as a result of smartphone use in children and adults. There are certainly instances where it can be detrimental to normal cognitive functioning. For example, decades of research confirm that distractions caused by mobile devices can have devastating short-term consequences for our attentional capacity. In the opposing corner lies research that aims to use smartphone technology directly to better understand cognitive function. This sub-discipline of psychology has historically been quick to adopt the latest advances in technology, and this is reflected in the methodological training many psychologists receive during their doctoral studies. Journals like *Behavior Research Methods* and *Psychological Methods* have often documented the refinement of new methods and analytical routines that are closely aligned with cognitive measurements. However, while mouse and keyboard inputs continue to be developed for lab-based behavioural experiments (e.g., Kieslich et al., 2019), smartphones offer a variety of new ways to measure participants' responses (Stieger, Lewetz and Reips, 2018). To date, a number of standard psychophysical experiments and reaction time tasks have been ported in the form of experimental apps. Combining advanced graphical abilities with gamification, various cognitive tasks have also been validated to assess working memory, attention and decision-making (Paletta et al., 2014; Wilmer, Sherman and Chein, 2017).

The structure of this chapter reflects the above chasm. First, I will critically consider research that documents the potential cognitive impact of smartphone use in children and adult populations. A second section will then explore how smartphones are being repurposed to improve our understanding of cognition in more ecologically valid settings. Ironically, while considered separately in the literature, understanding the impact of smartphones on cognition will involve merging these two areas of research together. Only then can the cracks be repaired.

5.1 Cognitive Development

Millennials (those born between 1981 and 1996) are well accustomed to high-speed internet access and associated technologies. However, a distinctive feature of childhood development today is the integration of digital technologies from a very early age (Houghton et al., 2015). Entire books have been devoted to the potential impact modern technology is having on generations of children (Carr, 2010; Twenge, 2017). Children will often gravitate towards new technology with little fear of failure, and many prominent scientists have made alarming claims in response. David Bolt and Ray Crawford (2000) raised sensible concerns regarding computing in previous decades, but a societal increase in the use of any new technology, including video games, mobile phones and tablets, by the young is often viewed negatively with few redeeming features. Concerns tend to range from the notion that the shared family experience is under threat to the death of imaginative childhood play. The latter is slightly confusing given that many video games encourage imaginative play (e.g., Minecraft) (Mavoa, Carter and Gibbs, 2018). Others go further to suggest that screens are reprogramming children's brains and silently shaping the future evolution of Homo sapiens (Greenfield, 2015). This includes the notion that modern technology is causing an epidemic of neurodevelopmental pathology, including attention deficit hyperactivity disorder (ADHD).

While Greenfield and others have become quieter in recent years, their impact has been significant and more loud voices are always around the corner irrespective of the technology. Their thesis follows that social relationships are fundamentally damaged by screen-based technology, which may affect cognitive development in children. As considered in previous chapters, book reading is also a socially isolating activity, but smartphone use is often singled out as specifically problematic – possibly because it provides so many potential distractions.

All this has to be squared with evidence to support the beneficial use of technology, including early learning, exposure to new ideas and knowledge, increased opportunities for social contact and support, and new opportunities to access health promotion messages and information (Chassiakos et al., 2016). While some researchers suggest that 'passive' use of technology (such as background television) has negative impacts on children's behaviour, others argue that use of interactive devices and gaming platforms in a social setting might enhance a broad range of perceptual and cognitive mechanisms (Courage, 2017; Fikkers et al.,

2019). Thus, a different take on the above could be that the children's brains are being loaded with new knowledge and capacities that will ultimately enhance educational outcomes by improving cognitive flexibility. Recent work from Przybylski and Weinstein (2019) focused on links between well-being and screen time in children, which includes the use of smartphones. They found little to no support for harmful links between screen use and well-being. Of course, this does not rule out costs to physical health or executive functioning (Chassiakos et al., 2016; Costigan et al., 2013). However, Taylor et al. (2018) observed no associations between mobile device usage and language development in children. Cohort designs have also observed no evidence that parents or teachers rate children's face-to-face social skills as worse after accounting for screen time use (Downey and Gibbs, 2020). As with studies reported in earlier chapters, designs that have been pre-registered or rely on objective methods are less likely to observe links between general technology use and poorer cognitive development in children.

5.2   Adult Cognition

As with childhood development, fewer papers focus specifically on the direct cognitive impacts of smartphone use in adult populations. Rather, research often considers areas that are analogous to specific smartphone functions. This includes how single phone calls might distract attention or if repetitive photo-taking impairs memory. Therefore, rather than concentrating on potential 'problem' behaviours associated with smartphone technology as discussed in Chapter 1, I will specifically consider evidence as it pertains to cognitive consequences following typical everyday smartphone use before discussing the merits and limitations of research that considers child and adult populations.

5.2.1   Attention

One impact of using smartphones that has been demonstrated consistently is their ability to provide a cognitive distraction that can interfere with ongoing mental tasks. Wilmer et al. (2017) suggest that such distraction can come in two forms: endogenous or exogenous. The first, which is more challenging to study, involves an individual's thoughts drifting towards the device, whereas exogenous distractions involve the capturing of attention by hearing the sound of a smartphone or feeling it vibrate. Marty-Dugas et al. (2018) have made a similar distinction between general and absent-minded

activities. In terms of general usage, one study demonstrated that participants who were unable to answer a ringing iPhone were slower to complete
a puzzle (Clayton, Leshner and Almond, 2015). Receiving notifications can
also lead to poorer performance on tasks that require significant concentra-
tion (Stothart, Mitchum and Yehnert, 2015). Similar results have been
observed with the mere presence of a device, but this only appeared to
impact more demanding tasks (Thornton et al., 2014; Ward et al., 2017).
Other research, however, has found that smartphone cues (e.g., Facebook or
Twitter icons) associated with high social rewards did not capture attention
or impair visual search tasks (Johannes, Dora and Rusz, 2019). The same
authors also observed, somewhat in contrast to previous findings, that
participants who were deprived of their smartphone were faster to respond
than those who were allowed to keep possession of their device. However,
there is very little to suggest that resultant changes are specific to the
separation or presence of a smartphone or whether an identical effect
would appear when participants are separated from something else of
equal monetary value (e.g., their wallet). Recent reviews regarding the
impacts on attention in the laboratory conclude that the literature is still
in its infancy (Wilmer et al., 2017).

Irrespective of laboratory-based research, there is no denying that smartphones can provide a harmful distraction, at least in the short term. For
example, several studies have considered everyday smartphone use in the
context of attentional lapses and mind wandering, which are of an arguably
greater concern to public health. This includes phone use that can demonstrably interfere with driving or walking (Ioannidou, Hermens and
Hodgson, 2017; Marty-Dugas et al., 2018). For example, a sixfold increase
in pedestrian injuries related to mobile phone use was found during the rise
of smartphone technology (between 2004 and 2010; Nasar and Troyer,
2013). Talking on the phone has also been found to increase unsafe crossing
at crosswalks (Nasar, Hecht and Wener, 2008). Phone users also walk more
slowly, change direction more frequently and notice unusual activities less
often (Hyman et al., 2010). These findings have been replicated during
virtual reality road crossing. Here, phone use distracted attention away
from traffic, led to unsafe crossing behaviour and more collisions and close
calls with upcoming traffic (Stavrinos, Byington and Schwebel, 2009).
Video recordings of pedestrians also revealed that 20 per cent were using
their smartphone while crossing the road. Overall, they observed that
smartphone users generated more critical events compared to non-users
(Horberry, Osborne and Young, 2019). However, the effects were not
completely homogeneous. For example, while smartphone users were less

likely to be looking ahead, they were also less likely to cross at the wrong time when compared to non-smartphone users. This suggests that potential interventions to reduce risk might need to target specific behaviours accordingly.

Again, other activities that existed before smartphones – for example, listening to music while walking – can provide similar distractions, but can often be more passive as usage is not essential (Schwebel et al., 2012). Ioannidou et al. (2017) specifically examined how smartphone use distracted visual attention when climbing stairs using mobile eye trackers. Again, they found that mobile phone use strongly attracts attention away from the stairs, but when people looked away from their phone, they distributed their attention similarly to when no phone is used. This may mean that people are relying on memory from earlier encounters of the stairs or looking closely at their intended path before walking (Rosenbaum, 2009). However, they also point out that this is at odds with other research by Miyasike-daSilva, Allard and McIlroy (2011), who found that a preview of stairs and repeated ascent and descent did not influence gaze behaviour.

Using a smartphone in other circumstances, including while driving, is a criminal offence in many countries. This includes making or receiving a call without a hands-free device, or performing an interactive function, including texting or reading a text. While driving, the risks associated with smartphone use have been researched at length, possibly because of the direct danger this poses to other road users and pedestrians. Even before the advent of smartphones, field research has considered the impact of making a call while driving. The risk of a collision when using a traditional cellular telephone was four times higher than the risk when a phone was not being used (Redelmeier and Tibshirani, 1997). Even hands-free systems are not without their distractions, possibly because this can still involve some interaction with a device. The same authors on that occasion found that systems that allowed the hands to be free offered no safety advantage over handheld units. There is no doubt that these activities distract attention from driving. This makes accidents more likely and remains a major public health challenge (Engelberg et al., 2015). Despite this, many drivers continue to report using their smartphone while driving (White et al., 2010). However, as with other comparisons between smartphone usage and self-report (Andrews et al., 2015), young drivers underestimate their smartphone usage while driving (Albert and Lotan, 2018). For example, one naturalistic study asked young drivers to install a research-oriented smartphone app which continuously monitors smartphone interactions while driving. Albert and Lotan (2018) examined thousands of trips and observed that young drivers touched their smartphone screen on average 1.6 times per minute of driving. More than half of the screen-touches were performed while the vehicle was in motion, and often occurred while using WhatsApp.

In terms of the impact this might be having on accidents directly, Owens et al. (2018) took advantage of data from the 'Second Strategic Highway Research Program Naturalistic Driving Study'. This included data from thousands of participants who had had their driving monitored using in-vehicle video and other data collection equipment for several months. A case-crossover study design considered a driver's cell-phone use in the six seconds immediately prior to a crash, which was compared with the same driver's cell-phone use in up to four six-second segments of ordinary driving under similar conditions (time of day, weather, locality, lighting and speed) within the three months prior to the crash. Cell-phone use, crash involvement, and traffic and environmental conditions were assessed using in-vehicle video. The researchers could control for many additional factors that can also lead to an accident. Their results reflected similar patterns to previous studies, with visual-manual tasks (particularly texting) associated with significantly increased crash risk.

In summary, the evidence for the short-term impacts of smartphone use (in some situations) on attention is compelling but not unique to smartphones. Long-term impacts on attention are unknown. Even in the case of distractions caused by driving, entertainment systems including radios often provide a similar distraction (Stevens and Minton, 2001). Many of these issues may also extend to the use of smartwatches, but there is less research in this area (Giang, Hoekstra-Atwood and Donmez, 2014). This has led to some innovative technological enhancements following applied research outlined above. For example, smartphones can switch into a specific mode while driving or sleeping to remove additional distractions. Automatic replies to any incoming texts or calls are available to most users, but these of course can be overwritten at any time.

5.2.2   Memory

Despite the ability for smartphones to generate and access knowledge, many have suggested that our autobiographical memory is being disrupted by an over-reliance on devices that store large amounts of information about ourselves and others (Frith and Kalin, 2016). However, even less research in this area is specific to the use of smartphones (Wilmer et al.,

2017). Instead, associated digital services or systems which can easily be accessed via a smartphone are the focus of research. For example, individuals who believed a computer would remember access to typed information performed more poorly on a later recall task when compared with those who were told the information would be erased (Sparrow, Liu and Wegner, 2011). Remarkably, being told to remember the information versus not being told to remember had no effect on recall. This perhaps reflects the cognitive miser principle. Specifically, people will gravitate towards thinking and solving problems in simpler and less effortful ways wherever possible (taking shortcuts) regardless of intelligence (Fiske and Taylor, 2013). Adapting and remembering how to use more technology that can access information is preferable to devoting cognitive resources that store readily available information. This notion of 'memory externalisation' that many research designs focus on is certainly not a new issue (Wilmer et al., 2017).

Somewhat parallel to these findings, but taking the extended self-concept further, Barr et al. (2015) frame the smartphone as a tool that allows people to extend their mind based on the same notion that people tend to be 'cognitive misers' (Kahneman, 2011). They argue that people's reliance on mental shortcuts leads to the regular use of search engines as a substitute for deeper cognitive thinking. Heavier self-reported smartphone use was associated with a reduction in analytical thinking styles. Irrespective of existing issues regarding technology measurement and the correlational nature of the design, Wilmer, Sherman and Chein (2017) point out that these results could be interpreted in the opposite direction. Specifically, seeking out information is associated with fluid intelligence (Fleischhauer et al., 2010) and those with improved analytical thinking processes may be more efficient in their use of search tools.

Other research has focused on the impact on memory when taking photographs or using navigational systems. The practice of taking pictures and videos for some is a consequence of both smartphone ownership and the popularity of apps like Instagram and Snapchat. Taking photographs appears to have an impact on memory (versus simply observing objects). Henkel (2014) observed that people were worse at recalling objects they had photographed with a digital camera. Another experiment in the same paper showed that this effect was mitigated by asking the participants to zoom in on specific features of the objects that they were viewing before taking the picture. One wonders if identical effects would appear if an analogue camera and zoom were used. Of course, taking and sharing photos have become more prevalent, and this could change the way in which memories are encoded. A smartphone, however, records more than just the photo-graph. Qualitative research documents personal accounts whereby the 'check-in' capability of some social media apps alongside photos can establish a topographical memory. This could both supplant and augment the memory of surroundings and experiences (Özkul and Humphreys, 2015).

While Wilmer, Sherman and Chein (2017) point out that little is known about specific effects of ephemeral photo-sharing tools on memory for events, Piwek and Joinson (2016) demonstrated that people are perfectly able to recall the last photograph sent and received via Snapchat. Perhaps a sensible avenue for future research in this area could compare the effects on memory following the use of specific smartphone apps, standalone digital cameras and analogue devices when contrasted with an observation condition used by Henkel (2014).

GPS systems have also been suggested as another way people can offload semantic memory because it interferes with the development of spatial representations. Some experiments, for example, show that when partici-pants are allowed to study a map for longer, their spatial knowledge of a journey is better when compared to those who studied a map for less time and were provided with a voice navigation system (Burnett and Lee, 2005). However, as with photographs, spatial knowledge can be improved if participants are encouraged to mentally rotate images (Boari et al., 2012). While modern smartphones allow for actual rather than mental rotation of maps, Boari et al. (2012) observed that spatial tasks were performed faster, and just as accurately, when participants relied on mental abilities rather than interaction techniques to perform 3D rotations. However, their spatial task was comparatively different to reading a map. It is worth noting that traditional map use and smartphone GPS mapping are cogni-tively very different tasks that require a somewhat separate set of skills in order to be successful.

One might conclude that the available evidence suggests that if we rely on other devices or services, we remember less from these experiences.

> Creating a hard copy of an experience through media leaves only a diminished copy in our own heads. (Tamir et al., 2018, p. 167)

However, none of this is specific to smartphone technology and appears to apply to various forms of media (Tamir et al., 2018). Exactly why these effects occur remains unclear. It might be due to distractions from multi-tasking or simply externalising an experience. These may interact or combine and likely depend on other contextual factors. For example, sharing or interacting with different audiences is already known to impact other psychological phenomena (e.g., social comparisons). This makes future research in the area challenging as the specific activity is likely to be of equal importance to the intended audience and surrounding environment.

5.2.3   Delay Discounting

Delay discounting is based on the notion that adults and children are less able to wait for rewards in comparison to previous generations. Wilmer and Chein (2016) observed that people who self-reported heavier use of mobile technology were more likely to accept a smaller, immediate reward than wait for a substantial delayed reward. The correlation between technology habits and delay of gratification was mediated by individual differences in impulsivity, but not in reward/sensation seeking. These findings replicate earlier investigations linking media use and impulsivity (Sanbonmatsu et al., 2013). However, this could be because people who naturally gravitate towards immediate gratification and give into impulses more easily also use their mobile devices more often (i.e., there may not be a causal relationship from media use to discounting behaviour).

Pilot experimental work has considered whether non-users of smartphones would exhibit a change in their reward processing capacity after being provided with a smartphone for the first time (Hadar et al., 2015). Participants were split into three groups: heavy smartphone users, smartphone non-users and smartphone non-users who were given a smartphone for the first time (the latter two groups were assigned randomly). The heavy smartphone users showed higher scores for impulsivity and hyperactivity on a questionnaire that was administered at the beginning of the experiment. However, after a three-month exposure to smartphones, the non-users who were given a smartphone were found to have become more immediacy oriented in the delay discounting measure, whereas non-users' orientation did not change. One might conclude that heavy smartphone usage might causally reduce an individual's capacity (or at least tendency) to delay gratification in favour of a greater reward in the future. While these findings are strengthened by the study's experimental design, the sample sizes are far too small to allow for strong conclusions. These results have also been somewhat refuted by larger studies in recent years that have considered both delay gratification and higher-order effects (Frost et al., 2019).

5.2.4   Collective and Higher-Order Effects on Cognition

A final area of research has considered trickle-down effects that cut across multiple cognitive domains. This can also be considered in the context of previous examples. For example, driving behaviour has been shown to be affected by mobile phone use (Engström, Johansson, and Östlund, 2005; Törnros and Bolling, 2005), which may impact on the distribution of overt attention (Konstantopoulos, Chapman and Crundall, 2010), recognition memory (Strayer, Drews and Crouch, 2006) and reaction times to the slowing of a car ahead (Lamble et al., 1999). Therefore, multiple effects occurring in specific domains may be reflected in higher-level cognitive functioning (Bauerlein, 2011; Marsh and Rajaram, 2019). This can quickly become complicated to understand in an applied context. While it seems sensible to assume that the internet alone may provide a route to cognitive enhancement in many circumstances, this requires a new set of skills given the volume of information available, which will vary in quality (Buchanan, 2011; Voinea et al., 2020). At the same time, being permanently connected allows people to access information at any time, but provides additional distractions. For example, a sizeable body of research has associated smartphone use with poor academic performance (e.g., Lepp, Barkley and Karpinski, 2015). Researchers have also directly investigated the relationship between mobile technology/media multitasking habits and executive functions that are thought to be essential to academic performance (Seo et al., 2016). Less research has considered academic performance in the context of actual device usage longitudinally. The *studentlife* project did predict students' grade point average (GPA) from behaviour derived from a variety of on-board smartphone sensors, but app usage was not a factor (Wang et al., 2015). On the other hand, small correlations between usage and academic performance have been observed in other objective studies (Felisoni and Godoi, 2018; Giunchiglia et al., 2018).

Experimental research, however, suggests that smartphones are unlikely to be the causal factor. In one of the most comprehensive studies to date, Frost et al. (2019) explored the lingering effects of smartphone use on cognition after manipulating usage experimentally. An initial study again observed a negative relationship between self-reported smartphone use, social problem-solving and delayed gratification. However, a series of experiments asked participants to increase or decrease their usage, which was cross-referenced with phone-tracking apps. While they observed that the ability to extract the deeper meaning of information was influenced by heavy, daily smartphone use, this only occurred for a limited amount of time (for about no more than a month after increased use). These effects could potentially also take place following any new intensive activity that disrupted normal habits. However, we know that smartphone use is remarkably consistent day to day (Wilcockson, Ellis and Shaw, 2018). As observed previously, when careful experimentation and objective measurement are aligned, the effects of mobile technology on higher-order cognition dissipate.

That said, many questions remain regarding the impact of smartphones on productivity, especially when it may become difficult to disconnect from occupational demands. For example, many people feel that the boundaries between home and work have become completely intertwined (Bright Horizons, 2020). This may be a cause of employee burnout, and psychology research has, perhaps in response, focused on the notion of Cyberloafing. This term is used to describe the actions of employees who use internet access for other activities while pretending to do legitimate work. Derived from the term 'goldbricking', this originally referred to applying gold coating to a brick of worthless metal. However, like phubbing, which involves snubbing others in social situations and focusing on a smartphone instead (Haigh, 2015), there may be several other reasons why people engage with such behaviours that have little to do with the technology itself. A variety of indirect effects may explain other cognitive impacts associated with smartphone use.

Cyberloafing may simply be a coping mechanism for boredom rather than a form of counterproductive behaviour (Pindek, Krajcevska and Spector, 2018). Motivational models would argue that boredom and fatigue may reduce after short periods of use, but these interactions may instead enhance existing fatigue further (Dora et al., 2020; Inzlicht, Schmeichel and Macrae, 2014; Westgate and Wilson, 2018). Alternatively, Cyberloafing could simply be the result of sleep disturbances or other pre-existing conditions (Cain and Gradisar, 2010). The direction of any effect remains unclear: poor sleep in general may lead to increased screen time. On the other hand, exposure to smartphone screens, particularly around bedtime, may negatively impact sleep and cognitive functioning (Christensen et al., 2016). In support of the first explanation Wagner et al. (2012) demonstrated that during the annual shift to daylight saving time and its accompanying loss of sleep, employees spent more time than normal surfing the web for content unrelated to their work. These findings were also replicated in an experiment where sleep was interrupted the night before.

Related behaviours could be further explained by the ego-depletion model of self-regulation. This argues that all acts of self-regulation draw on the same group of resources (Baumeister, Muraven and Tice, 2000). This pool of resources has a limit, but is renewable. Imagine writing an essay and engaging in self-control to not watch your favourite Netflix series. Engaging in episodes of self-regulation or when concurrently engaging in multiple tasks that require self-regulation, the self-regulatory resource is drained, resulting in a state of diminished regulatory ability, or ego depletion. Sleep has been proposed as one way in which these resources can be recovered and so when this is limited for any reason, Cyberloafing is more likely to occur in this instance. The notion of ego depletion, however, remains the subject of considerable debate and has, in recent years, failed to replicate at least in laboratory conditions (e.g., Vadillo, Gold and Osman, 2018). Other related explanations may instead focus on the notion that sleep helps structurally generalise information across different problems, and a lack of sleep therefore would encourage less efficient use of the internet when attempting to solve a problem (Monaghan et al., 2015).

5.3   Limitations and Future Research

Decades of research has focused on how smartphones limit rather than extend cognitive capacity and largely ignores or glosses over how devices extend the possibilities for learning and knowledge exchange (Chassiakos et al., 2016). Alternative explanations appear to provide a more robust account as to why specific results might be occurring, and the latest evidence casts further doubt on how smartphones might interfere with basic cognitive processes in the first instance. Irrespective of whether the net gain is positive or negative, our current understanding of how technology impacts the cognitive development of children or impacts adults is hindered by several major barriers that are worthy of further discussion.

Longitudinal data sets with robust cognitive and technological metrics are lacking, especially studies including children under the age of six and older adults. Research again appears to be struggling to keep pace with technological development. This can also lead to knowledge redundancy for technologies that have become obsolete. Existing evidence does not measure behaviour or interactions with technology directly but relies on self-report using slightly different scales to those outlined in earlier chapters.[1] These continue to be developed despite failing to report or

---

[1] A few exceptions are studies that have measured the impact of smartphone use on driving (e.g., Albert and Lotan, 2018) and the lingering effects of smartphone use on cognition (e.g., Frost et al., 2019). Communication scholars have devoted more resources to describing multitasking across single and multiple devices (e.g., Yeykelis, Cummings and Reeves, 2014).

follow standard psychometric development procedures (Carpenter, 2018; Hawi, Samaha and Griffiths, 2019). Media multitasking questionnaires remain particularly popular (Baumgartner et al., 2016; Ophir, Nass and Wagner, 2009). However, given how poor single survey instruments are at predicting behaviour from one device, one would speculate that multitasking questionnaires will provide an even weaker alignment with ground truth (Ellis, 2019). This has not prevented researchers from associating frequent media multitaskers with a variety of cognitive deficits (e.g., poorer working memory and diminished long-term memory) or benefits (e.g., improved multisensory integration) (Lui and Wong, 2012; Uncapher, Thieu and Wagner, 2016). Relatedly, specific evidence for causal effects of technology use on brain function is lacking. Neurological evidence is often underpowered (Gindrat et al., 2015) and also lacks objective technology measurements (Moisala et al., 2016). Neural responses to specific digital events and behaviours may provide a promising way forward in the first instance; however, it is not clear how any of these could be feasibly linked to specific technology use in the long term (Crone and Konijn, 2018; Sherman et al., 2016).

Existing associations are equally likely to arise due to an increased propensity for certain individuals to engage with new digital technology, including video games and social media. In terms of ADHD specifically, while some meta-analyses have demonstrated small associations between screen-based media and ADHD symptoms (e.g., Nikkelen et al., 2014), the directionality of this relationship is unknown and unrelated to a specific use of one technology. Technology use may increase the prevalence of ADHD symptoms by impacting development. However, increases in frequency and severity of symptoms are equally likely to be an artifact of changing diagnostic criteria and enhanced awareness (Russell et al., 2014). Alternatively, those with a diagnosis of ADHD might use digital media more anyway. To further complicate matters, transactional media-effects models propose that ADHD symptoms in children may not only impact how they use media but also partly shape any effects following the use of such technology (Beyens, Valkenburg and Piotrowski, 2018; Ra et al., 2018). Considering how those with a diagnosis of ADHD use technology would help differentiate these associations between those without a diagnosis further.

The science has simply not caught up with the grand claims. Selective reporting dominates the discourse from prominent scientists in the area. While considerably more research has been conducted in adult populations, this has not prevented some countries setting health guidelines on restricting screen time for younger children (Przybylski and Weinstein, 2019), even when large studies and systematic reviews continue to support the notion that more research is needed (Stiglic and Viner, 2019). Surprisingly, developmental work concerning new technology rarely involves children in the research process. Children are often treated as passive subjects rather than active collaborators and designers in the scientific process. There is an opportunity to reframe research questions so they become more relevant and impactful to children's lives. Lessons could be learnt from patient involvement with clinical trials in other areas.

5.3.1   Cognitive Biases: The Kids Are All Right

Many attempts at explaining causality appear plausible, at least from a 'folk psychology' perspective. However, it remains surprising that many professional psychologists and other scientists drift into this territory without first considering the evidence as it stands. The idea of smartphones causing 'brain drain' or impacting heavily on neuroplasticity will struggle to square with a scientific perspective. Instead, these are drawn from anecdotal explanations (e.g., Carr, 2008, 2010). Specifically, this is built around casual observations of people we know, sometimes students who are taught by academics. Of course, even if an individual observes the behaviour of everyone they know, the average person will only know about a dozen people well (see Dunbar, 1992) and a few hundred in extreme cases. That prevents any form of assumption or analysis, especially when most of us only know a fairly restricted kind of person. For example, many academics know many other academics but fewer students.

Building on this argument, recent research has confirmed that people typically compare their biased memory to the present, whereby a decline appears when reflecting on children today (Protzko and Schooler, 2019).

> Authoritarian people especially think youth are less respectful of their elders, intelligent people especially think youth are less intelligent, and well-read people especially think youth enjoy reading less. (Protzko and Schooler, 2019, p. 1)

These effects may be even stronger in academics who are likely to meet at least one of those criteria. Protzko and Schooler (2019) suggest that two mechanisms contribute to this illusory effect: a person-specific tendency to notice the limitations of others where one excels and a memory bias projecting one's current qualities onto the youth of the past. The authors also note that while their results do not rule out that in some domains children may have genuinely been in decline, in many areas children are improving, including on measures of intelligence. If this has continued over time, then they identify no other reason why more intelligent people would falsely believe the opposite.

Moving beyond what may happen in one person's head to the influences and associations across an entire population is therefore not possible with explanations provided by many leading voices as to how children specifically are cognitively worse off as a result of new technology. In contrast, those in medicine would never allow such a weak basis for mechanisms to drive subsequent study (except maybe homeopaths). What cannot be denied, however, is that children grow up while continually surrounded by a variety of digital devices and smartphones have become increasingly prevalent. Similarly, whether engaged through computers, tablets, smartphones or televisions, technology will remain a fixture of modern childhood and adult life (Houghton et al., 2015). This already makes for a challenging research environment because controls are not readily available. Despite this, researchers still have a duty to identify any mechanisms and the extent to which mobile and other screen-based technology might influence children.

While some research concerning potential cognitive impacts relies on explanations that fall foul of pre-existing biases, these may also affect research designs directly. Specifically, researchers appear to actively avoid using the technology they aim to understand. There is an under-explored opportunity to build experimental paradigms into smartphones directly. This would provide a more complete understanding of cognitive impacts as they align with technology use in situ. Remarkably, all the above research sits separately from psychologists who are using the very same technology to build exactly those platforms. These alone can bring cognitive testing from the laboratory into the real world in ways that can engage millions of children and adults.

5.4   Smartphones as a Platform for Cognitive Science

Research concerning the impact of smartphones on cognition largely ignores cognitive research that uses smartphones as a research tool. Nevertheless, the notion of studying cognitive processes in the real-world including how memories are stored and curated is not a new idea, but it was previously methodologically challenging (Neisser, 1985). The studies outlined in the following pages demonstrate that cognitive abilities can be assessed accurately and better understood in large samples outside the laboratory. Despite previous appearances, cognitive science has been engaging with and adapting smartphone functionality for some time. Cameras, motion sensors and location-tracking abilities have recently been combined with traditional lab-based approaches. For example, a small body of research has started to repurpose smartphones as wearable devices to better understand how people encode and retrieve autobiographical memories in their everyday life (Nielson et al., 2015). In one study, participants wore a smartphone that took photos of their daily life as well as recording location and time. The same participants were invited to a test session where they were presented with these photos while in an MRI scanner. The results showed that the left anterior hippocampus represents time and space up to a scale of a month in time and 30 km in space. These results replicate previous laboratory experiments that involve much smaller timescales (up to a few minutes) and suggest that the anterior hippocampus may help scaffold or represent time and space in everyday life (Dennis et al., 2017; Nielson et al., 2015).

Similarly, ecological momentary assessment has benefited research concerning a variety of other memory processes (e.g., presenting recall tasks), emotional regulation and emotional development. Emotional regulation specifically is a central process that underpins adaptive social and emotional development. However, like psychology more generally, the field has struggled with conceptual and methodological challenges in operationalising and investigating such a topic over time, in different contexts and with multiple measures (Cole, Martin and Dennis, 2004). Recent studies using smartphones have, however, started to demonstrate more within than between variation in emotion regulation strategy, suggesting that contextual factors are important (Benson et al., 2019). For example, depressed and non-depressed youths continue to rely on adults to help regulate emotion for about half the negative events reported by adults (Waller et al., 2014). However, the authors also observed that the social context's impact on emotional regulation may be moderated by other individual differences, including symptoms of pathology. Smartphone sensing methods introduced in Chapter 2 may be beneficial to future research in this area for both understanding and delivering interventions (Silk, 2019).

In other instances, cognitive research has developed interactive apps that mimic experimental tasks. As with other studies involving data collected remotely, these apps can then upload data sets to the cloud. Although in principle this is likely to be noisier than small-scale laboratory studies, these have the potential to uncover subtle effects such as individual differences, temporal trends and the influence of lifestyle and demographic factors on cognitive performance. In addition, one could make the argument that tests conducted outside the laboratory are a closer approximation to the truth as real-world *noise* is a key component of everyday cognitive processing. The potential to share cognitive data collected directly from devices also opens up avenues where experimental findings can be replicated, challenged or linked to other data sets. For example, linking cognitive performance with clinical records can allow for the analysis of unprecedented amounts of data from increasingly large numbers of research participants (McQueenie et al., 2019).

Complete systems can also provide a public engagement loop whereby participants can be informed of publications, press releases and even how their performance might compare to others in a sample or population. Sometimes termed 'citizen science', these projects often harness the goodwill of participants to undertake a variety of tasks. Such an approach often shares the documented advantages of web-based research (Birnbaum, 2004); however, smartphone apps are often more enjoyable, easier to use and can build trust and mutual understanding between researchers and the public. As with other areas these can also transcend issues concerning a lack of diverse samples and help recruit difficult or hard-to-reach, culturally diverse populations. For example, a variety of researchers have built specific apps to successfully consider the effects of ageing on cognition (McNab et al., 2015; Teki, Kumar and Griffiths, 2016).

The Great Brain Experiment was one of the first large-scale studies to demonstrate the validity of smartphones as a suitable platform to collect cognitive behavioural data outside a laboratory environment. Standard cognitive paradigms were recreated in a way that made them quick and enjoyable to complete (see Lumsden et al., 2016, for a review on gamification of cognitive assessment and training). Four paradigms were chosen that covered several cognitive domains, including perception, action inhibition, decision-making and short-term memory (see Figure 5.1). The authors were able to collect data from over 16,000 participants in a single month. Participants could also compare their scores against others and read information about the background and significance of each psychological paradigm (Brown et al., 2014). Effect sizes were broadly similar to tasks conducted in a laboratory environment with a larger number of participants allowing researchers to detect smaller effects in some instances.

Other designs have focused on more specific aspects of cognition. For example, Zimmerman et al. (2016) confirmed previous lab research that documented population-level abilities in subtraction and addition. In recent years there has been a mini explosion in the development of specific

Figure 5.1 A gamified version of the stop-signal reaction time task (Brown et al., 2014).
Note: Fruit fell from the tree and participants were asked to tap simultaneously on
both sides of the screen as the fruit passed through the circles. If a piece of fruit turned
brown during its fall, participants had to inhibit their response on that side
Brown, H. R., Zeidman, P., Smittenaar, P., Adams, R. A., McNab, F., Rutledge,
R. B., & Dolan, R. J. (2014). Crowdsourcing for cognitive science – the utility of
smartphones. *PLOS ONE, 9*(7), e100662.

apps that can present stimuli over longer timescales (Mack et al., 2019) and conduct vigilance tests (Grant et al., 2017). This also extends to apps and analysis routines that aim to quantify other behaviours known to impact on or correlate with cognitive functioning, including sleep and heart-rate variability (Brunet et al., 2017; Matsumura and Yamakoshi, 2013).

Researchers have also persevered with the notion of gamification further to encourage participant engagement. Coutrot et al. (2018) used a mobile app to test the spatial ability of over 2.5 million people around the world. However, their analysis only focused on around half a million participants who had completed at least nine levels of the game. This game (Sea Hero Quest) involved navigating a boat to search for sea creatures. While game based, the aim was to capture a wide range of abilities and processes required for successful everyday navigation. As expected, spatial ability declined with age. However, after linking this data with other metrics they also observed that spatial ability was strongly correlated with a country's economic wealth, with gender differences reflecting gender inequality in a specific country. Performance in the game also appears to be predictive of real-world behaviour in small samples when tracking location patterns via the GPS sensor (Coutrot et al., 2019). In addition, people who are genetically predisposed to developing Alzheimer's disease can be distinguished from healthy individuals using specific features and levels of the Sea Hero Quest game. In contrast, standard memory assessment tests struggle to distinguish between these two groups (Coughlan et al., 2019; Hudson, 2019).

Global cognitive deficits are a major world health issue and their impact cascades across the lifespan. As with work concerning physical health and personality, smartphone games and sensor-tracking technologies could be used to diagnose and track cognitive function over time in large sections of the population (Hudson, 2019). Modelling cognitive decline specifically already appears possible between participants. Other researchers have pointed towards the variety of data generated from related devices and commercial games, which could assist with other diagnoses based on cognitive performance and fine motor control (Gielis, 2019). For example, Apple has recently added a new application programming interface (API) to its open-source ResearchKit framework. This allows the Apple Watch to continuously monitor Parkinson's disease symptoms (Apple, 2016). Similarly, games publishers already provide access to APIs that would allow researchers to access player data. However, many questions remain as to how these might work in practice (Mandryk and Birk, 2019). Even if game metrics were readily available, these would need to be extensively validated against standardised cognitive batteries or expert observation. The risk of false positives is also likely to be high. Going forward, researchers developing new paradigms or games might want to follow Sea Hero Quest's example, as it appears to have been developed carefully and tested incrementally across multiple populations and contexts. Collectively, this avenue of research provides yet another collaborative avenue for human–computer interaction researchers and psychologists.

5.4.1   Limitations and Future Research

Conducting cognitive research on a larger scale is possible by systematically shifting more laboratory work into the real world. The utility of smartphones and associated wearable devices in this domain will grow as more people across the world have access to the technology. Rather than being viewed as a noisy alternative, the interface provided by a modern smartphone may, for some tasks like the Stroop, be superior when used in certain populations (Spanakis et al., 2019). That said, drop-out rates can be high for some of these designs; however, the statistical power afforded by a larger subject pool can compensate as demonstrated in web-based research previously (Birnbaum, 2004). In addition, it is often more straightforward to reward participants financially or encourage them via gamified approaches to interact with a task for longer periods of time to rectify this issue (Lumsden et al., 2016).

Brown and colleagues argued in 2014 that data collected from smartphones will struggle to offer a perfect mapping of users to devices. It is true that more than one person might use a device and poor internet coverage may lead to some data loss. However, this ignores improvements to authentication practices and the reliability of cloud-based systems. Further, a cloud-based approach to data collection may not be necessary once an app is installed. Local collection remains possible for many designs with encrypted data being transmitted via email or personal cloud systems (Geyer, Ellis and Piwek, 2019). Irrespective of data-sharing issues, complex video-game-based designs will continue to rely on intensive processing pathways to make data useful. For example, Coutrot et al. (2018) defined overall performance in Sea Hero Quest as a metric that captures different aspects of navigation abilities while correcting for video-gaming skills. While full data sets are sometimes available, the code for developed apps and analytical processes are not mentioned in the vast majority of papers. This raises issues of replication and reusability that are analogous with incomplete data sharing (Turner et al., 2019). Developing apps remains time consuming and technically challenging, especially when compared to other software used to build cognitive experiments for use in laboratories (e.g., *SuperLab*, *PsychoPy*). The process often has to be outsourced. On the other hand, many research-ers are regularly developing interdisciplinary collaborations. Doctoral train-ing in psychology also appears to be encouraging more students to develop skills traditionally associated with computer science.[2]

Software that allows researchers to build experiments and create an executable file that can be uploaded to an app store would support future research. These would need to be kept simple in the first instance and allow for the straightforward collection and transmission of data. However, hardware and software changes are inevitable and so any toolbox or development library may require constant development if it was to remain future-proof. The creation of more advanced 3D environments using systems like *Unity* requires even more specific knowledge, but several researchers in psychology are already building simple virtual environments from scratch to better understand perception and action (Linkenauger, Weser and Proffitt, 2019).

Technical challenges may lessen over time, at least for simple designs – for example, *PsychoPy* experiments can now be deployed online via web browsers. A smartphone app in theory could simply point towards a URL; however, performance may be inconsistent (Peirce et al., 2019). Commercial providers have been quick to identify gaps in the market when existing software already runs on similar devices. For example, several organisations can combine experience sampling with objective sensor data (e.g., *MetricWire*) or supply cognitive tasks for tablet devices (e.g., *Cambridge Cognition*). However, even if all these options were readily available, the consistent delivery of some stimuli may forever be problem-atic given the variety of devices, especially for psychophysical experiments (Brown et al., 2014).

5.5   Conclusion

As alluded to in previous chapters, the experimental power going forward comes from looking beyond what psychology alone has become fixated on – harm (Haslam, 2016). Cognitive science alone provides convincing explanations as to why people often think children are worse off than previous generations; however, these do not fully explain the current predicament (Protzko and Schooler, 2019). There is a strong sense of

---

[2] At least in psychology departments known to me.

separation throughout this literature. Scientists who argue that new media is damaging childhood development or adults' cognitive abilities appear to have very little understanding of the technology itself. As before, resources devoted to the technology from a psychological perspective focus on surveys with little regard for objectivity (e.g., Hutton et al., 2019). On the other hand, those who are developing smartphone paradigms to assess cognition directly have very different research priorities and appear unaware of those who wish to understand the impact of said technologies on people and society. Looking ahead, methodological advances from this second group of researchers has now reached a point where smartphones can be easily linked with other recording devices. These can operate at increasing levels of temporal resolution and include physical movement, eye-tracking and event-related potential (ERP) methodologies (Brown et al., 2014). Being more optimistic still, several developmental researchers have recently acknowledged that smartphone use may provide important information about the social context of emotion regulation given that the emotional life of preteens and teens often revolves around smartphones (Silk, 2019).

Psychological science has struggled to assess dynamic behaviours and cognitions in the real world, which can be influenced by temporal or situational factors. However, many argue that this is now feasible (Kaye, Monk and Hamlin, 2018). This can include the impact of technology use itself. Bringing both strands of this chapter together, smartphones themselves are best placed to answer questions regarding how they impact cognitive abilities. Web-based systems have already been used to better understand positive associations between daily activities and cognitive assessments. Specifically, Bielak, Mogle and Sliwinski (2017) found that participants' working-memory performance and response times became faster on days where they also engaged in more social activities with people they knew. Interestingly, physical activity showed no effect on cognition; however, this study did not make any distinction between computer-mediated or face-to-face communication.

Similar work might examine cognitive functioning as it relates to objective smartphone use throughout the day. This could also understand any effects in the context of other, well-established variables that affect cognitive and neurological development, including social deprivation (Mackes et al., 2020). However, while smartphones can deliver cognitive tests, understanding someone's entire human–computer footprint (or total screen time) across multiple devices remains challenging. This will require access to multiple systems or wearable devices to record precise usage patterns that might include elements of active and passive use. Of course, if the effect sizes in recent epidemiological studies are replicated, one might question if the above is a sensible next step given the many other pressing issues known to impact cognition and health worldwide. Regardless, psychology is sitting on resources to start answering the cognitive questions that matter.

Useful Resources and Further Reading

Coutrot, A., Silva, R., Manley, E., De Cothi, W., Sami, S., Bohbot, V. D., ... & Spiers, H. J. (2018). Global determinants of navigation ability. *Current Biology*, *28*(17), 2861–2866.
Demonstrates the power of gamifying a cognitive task involving millions of participants from across the world.
Protzko, J. & Schooler, J. W. (2019). Kids these days: Why the youth of today seem lacking. *Science Advances*, *5*(10), eaav5916.
Presents multiple, preregistered designs that help explain why people often believe children are deficient relative to those of previous generations. Their findings can be applied to how scientists discuss the cognitive and wider impacts of technology on children.
Wilmer, H. H., Sherman, L. E., & Chein, J. M. (2017). Smartphones and cognition: A review of research exploring the links between mobile technology habits and cognitive functioning. *Frontiers in Psychology*, *8*, 605.
A comprehensive review of research that focuses on three key areas of adult cognition that may be impacted by mobile technology – attention, memory and delay of gratification. It also considers some broader issues relating to everyday cognitive functioning. This helped inform the structure of discussions that appear earlier in this chapter.

CHAPTER 6

Safety and Security

Smartphones and associated digital services have become essential for everyday activities. At the same time, increased levels of personalisation and improved functionality provide new avenues for harassment or criminal activity, which can compromise the secure storage of sensitive information. Mobile data also supports a range of corporate activities, and this hyperconnectivity brings with it a variety of complex cybersecurity challenges. On the other hand, the very same digital traces can be a vital source of evidence in criminal cases. For example, Harold Shipman is the only doctor in the history of British medicine to be found guilty of murdering his patients. Evidence at his trial included hidden computer files that proved he was modifying medical records after patients had died to avoid a post-mortem that would reveal their true cause of death – a fatal overdose of diamorphine administered by Shipman himself (BBC, 2000). While this evidence came from a desktop computer, smartphone data has quickly become a routine source for evidence in the previous decade. For example, several cases have used usage data or data collected by a motorist themselves (e.g., self-captured video) to secure convictions for dangerous driving. Related data can also be used to assist with covert surveillance (Scully, 2019). While such information can be invaluable, detective work has been made more complex due to the volume of material from smartphones and other devices, which can of course be manipulated by criminals to deceive law enforcement agencies (Pieterse, Olivier and van Heerden, 2019).

Despite the majority of devices holding large quantities of personal information, many people simply ignore advice when it comes to securing their device. The popularity of smartphones provides yet another digital outlet for illegal data capture, and the first part of this chapter will consider why, despite multiple security concerns, the majority of smartphone users and even large organisations are often unable to recognise the importance of developing sound security practices. Similarly, I will review how researchers are trying to better understand and improve hyperconnected systems for people who manage and interact with them on a regular basis.

While data collected as part of a research project often pales in comparison to what is transmitted to third-party apps (Van Kleek et al., 2017), much of the work considered in previous chapters has relied on participants who are willing to trust researchers with sensitive data. If this is compromised then many people may opt out. Alternatively, devices may become deliberately less accurate in how they track sensitive metrics (e.g., location) to protect privacy (Szot et al., 2019). Either or both outcomes would have a detrimental impact on future research. Unfortunately, existing ethical frameworks for psychological research were designed around the notion of capturing single measurements, but a move towards real-time data collection poses new challenges (Ellis and Piwek, 2016). Therefore, this chapter will conclude by exploring how researchers can develop systems and data collection methodologies that are trusted and secure. These developments can raise awareness and provide solutions to ensure data remains secure even when attempts are made to compromise, distort or disrupt technology that has become essential for everyday functioning.

6.1   Safety and Digital Harm

Previous chapters have touched on potential issues of harm where the research base is far from conclusive. Even issues that one might expect would always lead to harm are rarely universal. For example, making social comparisons is often assumed to be problematic because it can impact on well-being; however, how these are made alters the outcome. Specifically, a social comparison that involves comparing oneself to a body image that is unrealistic and potentially unhealthy can lower mood (Tiggemann and McGill, 2004). Opinion-based comparisons, on the other hand, can reaffirm and help people feel optimistic (Yang, Holden and Carter, 2018). Despite a confused literature base when it comes to understanding the direction of harm, there are areas concerning safety and security which, while straightforward to acknowledge and quantify, remain difficult to address.

As with the impacts of smartphones on social interaction, cognition and well-being, much of the literature tends to focus on safety issues pertaining to children and adolescents. For example, parents often report concerns about who their children are interacting with online.[1] However, research

---

[1] This assumes that most adults understand and take more steps to protect themselves online and lead by example (Alsaleh, Alomar and Alarifi, 2017; Annansingh and Veli, 2016). Gaps in adult knowledge may be similar to those observed in adolescent populations and require further investigation (Macaulay et al., 2019). This lack of or inaccurate knowledge may amplify existing safety concerns.

tends to show that offline and online networks are actually very similar (Boyd and Hargittai, 2013; Gross, 2004). Nevertheless, this raises a genuine safety concern that can lead to harm. Other research has focused on specific interactions with many adolescents reporting that they have, at some point, sent a sexually explicit photo of themselves (Rice et al., 2012). Estimates within adult and adolescent populations vary between studies depending on how *sexting* is defined. However, irrespective of age, many people share intimate details about themselves readily. Beyond being a risk to personal privacy, these can sometimes be unwanted by a recipient (Klettke et al., 2019).

Cyberbullying and trolling can also occur across child and adult populations (Lowry et al., 2016) and domestic abusers can exploit technology to inflict harm irrespective of physical proximity (Woodlock, 2017). This can also have serious psychological consequences for victims (McKenna, 2007). Smartphones also allow for the proliferation of online dating scams as their availability enables relationships to develop more quickly (Whitty, 2018; Whitty and Buchanan, 2016). In terms of physical health, smartphones may encourage sedentary behaviour, and physical injuries from distracted walking are increasingly common as mobile devices have become more popular (Povolotskiy et al., 2019).

Much of the above can be augmented alongside harmful content and misinformation that can be readily accessed online via smartphones. Some concerns focus on a variety of questionable online content, particularly if it advocates self-harm or suicide. This includes high-profile cases involving popular smartphone apps, including Instagram and Facebook (Metz and Satariono, 2019; Talbot et al., 2017).[2] Being exposed to more extreme, traumatic content can also lead to increased levels of stress and post-traumatic symptoms (Holman et al., 2019). Similarly, extremist movements can also use these platforms to help spread harmful ideologies (Aly et al., 2017). This includes the use of deepfakes that can change a person's appearance or voice (Korshunov and Marcel, 2018).

Systems that attempt to recommend content can have unintended consequences. Specifically, algorithms that control content often lead people down wormholes that confirm biases and stereotypes that might already be inaccurate. Recent examples include anti-vax movements, climate change denial and other political misinformation on a global scale that

---

[2] At the time of writing, Instagram is reportedly about to start warning users if their captions on a photo or video could be considered offensive.

harms people and society (Grinberg et al., 2019; Hviid et al., 2019; Lazer et al., 2018; Schäfer, 2012). Other findings, however, have suggested that social media and news portal browsing, when measured objectively, does not contribute to the avoidance of news or restrict diversity (Scharkowa et al., 2020). This suggests that confirmation bias may be driving many of the above effects rather than the availability of information alone. Regardless, these results do not mitigate potential harm following any exposure to misinformation.

While hate-crime content has long been found on the internet, there is a concerted effort to remove such speech through increased moderation. However, many questions remain regarding what the role of law and government should be in this area as illegal online activity can quickly move to different websites or sections of the internet (e.g., the dark web). Criminal activity often relies on technologies (including smartphone apps) that allow groups to communicate anonymously, operate at scale and, in turn, avoid detection. Devices or systems can be difficult to trace when, for example, they are encrypted or not indexed by search engines (Chen et al., 2008). However, there is an element of cat and mouse when it comes to the proliferation of harmful information and online criminal activity as security researchers develop new innovations that can automatically detect such activity and bring it to the attention of law enforcement agencies (Yang, Li and Lyu, 2019). Criminals, in turn, change their behaviour or devise new ways to remain hidden.

Many issues pertaining to digital safety are certainly not unique to smartphones and appear as reflections of how people behave offline (George and Odgers, 2015). Whether the harm is radicalisation or the illicit selling of drugs, these happen where life happens – online, in books and in person. When it comes to childhood specifically, adverse experiences are a very strong predictor of negative life outcomes. Some of these could come via the use of technology, but this same technology can also act as a safety blanket (Williamson et al., 2020). Many other potential harms can become magnified and intertwined as mobile technology is always available. For example, there are well-established links between cyberbullying, offline bullying and sexting (Ojeda, Del Rey and Hunter, 2019). Adolescents who bully others offline also engage in online abuse. Victims of abuse online are more likely to be victimised offline (George and Odgers, 2015).

While it is beyond the scope of this book to consider all potential digital harms in detail, these examples alone document clear risks. However, these are discussed less by psychological science because the majority of existing literature associates everyday usage with emotional harm, poor cognitive functioning or disrupted social interaction – perhaps because many of the potential harms outlined above affect smaller numbers of people. Indeed, for most members of the public, their perception of smartphone security plays a larger role when determining digital safety on a daily basis.

6.2   Security Perceptions

While parents worry about children and teenagers, security and privacy are often not reported to be a concern among the general public, regardless of any acknowledged risks (Alsaleh et al., 2017). For example, permissions provide apps access to specific streams of data or hardware features. This may include real-time location tracking or activating the camera. However, most people do not understand the implications of giving apps permissions to access specific sensors or sensitive data from other apps (e.g., medical data). Indeed, some studies suggest that many app developers themselves do not fully understand permissions. Felt et al. (2011) observed that many developers who create apps request permissions that they often do not require. Similarly, many people incorrectly assume that controlled app marketplaces (e.g., Google Play Store or the App Store run by Apple) will only provide access to secure software (Mylonas, Kastania and Gritzalis, 2013).

There appears to be some consistency in how people describe their smartphone security behaviours specifically. Alsaleh et al. (2017) asked participants about a variety of different security features, including locking mechanisms, application repositories, smartphone location services and mobile instant messaging. Following a series of interviews, they concluded that those who do not lock their phones at all still keep personal information on the device that is often not backed up. People often misunderstand what the data on their phone can reveal about them and view locking the device as an inconvenience (Alsaleh et al., 2017). A range of other behaviours were identified that people do not view as risky but which could potentially compromise their device. This might include chatting with unknown people, archiving WhatsApp conversations, using messaging app location services, sharing location information in online social networking sites, saving personal photos in gallery apps, syncing photos to the cloud and connecting to public Wi-Fi networks. On the other hand, people were able to consistently rank risks and the sharing of data by third-party apps that they would find more concerning. Surprisingly, improper location sharing was not viewed as especially risky (Alsaleh et al., 2017). Previous research however, suggests that these concerns can change depending on the specific app and over time with people being more concerned about theft and data being compromised before the widespread development of remote recovery services for example (Chin et al., 2012).

In a similar vein, researchers have theorised to try to better understand what factors drive users to protect themselves (or not). For example, social cognitive theory argues that people learn from their environment (e.g., family members) and mimic those behaviours (Bandura, 1986). However, the majority of research concerning security behaviours revolves around a number of alternative frameworks, including the theory of planned behaviour (TPB), technology threat avoidance theory (TTAT) and protection motivation theory (PMT) (Ajzen, 1991; Liang and Xue, 2009; Rogers, 1975; Tsai et al., 2016). These attempt to explain how people perceive and manage security and privacy risks. Based on the principles of TTAT and PMT, decisions to undertake protective actions against threats follow a subjective assessment of how harmful those threats are and their likelihood of experiencing them (Liang and Xue, 2010; Tsai et al., 2016). The premise is that the more someone feels threatened, the more likely they are to engage with protective strategies (Liang and Xue, 2009). As before, if people do not view security as a major concern, they will fail to act.

The technology acceptance model (TAM) has also been used to explain these behaviours. This is an information systems theory that attempts to better understand how people come to adopt and use a technology (Adams, Nelson and Todd, 1992). For example, Ng and Rahim (2005) found that perceived usefulness, peer and media influence, and self-efficacy strengthened users' intentions to adopt backups, anti-virus software and personal firewalls. However, results are somewhat inconsistent as psychological explanations relating to social norms have been reported as more important than perceived usefulness (Jones et al., 2010; Thompson, McGill and Wang, 2017). Regardless, many of these findings can also be considered within a health belief framework (Ng, Kankanhalli and Xu, 2009). Specifically, one can draw links between a protective security behaviour (e.g., using a strong password to prevent data breaches) and preventive health-care behaviour (e.g., adopting a healthy lifestyle to avoid heart diseases).

It is debatable how useful many of these theories are in practice given the ubiquity of mobile digital services. Theoretical approaches more suited to uncovering psychological mechanisms and processes involved in privacy management in the digital age may be better placed by considering privacy in social and group relations, as digital platforms capture large quantities of information about people and places that are directly tied to the end user

(Stuart, Bandara and Levine, 2019). Perhaps in response, recent developments have focused more on what people share about themselves on different communication platforms. For example, the Privacy Calculus theory shares some common ground with TTAT and PMT models as this states that people will self-disclose personal information when the perceived benefits outweigh any perceived negative consequences (Krasnova et al., 2010). This has also recently been extended and appears to generalise across a variety of different contexts (Dienlin and Metzger, 2016; Trepte, Scharkow and Dienlin, 2020). Despite this, communication research often refers to the privacy paradox – originally coined by Barnes in 2006. This states that people's concerns or worries about digital privacy are unrelated to the way in which they share personal information. In other words, even when people explicitly state that they are concerned about privacy in a variety of online contexts, they will continue to share personal information on multiple online platforms (Acquisti, Brandimarte and Loewenstein, 2015). This can also be considered as a misalignment between attitudes and behaviour (cognitive dissonance) and should lead to changes in the behaviour or the attitude (Festinger, 1962). Researchers have pointed out that this concept is slightly puzzling given previous evidence and well-publicised breaches of sensitive data. Some literature speaks directly against such a notion, which typically concerns between-individual data rather than looking at the same people over time (Baruh, Secinti and Cemalcilar, 2017; Dienlin and Trepte, 2015).

Dienlin, Masur and Trepte (2019) recently considered how these behaviours might change over time within participants. They demonstrated that when a person's privacy concerns increased, the same person shared slightly less information online than they did previously. They also observed that people who developed more positive attitudes towards the online sharing of personal information then shared substantially more personal information online. This suggests that at a within-person level the privacy paradox does not appear to exist. Perhaps more importantly, it confirms that online and offline behaviours are not ontologically different. In offline contexts, concerns relating to health, for example, are often not closely aligned with behaviours. People are aware that poor diet will contribute negatively to their health but continue to overeat regardless (Brownell and Horgen, 2004). Despite such a discrepancy, fostering concern about health in the first instance can drive behaviour change. Therefore, acknowledging that the sharing of personal information is not paradoxical and that concerns about online privacy are impactful might leverage responsibility and change behaviour (Dienlin et al., 2019). Such insights align with previous research that established relationships between password choices and shifting perceptions of security (Creese et al., 2013). These results, alongside other theoretical conceptualisations, suggest that existing attempts to change perceptions of existing security behaviours are worth pursing further (Williams, Beardmore and Joinson, 2017).

To summarise, when attempting to improve security within smartphones or designing new features, it is crucial to better understand users' perceptions and misconceptions about these very systems. Many other theories attempt to explain how people understand their own security practices but remain challenging to apply because while the underlying concepts of privacy and security are not new, societal concerns are constantly evolving (Houghton and Joinson, 2010). Similarly, from a technical perspective the landscape continues to shift and it remains equally important to understand exactly how smartphone systems might be compromised. This will, in turn, help researchers develop mechanisms that preserve the confidentiality, integrity and availability of data stored across billions of mobile devices.

6.3   Smartphone Security Threats

Irrespective of perceived risks, smartphones continue to face a variety of real security threats (Table 6.1). Some of these are more likely if an end user does not follow specific precautions (e.g., not locking a device), but others rely on user actions that have good intentions. Irrespective of malicious intent, this can include downloading content that could comprise personal data by, for example, installing poorly secured software (Leavitt, 2011). Early mobile phones were of limited interest to hackers or criminal gangs because they were a niche product and had comparatively limited functionality with far fewer on-board sensors to track behaviour. However, the more popular a technology becomes, the more attractive it is for criminals. Similarly, threats become more alarming as the quantity and quality of data captured by smartphones continues to increase. For example, smartphones are frequently used to handle sensitive financial transactions and record intimate patterns of behaviour, which can be used to blackmail individuals and organisations. Links between work data and personal data are further intertwined as smartphones are used for dual purposes (Flynn and Klieber, 2015; Kearns, 2016).

Psychological research has traditionally focused on understanding phishing as it applies to emails and text messages, which provides a pernicious threat to security for smartphone users through a variety of other services. For example, an attempt to gain unauthorised access to data can come from specific pop-ups within apps that request

Table 6.1 *Examples of security threats that could lead to sensitive smartphone data being compromised*

Threat	Description	Prevention strategy
Bluetooth	Unsolicited connections can steal information or execute software.	Use only trusted devices.
Botnets	An infected 'zombie device' is controlled by hackers.	Protect devices with anti-virus and firewall software.
Malicious Apps (Malware)	Apps available on popular online stores can steal information.	Only download 'trusted' apps. Use software to check permissions requested.
Phishing	Clicking on a malicious link that can be delivered by a variety of means. Can be included within apps, social media or email.	Flagging systems/behaviour change interventions to help pinpoint spam and likely phishing attacks.
Physical Access	Physical theft of devices can lead to data being compromised.	Lock device and encrypt all data.
Spyware	Software can monitor usage and other behaviours (e.g., location or conversations). Available commercially.	Ensure device is locked when not in use. Use software to check permissions requested.
Wi-Fi	Hackers can intercept communications. If a person's location or Wi-Fi access point is disclosed, then it could put their physical safety at risk. More vulnerable on public (hotspot) connections.	Use only trusted Wi-Fi access points.

information or permissions. Therefore, much of our current understanding is derived from research that has considered an individual's propensity to online influence or susceptibility to phishing (Williams et al., 2017).

Williams, Hinds and Joinson (2018), for example, used secondary data to consider contextual factors that might lead to a response. Their results demonstrated that authority cues increased the likelihood that an individual would click on a link embedded in an email. These findings support several existing models, including the information processing model of phishing susceptibility (IPPM), which suggests that the likelihood of an individual responding is influenced by the content of a message. This might include cues that suggest authority or urgency (e.g., official email signatures) (Vishwanath et al., 2011). In turn, attentional resources are hijacked by particular techniques that might include mentioning an urgent deadline. Focus groups conducted as part of the same research design also suggested that individuals were often unaware that these factors might influence their behaviour. This is also in line with what one would expect, as the IPPM argues that people rely on relatively automatic forms of information processing (heuristic processing) when specific authority or urgency cues are present and will not engage in more in-depth consideration of the legitimacy of the message (systematic processing) (Vishwanath et al., 2011, 2018).

Taking a complementary experimental approach, Jones et al. (2019) explored how individuals differed in response to a phishing email decision-making task. Participants had to rate the legitimacy of multiple emails and also completed a battery of cognitive tasks. They observed that sensation seeking and cognitive reflection were modest predictors of the ability to discriminate email messages. Personality constructs, despite their predictions, were not systematically linked to performance. Their data alongside previous research suggests that psychological markers, including cognitive and social factors, can help explain individual and group vulnerability to making erroneous email decisions. Such results may apply to other general attacks within a smartphone environment. Future experimental work should now consider how different factors across multiple contexts (e.g., locations, devices and services) translate into changes in detection ability. While this research is in its infancy, such work will improve our understanding of the decision-making processes associated with lapses that lead to security breaches (Jones, Towse and Race, 2015). This has simultaneously led to a growing realisation that psychological research can help optimise training or intervention programmes.

Beyond phishing, other issues originate from failures during the development of specific software or the compromising of existing security protocols. For example, the development of malware evolved comparatively quickly to extract data as experienced coders took what they had learnt from decades of developing similar software for personal computers and applied this to mobile development (Khan et al., 2012). A whitepaper from Symantec (2014) further highlights that data collected by self-tracking devices and apps can be easily intercepted. Specifically, transferring data between smartphone and a cloud via Wi-Fi, Bluetooth, cellular network or near-field communication (NFC) may put it at risk of traffic sniffing (allowing attackers access to all transmitted data) and re-direction attacks (which would see data sent to the wrong server). Once stored in the cloud, data is again susceptible to a larger number of attacks. Finally, smartphone operating systems have specific vulnerabilities, and while vendors push such updates to users, many devices are often not running the latest version. This alone can leave smartphones open to malicious code.

In summary, smartphones remain attractive targets if not suitably protected (Leavitt, 2011). However, their continual popularity has led to a comparatively new wave of research that not only aims to understand the threats but also now applies this knowledge to solve these widespread problems. Specifically, research within psychology and computer science has started to consider how smartphone systems and software can be modified in response to evolving privacy and security concerns.

6.4   Improving Security

Smartphones can benefit from commercial anti-virus and firewall products, but these are not widely available or used (Jeon et al., 2011; Ramachandran, Oh and Stackpole, 2012). This software can also struggle to protect against malicious code (Nguyen, McDonald and Glisson, 2017). A variety of other technological innovations to improve smartphone security are, however, widely available that can help users track how data is being used and collected by different smartphone apps. This is otherwise difficult if not impossible to track by a user, and apps can help consumers manage various permissions. Specifically, the Guardian Firewall app runs in the background and stops data and location trackers while compiling a list of times when apps attempt to deploy them (Newman, 2019). This means that while apps still function, Guardian Firewall reveals what specific apps are doing behind the scenes. The app itself does this without transmitting any data or even collecting a person's IP address. Other recent modifications to smartphone operating systems have also started to alert end users to the continual or occasional collection of sensitive data. For example, newer versions of iOS alert users that specific apps are collecting data in the background and ask for confirmation that this can continue. However, these approaches tell users almost nothing about what the information is being used for or if it is being shared more widely. They also do not distinguish between different types of data that may be more or less sensitive (Felt, Egelman and Wagner, 2012).

While there are only a few software products that encrypt all data, manufacturers have also built this into existing devices. However, like apps that track permissions, these are unable to prevent attacks caused by user error or poor security practices. Further progress here may require radical changes to how all software is developed. On the other hand, behavioural science alone has already proposed several improvements that could be incorporated into existing programmes or systems. Many questions remain, but applying our understanding of psychological processes to current security practices in the previous decade has provided some valuable answers and generated entirely new arenas of research.

6.4.1   *Playing to Psychological Strengths*

Cognitive science specifically has explored how security systems can play into human factors that make security not only more straightforward for the end user but also more secure in itself. Many existing interventions rely on the assumption that a person has secured their device with some form of passcode or screen lock in the first instance. For example, the majority of smartphones (and a variety of other digital systems including debit cards) are still secured using four-digit PIN numbers. These codes, however, are easy to guess or crack due to the limited number of combinations available. Looking over someone's shoulder or analysing the oily residue from a person's fingers can also provide clues (Aviv et al., 2010).

While it is possible to increase the length of a pin code or rely on a random sequence of symbols, these are difficult to remember. Other graphical systems do exist – for example, Brostoff and Sasse (2000) used photographs of faces. However, these are also vulnerable to attack as someone can secretly watch a user during authentication. Jenkins, McLachlan and Renaud (2014) took this one step further by applying insights from cognitive psychology. Specifically, several decades of psychological research confirm important distinctions between faces that are familiar and unfamiliar (Jenkins and Burton, 2011). When a face is familiar, it can be identified from a variety of photographs even when the image quality or lighting is poor or distorted (Burton et al., 1999). On the other hand, our ability to correctly identify unfamiliar faces is poor with different photos of the same person often being viewed as different people (Burton, Jenkins and Schweinberger, 2011; Jenkins et al., 2011). While this can often be a problem in other applied domains (e.g., identifying a criminal from a line-up), it provides opportunities to enhance privacy in a security context. Participants were first asked to provide multiple photographs of faces with which they were familiar. In an experiment, they were then presented with several grids that included nine faces. The task was to select a photo of a familiar face from this grid that they recognised. One image (the target) was a random photo of a person selected at random from that account holder's pool of target names. The other faces were random photos taken from a separate database. Identifying the correct image in four grids resulted in successful authentication. This system would make it very difficult for an attacker to gain entry, which was confirmed in a second study.

This proof of concept provides a powerful demonstration, but there are challenges associated with transferring these developments into applied contexts. Perhaps too much onus is placed on the user at the outset as they are required to source multiple photographs of familiar faces. Smartphone vendors in recent years have instead focused on developing new security features that rely on other biometric features. These allow users to unlock phones using a fingerprint or the owner's face, as an alternative to passwords. Related face perception research has, in turn, attempted to understand how biometric systems can become more secure. This often involves trying to understand what exactly is 'being matched' by reverse-engineering face recognition systems. However, the algorithms in smartphones use 'black-box', proprietary approaches to process images and so it remains unclear to researchers exactly how a system is operating.

Despite being unable to lift the lid on how these processes operate precisely, psychologists have proposed how such systems might be improved by again incorporating the advantages of face familiarity. Specifically, facial averages have been used to improve face recognition in other commercial settings (Jenkins and Burton, 2008). These, in part, also shed light on why people are so good at recognising familiar faces as they are based on multiple pictures of the same person and reduce the variability caused by different angles or lighting (Figure 6.1).

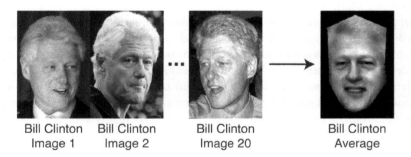

| Bill Clinton Image 1 | Bill Clinton Image 2 | Bill Clinton Image 20 | Bill Clinton Average |

Figure 6.1 Examples of individual images and an average on the right, which can be generated from multiple photos of the same individual.
Note: These techniques can further improve automatic recognition by reducing the large variability between different photos of the same person (Jenkins and Burton, 2008)
Jenkins, R. & Burton, A. M. (2008). 100% accuracy in automatic face recognition. *Science*, 319(5862), 435.

Most facial security systems work by storing multiple images of a user (the 'target'). These are then compared with images captured during unlocking attempts. Matches result in access being granted. Robertson et al. (2015) compared recognition performance for a target image comprising a photo (normal usage) with performance using a target image comprising of an average, derived from many photos of the target. To this end, they encoded the phone either with individual photos or the average face of a participant, who was then asked to unlock the phone using their face. They observed that people could unlock their phones more reliably when the device stored an average of the user's face instead of single images. This advantage was consistent across a wide variety of everyday viewing conditions. As with other work, the authors point towards how this could be built into existing systems where the average could be updated regularly with additional weight being given to more recent photos:

> We envisage that a new system might operate as follows: (i) Users would select seven digital images which provide an unobstructed view of their face. This is a relatively trivial requirement which could be accomplished through the user providing access to the image galleries in their Facebook or photo sharing applications; (ii) An automatic facial landmarking system would, for each image, mark the anatomical features required for averaging; (iii) Software would then create the person's average and encode it as the stored representation of their face; (iv) On each occasion authentication occurs, an image of the user's face would be captured and incorporated into their average. (Robertson et al., 2015, p. 9)

However, not withstanding additional privacy concerns, biometric systems remain low-security features because they can often be unreliable or be hacked. As a result, these security features can be removed with a traditional password (Prabhakar, Pankanti and Jain, 2003). It has even been recommended by some experts that biometric systems are deactivated to maximise security (BBC, 2019a, 2019b). While the passcode remains the last line of defence for now, it seems conceivable that if improvements proposed above were incorporated, they could at some point in the future become the new gold standard for smartphone authentication.

Beyond single biometric measures, others have proposed the use of transparent authentication (Crawford, Renaud and Storer, 2013). These privacy-enhancing technologies rely on data-rich human–computer interactions to create a pattern that can act as a baseline to support a comparison that confirms the current user is indeed the correct owner. Speed of typing and voice recognition are two potential streams of data that could assist with such a decision. While this remains computationally more intensive and not yet suitable for deployment in the wild without human input, early indications suggest that consumers like the idea in principle. However, removing all other security barriers at the same time, commonly cited as a goal in authentication research, may not have widespread appeal (Crawford and Renaud, 2014). Traditional systems that involve a strong element of user control are likely to sit alongside any new developments of this nature in the future.

While some of the above research provides novel avenues for improving existing systems, many of these have yet to be successfully commercialised. Most solutions still rely on people actively engaging with procedures that will help keep data safe and secure (e.g., two factor authentication), but less is known about how to encourage better security practices in the first instance. An important aspect of addressing security challenges therefore requires more knowledge of how people make cybersecurity decisions and why they behave in certain ways. Despite progress, comparatively little is known regarding how people think and conceptualise cybersecurity when making decisions and taking subsequent action. Therefore, it remains difficult to know how we might change attitudes and behaviour in relation to personal security practices. Simply making people aware of where data is going may help people make better decisions and reveal concerns (Van Kleek et al., 2017). However, more research is required to understand how existing and future behaviour change or training programmes can work effectively and remain valuable for different audiences (Annansingh and Veli, 2016; Williams et al., 2017).

> Do they reduce reliance on heuristic processing, enhance self-awareness and self-control, or increase suspicion? Understanding the mechanisms involved in reducing susceptibility to influence will not only enhance understanding of the processes involved in increasing it, but will also allow particular failures in resistance to be examined, such as how and why suspicious individuals may still succumb to scams. (Williams et al., 2017, p. 418)

Another way to address this gap is to explore how people understand cybersecurity via their mental models (i.e., expressions of how they comprehend an event, process or system). Gaining insights into these representations would help improve the security behaviour of individuals, organisations and society. Findings from recent studies involving children, for example, show that subjective knowledge, and not objective knowledge, predicted perceived safety online. This suggests that, like adults, young people are complacent in that their feelings of being safe are based on a possibly mistaken belief that they do enough to remain safe online (Macaulay et al., 2019). Understanding how much people have actually learnt following an intervention, or what they need to know before interventions are prepared, may need to involve the use of open questions as well as traditional quantitative assessments.

Perhaps the challenges associated with improving existing systems or understanding how to change security behaviours have led to a growing consensus that security should be considered in all phases of software development. This would ensure that resiliency against attacks is built in to all smartphones and associated software from the outset. Devices that are likely to have an even more profound impact in the future, sometimes in ways that are not yet clear, will have to put security front and centre. This will ensure that they remain valuable for people, society and researchers themselves.

6.4.2   *Commercial Software Development*

Despite proposed enhancements to smartphone security systems, device makers and wireless service providers have often relegated security to an afterthought (Khan et al., 2012). However, as mobile apps now provide essential links to highly sensitive data, many developers themselves now acknowledge that a lack of secure coding practices is a major problem (Ponemon Institute Research, 2015). Research has, in turn, started to consider the issue of security from the perspective of commercial developers by examining barriers that prevent best security practices when developing software (Balebako et al., 2014). In 2011 for example, one analysis of commercial Android apps found privacy issues in the majority (Enck et al., 2011), with the vast majority of vulnerabilities being the result of decisions made by developers (Weir, Rashid and Noble, 2016a). Alternative decisions would have made the software more secure. As a result, awards are often offered for spotting bugs, which is perhaps a reluctant acceptance from commercial developers that, given modern development environments, no software will ever be completely secure or bug-free.

Questions concerning security errors and what technical interventions might mitigate or reduce such errors are as much questions for computer science as for psychology. For example, Weir et al. (2016a) note that there is comparatively little literature on exactly how app programmers learn about security or even consensus on how to motivate programmers to engage with security techniques. In recent years, however, Lopez et al. (2019) have started to better understand what security practice looks like in professional environments, which was facilitated via workshops. They suggest that getting developers to move away from source code itself and use visual languages may help build more secure systems. Other attempts have been made to take motivating techniques developed by others and adapt these to upskill independent app developers (e.g., Weir, Rashid and Noble, 2016b). Gamification has also been trialled to increase developers' awareness of security issues associated with software development. Such an approach, which consists of turning a domain activity into a game, has been used in both software engineering and cybersecurity contexts; however, early results suggest that linking programming tasks with a game is inherently challenging (Maarek et al., 2019).

> Future research is needed to explore objectively the most effective ways to motivate app developers in different contexts to learn and use secure development practices. And research is required to clarify the best security practices in different app development contexts and to discover the most effective ways for programmers to learn. (Weir et al., 2016a, p. 7)

This line of research is almost certainly going to require more input from the social sciences. Following improvements to education, many of these projects aim to achieve a form of behaviour change, which has primarily been the domain of psychological science (Weir et al., 2016b).

Beyond commercial enterprises, developing software is no longer left to a handful of individuals with carefully crafted technical skills. Software engineers at any level can quickly become fundamental figures in the socio-technical systems that characterise and define modern society. The current community of smartphone developers are often young and less experienced (Van der Linden et al., 2018). This includes those who are using smartphone apps to assist with psychological research. Many apps handle increasingly sensitive information, but when using these directly researchers are reliant on the security practices of multiple third parties or participants and have little control over how data is collected or stored (Geyer, Ellis and Piwek, 2019). In addition, research that aims to answer specific questions often requires access to even more sensitive information albeit on a smaller scale. This includes monitoring participants remotely or delivering interventions. As with previous methodological innovations, psychology now must contemplate a series of new challenges to ensure that all research procedures remain safe and ethical.

6.4.3   *Ethical Practices for Psychological Research*

Data that researchers collect in the digital domain is extremely valuable, but it is also highly sensitive. Many researchers continue to raise concerns about the increasing availability of data in conjunction with advances in computational power (Wang and Kosinski, 2018). Seemingly innocuous data from a smartphone can be used to trace identity (de Montjoye et al., 2013), tell if the user is a parent (Seneviratne et al., 2014), or detect user mobility patterns (Song et al., 2010) or face-to-face social interactions (Osmani et al., 2014). A potentially more problematic issue when collecting data as part of a research project is the collection, transmission and storage of data. It is common practice for most smartphone data to be transmitted via Wi-Fi, Bluetooth, cellular network or NFC, and stored on a cloud server. For example, while it is often possible to recover significant amounts of apparently deleted personal information from a single device, smartphones can also be used to locate artefacts on linked cloud systems with several devices allowing for the recovery of more information (Glisson et al., 2011; Grispos, Glisson and Storer, 2015).

New prospects for research concerning smartphones and associated digital services pose ethical challenges that relate to people's privacy, security and trust. It provides more opportunities to use data in coercive or fraudulent ways and raises the question of what true informed consent might look like in the future (Hinds and Joinson, 2019). Countless examples involve the public release of non-anonymised data (Zimmer, 2018). However, anonymised data can still be used fraudulently or become vulnerable if it is cross-referenced with other systems (Barbaro, Zeller and Hansell, 2006). Cambridge Analytica, for instance, came under scrutiny after using approximately 87 million individuals' Facebook data for a new purpose without gaining additional consent. Psychological research in this area needs to avoid these pitfalls if it is to prosper.

Threats to privacy have serious implications because they can undermine trust and increase social inequality between large groups. While this has to be balanced against societal benefits, there are often winners and losers. Whether a person is taking part in ethically approved research or generating data across a variety of digital services, everyone should have the right to control their digital footprint. Psychologists should not be complicit or circumvent these rights, but this remains a challenge without any formalised standards. Traditional frameworks for research were designed around the notion of 'one-off' measurements, but the recent move towards real-time 'always-on' approaches to data collection poses new challenges for researchers, participants and policymakers. Psychology has often engaged with discussions regarding what ethics should look like, but much of this now appears dated (Gluck, 1997; Marks, 2018; Powell et al., 2014). Even existing ethical guidelines for internet-mediated research appear to be no longer fit for purpose (British Psychological Society, 2013).

When it comes to smartphones, many of the above challenges can be partly mitigated by developing apps by psychologists for psychologists. However, these will almost always rely on pulling data from functions under the control of a commercial operating system. In the short term, there are a number of steps that researchers can take that should already be integrated as part of existing research practices. First, data should be encrypted when stored on any device and while being transferred. This ensures that if data were obtained by unintended recipients, it would be difficult to access. Second, researchers should aim to minimise the quantity and quality (or resolution) of data that is collected where possible and avoid extracting every retrievable segment of information from a smartphone. Third, algorithms to process and analyse data should be transparent to the extent that participants can remain fully informed about what data is being collected and how it will be used.

Researchers also need to be cautious and honour the level of consent provided throughout. However, in order for participants to provide informed consent, it is important that they are fully aware of the data that is being collected. There are several problems with ensuring that this happens. Miller (2012) suggests that obtaining ethical approval is more difficult with smartphone research because people often ignore lengthy 'terms and conditions of use' that are necessary when signing up for other online and smartphone services and products. Indeed, a Fairer Finance survey (Daley, 2014) found that of those who did read the terms and conditions, only 17 per cent actually understood the information contained within. While it is unlikely that any information sheet within psychological research would be as complicated and confusing as a 30,000-word terms and conditions document, it is worth considering how participants are made aware of and understand what data will be collected about them, how the data will be stored, who will have access to it, and their rights should they wish to withdraw. One solution might involve asking participants (in both smartphone and lab-based research) to read an informed consent form, followed by several related questions. Doing so would ensure that they understand the information and provide authentic informed consent. Long-term developments, however, are likely to involve the creation of new guidelines for the use of smartphones within research.

A recent paper by Dennis et al. (2019a), however, gets closer to an ethical consensus regarding the collection of smartphone data using experience sampling, on-board experiments and passive sensor methods. There is though some conflict between the utility of open scientific practices that promote reproducibility and the rise of technologies that can collect large quantities of data passively (Dennis et al., 2019a). Specifically, it may be difficult to share sensitive smartphone data in its raw form, which contradicts open scientific practices. They argue that such data should always remain the property of participants whereby they can license that data to other researchers. For another researcher to be able to do that, however, they must be able to find that data. Similarly, participants should also be able to anonymously request that data is deleted post analysis, which would only be possible if researchers develop comprehensive search and visualisation interfaces (Dennis et al., 2019a). Of course, all this has to be balanced against a potential inability to reproduce some analyses in the future.

Proposals from Dennis et al (2019b) and others often involve the use of 'differential privacy', which aims to maximise the accuracy of queries from users' data while minimising the chances of identifying an individual by using 'statistical masking' methods such as hashing, subsampling and noise injection (Dwork and Roth, 2014). Synthetic data generation provides another promising method that can mimic real data sets by preserving statistical properties (e.g., the relationships between variables). It does so without running this risk of accidental disclosure because no record in the synthetic data set actually represents a real person (Quintana, 2019). Researchers can then ensure that results can be replicated and data sets explored while maintaining participant privacy. However, putting these methods into practice remains challenging and might ultimately reduce the value of some sensor data. For example, high-resolution location data is valuable to researchers, but sensitive for participants (James et al., 2016). Aggregated data will be less sensitive, but also less valuable.

6.4.3.1   *Methods in Practice: Building a Location-Tracking App for Psychological Science*

My own lab has started to develop smartphone apps that involve the collection of location metrics and other sensitive behavioural data (Geyer et al., 2019). For example, PEG LOG allows for the passive recording of GPS data, which is stored locally on the device. This can be exported on demand. We opted to avoid the use of a central server, in order to maximise usability; that is, researchers who want to use this app do not need to set up a cloud-based storage system, which assists with increased reliability and

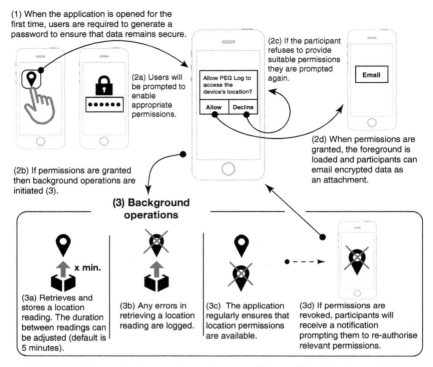

Figure 6.2 Infographic demonstrating foreground (1, 2a–2d) and background (3a–3d) operations of a smartphone location-tracking application designed to assist with psychological research (Geyer et al., 2019).
Note: The only aspect of the application accessible by participants is the main activity page, which requests the relevant location permissions (2a) and allows participants to read the documentation, change their password, view their location data and email files (2d)
Geyer, K., Ellis, D. A. & Piwek, L. (2019). A simple location-tracking app for psychological research. *Behavior Research Methods, 51*(6), 2840–2846.

longevity. This also ensures that participants are in complete control of their own data throughout the entire collection process (Figure 6.2).

On first launching our app, participants are presented with a brief information screen that specifies what information is being collected and how to stop data collection. This information, the terms of service and privacy policy can be recalled at any time from within the application. The app then instructs participants to provide a six-digit password to secure their data. This password has to be communicated to the researcher to allow any encrypted data to be accessed. It is not possible to start data collection without first defining a password. If a participant wishes to withdraw, he or she can choose not to submit their data or password. Participants who become uncomfortable with data collection or who no longer want to take part can simply uninstall the application. This will also delete any location files from the device.

To ensure that participants remain informed and aware of their active participation at all times, PEG LOG provides two visual reminders. First, the application displays a small icon in the top corner of the screen at all times. Second, a permanent text reminder will appear in the notification drawer, which explicitly states that the application is collecting location data. This has the added benefit of improving the reliability of the application as the Android operating system allocates more processing power for apps which declare that operations are running in the background (Android, 2018). During the collection phase, all location data are stored in a 256-bit Structured Query Language (SQL) cypher database. This ensures that even if the source code of the application were compromised, no data could be retrieved without the original password. Only PEG LOG can access this database. All exported data and associated error logs are encrypted with a 128-bit key. However, although the original password for the SQL database is fixed and cannot be changed, if the original six-digit code is forgotten, participants can modify their password via the main screen. This change will only apply to data after they have been prepared for export.

Location data can reveal activity patterns which participants may want to keep private (James et al., 2016). Although data can be anonymised, location coordinates are likely to reveal a person's place of work and home address with very little pre-processing. In line with Dennis et al.'s (2019a) recent guidelines, our app follows a number of their suggestions to help preserve privacy. However, as also suggested, we do not provide a visualisation platform to help show participants exactly what data is being collected beyond explaining how participants might visualise their own data. It would therefore be difficult for participants to anonymously request that data is deleted post analysis. If these data were to be shared openly with additional anonymisation, another option could involve the removal or masking of spatial data in sensitive locations (e.g., the home).

Ensuring that participants understand the granularity of the data collected will help guide subsequent sharing decisions. Location is but one example of sensitive data, and more work is slowly appearing to help guide the development of future apps (Dennis et al., 2019a). Many designs already generate even larger data sets from a variety of smartphone metrics (Harari et al., 2017; Piwek, Ellis and Andrews, 2016). With few exceptions, many of these apps are only available to researchers themselves and a handful of participants. Even if they are developed using open-source frameworks, being unable to view the raw code continues to make further comparisons difficult at the present time.

6.5 Conclusion

Smartphones can compromise our personal and occupational safety. While some of these issues are the result of technical weaknesses, many issues of genuine harm are caused by the way in which people choose to use the technology. This includes the oversharing of personal information, receiving abuse from others or falling victim to a phishing attack. Such harms are often not unique to smartphones, but sit alongside well-established threats to everyday safety and security. As hyperconnected systems are now essential for modern living, they will continue to attract attention from criminal groups.

The long-term implications for the sheer number of smartphones in existence are only now being realised. The law is slowly reflecting these developments. For example, General Data Protection Regulation (GDPR) allows some level of self-determination in Europe, including the right to be forgotten (Wachter, 2018). Many apps and associated services (e.g., Facebook) are simultaneously focusing on private communications, following scandals such as those involving Cambridge Analytica (Isaak and Hanna, 2018). In practice, this may mean a greater emphasis on closed spaces where members of the public are more in control of their data, but this could also make data more difficult to access for research. Facebook, Twitter and Instagram have already become more conservative with what data can be accessed for this purpose. Going forward, companies should engage directly with academics and set up data-sharing agreements with scientific research in mind, which is common elsewhere (Orben, Dienlin and Przybylski, 2019). However, the agenda of Facebook and others is not necessarily the same as that of researchers and the benefits of smartphone data may become less obvious if systems are closed off or provide limited access to the data psychologists would find the most valuable (John and Nissenbaum, 2019).

Existing data sets and methodological approaches are scattered among many groups, with uneven skills and different interpretations of what constitutes data security. If the notion of consent continues to be undermined within research, people themselves may start to show an element of restraint. While this may appear unlikely given recent examples and what we already know when it comes to the amount of data people share about themselves, psychology should be poised to set a good example. If researchers can leverage technologies that protect privacy while curating sensitive data essential for research purposes, these systems will prosper and deliver societal benefits. Security and safety may compete against or complement the need for privacy, but these are often studied separately and treated as trade-offs rather than considered in unison (Bansal, 2017). Despite privacy being historically neglected by psychologists, the discipline now has a key role to play alongside domains traditionally associated with security research.

When it comes to smartphone-related research specifically, good practice is likely to be incremental. Some streams of data on the face of it might appear more sensitive than others, but researchers should keep in mind that we often fail to realise the direct and indirect value of digital data until after collection. While researchers must continue to comply with all existing legal and ethical frameworks, organisations that represent psychological science – for example, the British Psychological Society (BPS), the American Psychological Association (APA) and the Association for Psychological Science (APS) – should be looking to develop new guidelines for research that will prevent future harms and encourage responsible research practices.

Finally, it is worth noting that many of the successful interventions or technical modifications that improve smartphone security have been derived by bringing multiple disciplines together, including criminology, computer science and psychology. Almost everyone currently working in security would agree that it is a multidisciplinary area. For example, the Centre for Research and Evidence on Security Threats (CREST)[3] is a national hub for maximising behavioural and social science research into understanding, countering and mitigating security threats. CREST brings together the United Kingdom's foremost expertise in understanding the psychological and social drivers of the threat, the skills and technologies that enable its effective investigation, and the protective security measures that help counter the threat in the first place. It does so within a context of significant stakeholder and international researcher engagement, and with a clear plan for sustained and long-term growth. Similarly, the Security, Privacy, Identity and Trust Engagement NetworkPlus (SPRITE+)[4] is an Engineering and Physical Sciences Research Council (EPSRC) funded digital economy network that brings together people involved in research, practice and policy with a focus on digital contexts. Finally, CyBOK aims

---

[3] https://crestresearch.ac.uk/   [4] https://spritehub.org/

to bring cybersecurity into line with the more established sciences by distilling knowledge from major internationally recognised experts to form a Cyber Security Body of Knowledge that will provide much-needed foundations for this emerging topic.[5] Therefore, while many security challenges are not specific to psychology, understanding and mitigating these threats will not only advance interdisciplinary research programmes but also deliver clear benefits for society as a whole.

Useful Resources and Further Reading

Dennis, S., Garrett, P., Yim, H., Hamm, J., Osth, A. F., Sreekumar, V., & Stone, B. (2019). Privacy versus open science. *Behavior Research Methods*, *51* (4), 1839–1848.
Considers how sensitive data collected via smartphone methodologies might sit alongside open science practices without compromising participant privacy.
Ellis, D. A., & Piwek, L. (2016). The future of . . . wearable technology. *CREST Security Review*, *1*, 4–5.
Provides a brief overview of how wearable technology could be utilised in a variety of security contexts.
Geyer, K., Ellis, D. A., & Piwek, L. (2019). A simple location-tracking app for psychological research. *Behavior Research Methods*, *51*(6), 2840–2846.
Documents the development of a smartphone application for research purposes. This freely available Android application logs location accurately, stores the data securely and ensures that participants can provide consent or withdraw from a study at any time.

---

[5] www.cybok.org/

Conclusion

Smartphones continue to provide many new opportunities for psychological science. Several years on from Miller's seminal paper 'The smartphone psychology manifesto' in 2012, these ubiquitous devices have started to appear with increasing regularity. The sheer number of individual researchers who have touched on this area is equally impressive and includes academics from almost every corner of the discipline. At the same time, mobile technology and computational power continue to evolve. Smartphones and associated methodologies are likely to reach even larger numbers of participants in the future.

Psychology became a science in the early twentieth century when it moved towards grounding itself in objective measurement (as opposed to introspection). This was further cemented by the widespread adoption of statistical analysis. Collectively, these generated new gold standards for the discipline. In a similar fashion, digitised data from smartphones should enable many psychologists to reconsider our current position in the digital age. Combining multiple streams of data, capturing individual and situational factors simultaneously, can now be achieved outside a laboratory environment. This is particularly pertinent when it comes to improving assessment and revealing the psychological mechanisms that underpin everyday aspects of cognition, social interaction and health. Even without contextual measurement, a single sample of an individual or group behaviour will provide considerable insight. Methodological agreement is unlikely to occur in psychology any time soon, but the smartphone is opening opportunities for people to make important discoveries given the variety of mobile methods at our disposal.

On the other hand, new technologies and research paradigms provide a host of new challenges for psychology and related disciplines. These should not be underestimated, and research that actually engages with these devices as research tools only applies to around 50 per cent of the work discussed throughout these pages. When not using smartphones to answer specific research questions or investigating how they might improve health, many psychologists focus on the negative impact they might have on well-being, cognition and social interaction. This often glosses over the fact that, in the vast majority of cases, effects are unlikely to be uniform. For example, the use of social media to facilitate social interaction can help develop skills for those who are shy but may also exacerbate a pre-existing mental health condition. Many investigations appear completely detached from the technology they claim to understand and suffer from serious theoretical and methodological limitations as a result (Ellis, 2019). They also detract from areas of genuine concern where psychologists could provide a stronger contribution, especially within health and security contexts. This extends to the social economic issues associated with the absence of modern technology that has become essential for daily life. Specifically, while mobile technology often appears ubiquitous, the digital divide remains a barrier for research and society as a whole. Almost 20 per cent of people in the United Kingdom are not online (Blank, Dutton and Lefkowitz, 2019). This presents a dilemma for governments that want to reach and support people as more public and health services move online. Identifying barriers to adoption should remain of equal importance when placed alongside research that aims to improve our understanding of what new technology can offer people and society as a whole.

When it comes to utilising mobile technology, progress across psychological science might therefore be described as slightly disappointing, but many issues reflect broader concerns across the field. In this final chapter, I consider what the future might hold for smartphones and their integration into psychological science. This includes a further exploration of what limits and drives research in this area before considering how the discipline can move forward productively. These discussions are not simply about new technical and methodological barriers faced by researchers but also speak to how we reward and encourage research that often places a sheen of impact ahead of the paucity we should expect from genuine scientific progress.

Future Smartphone Research

Methodological Development: Software

A number of recommendations throughout rely on the development or availability of smartphone software. The proliferation of mobile development means that many solutions are readily available to assist with research, provided psychologists are willing to explore the landscape. Even simple apps that collect minimal data have already shown themselves to be extremely valuable, and future work may wish to catalogue operating system features or apps in respective stores that are primed to assist with a variety of research designs. For example, the tracking of screen time and digital activities at a device level has previously presented several technical challenges (Orben and Przybylski, 2019), but this has now become more straightforward. Beyond specific apps, Apple and Google have implemented 'screen-time' tracking systems into their smartphone operating systems. This appears to replicate metrics developed by several researchers in the previous decade (Andrews et al., 2015; Oulasvirta et al., 2012). Specifically, these systems make distinctions between total usage time and 'pickups' (Gonzalez, 2018). However, the resolution of this data can be limited on iOS devices as it cannot be accessed by researchers via an application programming interface (API). Researchers instead must ask participants to report this data directly, which limits their utility for larger projects (Ellis et al., 2019). Other solutions in this domain have focused on the notion of capturing screenshots across multiple devices. Snapshot data could then be analysed using optical character recognition, image analysis or human observation (Reeves et al., 2019). However, such systems are unlikely to encourage mass participation in their current form given that participants are likely to have many privacy concerns. There is considerable work ahead when it comes to measuring technology usage accurately and ethically across the multiple devices and services people interact with on a daily basis (Wilcockson, Ellis and Shaw, 2018).

If existing software is not available or unsuitable, developing new apps can better meet the specific needs of researchers working in a variety of domains. Software development is an entire discipline in its own right, but many psychologists already write code or develop software in MATLAB (Brainard, 1997), Python (Peirce, 2007) and R (Li and Baron, 2012). These languages are used to create experiments, analyse data and visualise results. Multiple journals, in turn, publish a broad range of code, libraries and methods that are described in detail (e.g., Ellis and Merdian, 2015; Piwek, Petrini and Pollick, 2016; Sochat et al., 2016). Perhaps in response, a number of programming frameworks have been developed to facilitate the process of creating apps for research purposes. Unlike a fully featured smartphone app, many open-source frameworks are used to develop apps from scratch that can deploy surveys, send notifications, collect data from on-board sensors or wearable devices, or trigger context-related data collection depending on a researcher's goal (Ferreira, Kostakos and Schweizer, 2017; Runyan and Steinke, 2015). In theory, these aim to make life easier by providing free tools and resources for researchers, including tutorials, manuals and open-source code with example apps available in a repository (Apple, 2016). The value of open tools like these could be considerable because they ensure that the resources required to replicate findings will not become prohibitive to other labs (Epskamp, 2019; Poldrack, 2019). A recent UK Reproducibility Network primer also pointed out that open code facilitates collaboration and enhanced functionality.[1] For any intervention that aims to change behaviour, attitudes or thought processes, a lack of transparency is akin to not sharing exactly what drug was administered during a trial.

While it is possible to create a simple app with these tools and a basic understanding of programming, getting frameworks to work in practice remains a daunting task and will likely still require a software developer or computer scientist with the ability to program in, for example, Objective-C or Swift. In addition, while frameworks can support initial development, to be useful apps often require several other components that go far beyond these resources. For example, back-end components might include cloud computing services that manage the collection of data or generate push notifications. Other systems are also often required to manage capacity provision for larger designs and may rely on additional services to deliver analysis pipelines that manage the pre-processing of incoming data before it reaches researchers. An additional limitation concerns the fact that these frameworks sometimes collect processed data summaries from sensors rather than data in a raw format. This introduces a new challenge because it can separate the data-generating process from an analysis, making it difficult to compare data across devices or pool data across studies as the summary statistics will likely be different. For these and a variety of other reasons, many development kits have not been used widely within psychology, which continues to rely on custom-designed apps or closed-source commercial solutions that lack privacy assurances. Several other frameworks, apps or related technological solutions continue to be proposed, but authors often fail to provide any resources that would allow other researchers to take advantage of these methods. Security, consent and privacy also remain an afterthought (e.g., Reeves et al., 2019). This

---

[1] www.bristol.ac.uk/media-library/sites/expsych/documents/ukrn/UKRN_Primer_Open_Code_Software.pdf

represents the tip of the iceberg for replication and transparency across computational social science (Hutson, 2018; Peng, 2011).

Another possibility would be to form more interdisciplinary collaborations with computer science departments – who may be more skilled at developing the appropriate software. Otherwise, there is a dearth of programmers available to program a specific app. In the case of psychology, this often results in a researcher outlining their requirements, which a programmer then develops. It remains unclear whether this would result in the development of a research app that is correctly tuned to methodological and research requirements. Without the ability to see the inner workings of the app, however, it might be difficult to guarantee that an experimental design works as intended. Further, a complex smartphone application might take some time to develop, meaning that development costs run high (Formotus, 2016). Cloud services and storage, maintenance and bug fixes all require additional funding and continued development. Regular modifications to smartphone operating systems also impact functionality, which can be especially problematic when attempting to collect sensor data longitudinally. In the current economic climate, where researchers are increasingly required to demonstrate cost-efficient research, this might turn out to be an impossible long-term solution.

Other recent developments aimed at psychologists appear to be more promising. These range from individual apps that do not rely on a back-end services to complete systems that are becoming more concrete in how they handle privacy and consent. For example, the Unforgettable Me sensing platform can collect images, location, accelerometry and audio data. It can also link with other systems, including If This Then That (IFTTT). In theory, researchers could then collect streams of data from hundreds of different services and devices ranging from social media to wearable devices and household appliances (Dennis et al., 2019a). This essentially unifies multiple APIs (which vary in quality) that can be piped through one system.

In their system, data is collected by participants first who can then share this with researchers if they wish. However, researchers using the platform may be unable to use standard analysis platforms, including R and Python, for some variables to maintain privacy. Using IFTTT may also enforce additional limits on what can be retrieved without going to a specific external API directly. Whether researchers will be willing to work with such a system in the context of open science remains to be seen, but the developers acknowledge that there is a fine line to walk between maintaining the values of open science, while simultaneously ensuring participants' data remains secure and under the control of participants themselves throughout the research process (Dennis et al., 2019b).

Future solutions for app development will likely become more refined and accessible with 'out-the-box' options to deploy research apps that do not require a heavy dependence on software developers. A platform for all researchers to develop smartphone research tools that could be used across the research process is likely to be more akin to existing software that provides a graphical user interface (GUI) to devise experiments such as PsychoPy (Peirce, 2007) or SuperLab (Haxby et al., 1993). A GUI drastically reduces the complexity of creating, deploying and replicating any study but has yet to be developed when it comes to building smartphone apps for research purposes, but again this may need to provide support for other cloud-based components. However, we are perhaps already in the second wave of smartphone collection systems that require less technical expertise. This includes commercial purpose-built systems for experience sampling and limited sensor logging (e.g., MetricWire). Researchers at Harvard, for example, have developed the Beiwe platform that aims to help standardise data collection, which can include raw metrics from on-board sensors. Similarly, there is already a growing consensus on how researchers can increase their chances of high-quality data from web-browser platforms. A collection of commercial systems also now link data collection between web-browser platforms and assist with compensating participants, including Amazon Mechanical Turk and Prolific Academic (Buhrmester, Kwang and Gosling, 2011; Peer, Vosgerau and Acquisti, 2014). Some smartphone apps could simply point towards a website, but this may not be suitable for many research designs. In addition, the development of apps that alleviate issues relating to transparency and privacy may always require more specialised software using serverless designs (Geyer, Ellis and Piwek, 2019; Keil, Koschate-Reis and Levine, 2020).

While psychological science has spent vast sums of money on neuroimaging to understand brain function, a smaller proportion of funds have been devoted to ecologically valid measures of online and offline behaviour. For example, we would not dream of self-reporting amygdala activity, but researchers have little choice but to continue with subjective measures in other areas (e.g., Hutton et al., 2019). Social and personality psychology specifically may need to make its voice heard in order to generate the levels of funding required that can support some of the more ambitious programmes of research outlined in these pages.

Otherwise, analogous disciplines or commercial enterprise will drive this agenda forward regardless.

Methodological Development: Hardware

Without access to specific hardware, software emulation alone can reveal how data was collected from a device so that specific apps could be replicated as hardware evolves. However, sensor development is analogous to software. Building customised sensor systems for social research is now possible, but this is the exception rather than the rule at present within psychological science. Previous work has demonstrated the utility of sensors that exist within or beyond the smartphone ecosystem (Pentland, 2008; Taylor, 2013). For example, sociometric sensors provide a valuable new approach to product evaluation and measuring face-to-face social interaction. Similarly, radio frequency identification (RFID) tags alone can act as a proxy for social interaction (Elmer et al., 2019). In addition, many devices can remotely track physical and psychological health by incorporating measures of physical activity, heart rate, and location, which can support a variety of behaviour change interventions. Therefore, there is huge potential to take our understanding of smartphone sensors further and build custom devices for specific research projects. This can also help overcome limitations associated with proprietary devices like sociometric badges and other wearable devices.

First, these devices are often 'closed' to such an extent that we are unable to confirm the exact nature of each sensor output. As a result, it is also not currently possible to tweak the system to deliver specific research prototypes or flexibly scale a platform to introduce additional functionality (new components are always being developed). Devices that underpin interventions or remote monitoring systems also struggle to keep pace with technological innovation. Second, many devices are temperamental and, because they are closed, it becomes impossible to diagnose why this is the case. In testing situations where a device is given to participants for extended periods of time, reliability is essential. Finally, commercial devices are relatively expensive, which limits mass deployment and makes any 'loss' during testing unacceptable (i.e., one could not envisage giving them to participants where there was a significant risk of loss or damage). Therefore, acknowledging the limitations associated with sensors that are fixed to a smartphone or embedded in other commercial devices, psychological science could move beyond these ecosystems and build bespoke, inexpensive devices from scratch. Similar to commercial devices, these could integrate a variety of similar sensors depending on the research design. This might include accelerometers, microphones or Bluetooth sensors. For example, multiple sensors could provide data on how participants behave in a variety of different social interactions across multiple contexts. Prototype devices could then be validated against high-resolution lab-based systems. Of course, these would again require suitable software, but could rely on an open-source electronic prototyping platform, Arduino. Software that integrates with this hardware can be created in C and C++.

Researchers are starting to take advantage of related technology, and similar devices can, as with software, remain simple but powerful. For example, Tomko et al. (2019) have integrated similar technology into an electronic smart lighter than can accurately quantify cigarette smoking. However, while many wearable devices developed by academic groups have enormous research and commercial potential, the outputs are often siloed. Specifically, their design rarely involves end users or those who might, in the case of medicine, help deliver interventions into the health-care market and beyond. Maker Spaces would allow mobile and wearable hardware and software solutions to be developed quickly to support research programmes across multiple disciplines. While spaces are physical, online systems and public events would engage interested parties who, from our previous research, already have a limitless number of ideas on how this technology can be developed further in a way that escapes the confines of expensive 'off-the-shelf' research monitoring solutions and commercial fitness trackers. Beyond delivering societal benefits in the form of knowledge exchange, this form of co-design will also become essential when developing ethical artificial intelligence that is likely to rely on related services in the near future. Collectively, such an arrangement also allows end users and researchers to think critically about and mitigate privacy and security issues from the outset, which continues to limit subsequent impact. Such spaces can also act as a repository of ideas that would outpace the development of new technology. Mirroring a systematic approach that links personality or social processes to smartphone metrics (Chapters 3 and 4), the qualitative mapping of symptoms and health metrics onto specific sensors can help engage non-expert audiences. Finally, this would help support rapid commercialisation where research devices could quickly transition into start-ups that will be well placed for success in the not-so-new digital age.

There are many opportunities to develop programmes of interdisciplinary research by combining the expertise of psychologists and engineers. Like new methodologies developed following the cognitive revolution, similar devices could have far-reaching consequences for future research across psychological science. However, while the methodological possibilities across software and hardware are exciting, the field will struggle to embrace these if it is unable to provide strong foundations for knowledge generation in the first instance.

Theory and Measurement

Issues pertaining to transparency remain front and centre. The replication crisis is well documented across psychological science as an increasing number of research findings have not held up to further scrutiny (Open Science Collaboration, 2015). Many studies across social science continue to be underpowered (Lakens, 2015; Maxwell, 2004) and distorted by publication bias (Francis, 2012). At the same time, an alarming number of individuals have been less than reliable in psychology, specifically including Eysenck, Zimbardo and Rosenhan (Cahalan, 2019; Pelosi, 2019; Reicher and Haslam, 2006). Other problems, however, may reflect serious theoretical and methodological shortcomings that will not be overcome by embracing open science practices. While I have referenced or alluded to many theoretical explanations throughout, these are unable to fully explain a phenomenon, let alone generalise. Recently, this has been described as a gulf between qualitative claims made following empirical investigations and the statistical entities from which they draw breath (Yarkoni, 2019).

Considering the results or potential relationships discussed throughout this book, I have provided dozens of alternative explanations. Recent critiques have suggested that many authors rarely acknowledge or address these in subsequent investigations (Cohen, 2016; Yarkoni, 2019). Philosophers of science (e.g., Popper and Lakatos) would argue that theory is never a complete description of reality and will either require further development or be refuted completely. Psychology has certainly become slower at the latter (Phaf, 2020). Many areas appear to prioritise unsuitable theory irrespective of new evidence or critiques. For example, when concerning the impact of technology on people and society, we are quite far away from a generalisable model. A useful framework that might incorporate a variety of theories could reduce this space. At present, we appear to be running study after study that fails to get any closer to understanding the mechanisms that, for example, lead to positive or negative impacts in isolation (Muthukrishna and Henrich, 2019). Take work concerning health in Chapter 2 and compare this to the potential harms documented elsewhere. These all consider harms or benefits under completely different theoretical frameworks despite obvious overlaps in the application of the technology. They cannot all be winners. Once again, this is not unique to research involving smartphones or technology. Take cognitive dissonance theory, for example; it is difficult to directly connect this to other higher-level theories (e.g., the privacy paradox) – let alone challenge or support itself across multiple contexts.

Similarly, models that aim to predict the continued use of technology sit within a convoluted web of moderating and mediating variables, which makes them difficult to apply (Venkatesh et al., 2012, 2016). On the other hand, traditional models like the technology acceptance model (TAM) oversimplify complex relationships (Davis et al., 1989). Frameworks like these remain widely popular but often imply the existence of a phenomenon in such broad terms that it becomes impossible to falsify and open to misinterpretation. This also applies to the notion of utilising a behavioural addictions framework to explain technology use in the general population (Griffiths, 2005). For example, Kuss and Griffiths (2017) have argued that smartphone 'addiction' might relate to specific pieces of software running on the device rather than an addiction to the object. When applied to smartphone apps or digital services, however, these conceptualisations are unhelpful when it comes to understanding relevant psychological processes in both general and clinical contexts (Billieux et al., 2014; Brand et al., 2020). Unlike gambling or allied behavioural addictions, we know even less about how relevant physiological and psychological mechanisms would apply to technology. As a result, evidence to support the notion of addiction in this instance is disconnected from the original theory proposed. For example, the biological mechanism that would explain this operates in the order of seconds, not days, weeks or months of general usage measured in hours (Reeves et al., 2019). Eliciting attitudes towards usage or creating scales that appear to align with a components model of addiction will also struggle to reveal any mechanisms in this regard.

Technology addiction, even when attempts are made to defend it or explain the surrounding constructs, will slow progress because it allows researchers to generate a limitless number of pathologies off the top of their head. Like previous incarnations, including internet addiction, these conceptualisations become increasingly meaningless as the world becomes digitally intertwined (Ryding and Kaye, 2018). The term 'problematic usage' is no less problematic given that everyday technology use is habitual and routine. Therefore, while publishing highly powered, preregistered successful or failed replications will provide more information for some research areas, this may not address many underlying problems in this instance (Firth, 2019).

Theory certainly appears to mean different things across sub-disciplines within psychological science. If a theory is only used to simplify the phenomena under investigation and allow for an improved understanding, this serves a very different purpose to how it is often described. As a whole, psychological theory has not attained the same standards in elucidating mechanisms as the physical sciences. Klein (2014) suggests this is due to the discipline's tendency to investigate hypotheses via binary opposition rather than via quantitative manipulation. On the other hand, many theoretical models and the statistics that support them can make useful predictions provided they are developed in an iterative fashion where new data leads to genuine modification or replacement (Box, 1976). However, it is unlikely that anyone thinks these models are complete. In practice, the number and complexity of inter-acting entities remains high for most areas and will limit the formulation of perfect mathematical models (Phaf, 2020). This is not in of itself problematic because psychological theory and its underpinning statistical models should aim to tell us something valuable about the real-world and not an abstracted mathematical environment (Hand, 2014).

Theorising therefore remains vitally important because, without any theoretical reference, research may be driven even further by biases based on individual experience. At the same time, neglecting theoretical integration also risks increasing the current disarray further (Kim, Ployhart and Gibson, 2018). Practical theory development likely needs to run across multiple tracks simultaneously and include empirical assessment, quantitative modelling or analysis. This may even need to include crowdsourcing technology to develop causal models and improve inferences from blinded data (Rohrer, 2018), which will further ensure that theory is truly aligned with observed outcomes (Starns et al., 2019). This does not prevent theorising taking place after data has been collected, provided it occurs transparently and is not due to hypothesising after the results are known (Kerr, 1998; Phaf, 2020). In order to balance competing priorities, related discussions have considered how researchers might make a distinction between discovery-oriented versus theory testing. The former applies to the vast majority of psychological theory that operates within a very large space that is not specific enough to the concept under investigation. This would include theories outlined earlier that focus on the adoption of technology (e.g., the TAM or extended self theory) (Belk, 1988, 2013; King and He, 2006). Theory testing research, on the other hand, suggests a far tighter link between theory and a specific hypothesis. This distinction between discovery-oriented and theory-driven research could be considered as a continuum, but should be clarified within designs (Oberauer and Lewandowsky, 2019). Research that is discovery-oriented (or exploratory) must acknowledge that the state of theorising means authors cannot make strong inferences to hypotheses. While even the most sophisticated statistical analysis cannot control for all extraneous variables, we should capture that uncertainty, quantitatively or qualitatively (Oberauer and Lewandowsky, 2019).

Existing theoretical misalignments, however, may also lie at the root of methodological challenges that afflict the discipline because it is analogous with poor operationalisation when developing suitable quantitative measures to test hypotheses (Flake and Fried, 2019; Yarkoni, 2019). Again, this can be less of an issue for some sub-disciplines, but it afflicts the study and understanding of technology more generally. We often stop at face validity – a smartphone 'addiction' scale for example appears valid by name alone, so it must be valid. The same measurements are quickly generalised across the discipline to support an implausible number of theoretical conceptualisations and conclusions (Ellis, 2019; Yarkoni, 2019).

Appreciating the value of applied prediction provides one route forward that can aid theoretical development. This also encourages a move towards suitable operationalisations of constructs that have real-world value and can provide reliable answers to questions that carry critical implications for public policy (Hässler et al., 2020). However, many data sets in the digital domain are extensive, collected without a specific research question in mind and made available to many researchers. As a result, understanding how variable operationalisation and measurement error interact with advanced quantitative approaches is going to become even more important (van Smeden, Lash and Groenwold, 2019). For example, if errors can be quantified and subsequently controlled for it can help researchers make improved inferences from noisy, imperfect measurements deployed in the wild. Large-scale studies, for instance, that aim to investigate the impact of screen time or multitasking on well-being or cognition should not simply acknowledge that there are errors of measurement between self-report and objective assessment, but factor these misalignments into quantitative analyses using error correction techniques. Methods can include regression calibration, multiple imputation or latent class analysis (Ellis, 2019; van Smeden et al., 2019). This may ultimately encourage a further move away from the notion of general screen time with the development of new latent factors built around multiple contextual and individual technology-related measures. However, such an approach assumes that technology use cannot be observed (it can) and brings new methodological challenges. For example, the use of inappropriate latent variable measurement models can lead to even larger biases (Rhemtulla, van Bork and Borsboom, 2019). As discussed in several chapters, sensible avenues of research might combine small- and large-scale approaches to address similar errors associated with other smartphone sensing-based methods used to detect social interaction, or location for example (Szot et al., 2019). Researchers could first understand discrepancies using highly accurate measurement techniques in small studies before collecting or accessing larger quantities of sensor data.

Across applied research, issues of measurement validity and reliability continue to impact linear and non-linear methods including the widespread use of machine-learning algorithms (Rhemtulla, van Bork and Borsboom, 2019; Jacobucci and Grimm, 2020). Related concerns apply to measurement selection whereby a test or variable must be carefully aligned with a specific research question in the first instance. For example, many robust behavioural measures used to assess cognitive performance in the laboratory will struggle to produce reliable individual differences becuase that was never their intended purpose (Dang et al., 2020; Hedge et al., 2018; Parsons, Kruijt and Fox, 2019). When left unresolved, measurement error can further impact the development of predictive models because data collection protocols that reduce measurement error to a minimum do not necessarily benefit the performance of the model as the precision of measurements will not always be available during validation or in other applied settings. This is particularly relevant for research that attempts to predict personality or health-related outcomes. Luijken and colleagues (2019) demonstrate the following in a series of simulations:

> When predictor measurements are more precise at derivation compared to validation, model discrimination and accuracy at validation deteriorate, and the provided predicted probabilities are too extreme, similar to when a model is overfitted with respect to the derivation data. When predictor measurements are less precise at derivation compared to validation, discrimination and accuracy at validation tend to improve, but the provided

predicted probabilities are too close to the outcome prevalence, similar to statistical underfitting. (Luijken et al., 2019, p. 3456)

Perhaps before applied prediction, acknowledging the value of descriptive research can mitigate the forced testing of unsuitable theories that are poorly operationalised. Yarkoni (2019) argues that this has happened successfully in genetics where researchers accept that the world is noisy, but providing a description of what is actually going on has become far more valuable than engaging with small-sample candidate studies that produced spurious results, which were based around weak theory (Chabris et al., 2012; Nagel et al., 2018). Given the vast quantities of digital data now available, descriptive research can still be systematic and sit alongside other paradigms. It may even lead to more integrative theories in the long run. Specifically, there are many instances in psychology where multiple lines of research appear to examine different topics from a theoretical perspective, but describe a similar phenomena. For example, security and privacy can be considered two sides of the same coin. To bridge gaps and advance our understanding in the future, smartphones could help directly by utilising more apps that can collect structured data that combines automatic sensing with participant-generated inputs (Kubovy, 2019; Mondol et al., 2016). Examples of this potential are prevalent across several chapters including work that explores descriptive patterns of health-related behaviours (Chapter 2) and social interaction (Chapter 3). A similar approach using data from simulations (e.g., video games) or the real world would also allow researchers to determine the extent to which personality processes operate across different contexts (Chapter 4). Given a descriptive approach to health specifically, however, it seems even more unlikely that there will be a theoretical unification that encapsulates all existing theories that can help encourage people to improve every aspect of their health. Similarly, while previous work has considered general smartphone usage in hours, describing human–computer interactions in greater detail suggests that we have quite a distance to cover before achieving any form of theoretical unification (Ellis, 2019).

My lab (Psychology Sensor Lab)[2] and others are therefore developing new methods that can help describe sensor outputs and associated behavioural patterns longitudinally (Deng et al., 2019; Geyer, Ellis and Piwek,

---

[2] www.psychsensorlab.com

2019; Wilcockson, Ellis and Shaw, 2018). For example, behavioural interactions with technology are now being visualised and described in increasingly finer detail. This involves the use of purpose-built apps to capture complex patterns of usage from smartphones and has shifted from tracking general use (in hours) alongside single smartphone interactions (pickups) to aligning these metrics with specific apps and notifications. As our understanding develops with each additional level of description, it becomes possible to consider between versus individual differences in more detail (Wilcockson et al., 2018). Interactions can then be understood in terms of how any new or subsequent technology interaction is driven by a participant themselves (e.g., goal-directed or absent-minded) or after being prompted by a specific event (e.g., notification or external contextual cue) (Ellis, 2019). Looking at routine interactions across multiple screens is also becoming easier, which gets around problems associated with multitasking (Reeves et al., 2019). Specifically, understanding how one type of technological interaction can impact on another is of interest to psychology, information systems and marketing. Taken together, a deeper understanding of how technology interactions map onto psychological affordances will help researchers and practitioners distinguish between positive and negative outcomes across multiple domains. Of course, understanding how this links to people's thoughts, feelings and attitudes (including worries) towards technology is equally important. Qualitative research that involves co-creation could encourage participants to reflect on data provided by new quantitative measurements, which would support future development. I am therefore not suggesting a hard move towards a reformed behaviourism in the digital age. Rather than viewing these technological enhancements as removing the human element, we should focus on the fact that these methods ethically inform us about what people are actually doing with technology on a daily basis. This reveals a set of behaviours that are uniquely *human* (Davidson and Ellis, 2019a).

Going further, while there is very little understanding of how general usage alone might cause psychological distress, genuine digital harms can be aligned with different technology interactions. For example, 'misinformation', 'disinformation', 'fake news' and 'problematic content' are often used interchangeably, and the potential harm of such content is currently difficult to measure – as is the impact of any mitigations (e.g., removing content or fact checking). Descriptive strands of work would also help qualitatively define and quantitatively understand behavioural interactions as they relate to genuine psychological harms. For example, engaging with social interactions is vastly different to passively viewing content. Similar dichotomies equally apply to creating harmful content; for instance, writing a tweet is different from simply sharing an endorsement or viewing such material. This would, in turn, also act as a first step to help define and quantify online harm in other contexts by combining principles from psychological science, data visualisation and human–computer interaction.

Research involving smartphones and new technology has not caused and will not solve every problem related to measurement and theory, but long-standing issues are magnified. Technology, from a research perspective, has increased the quantity of scientific output. In reality, however, removing computational barriers has negated the need for slow and considered theorising. The gap between theory and application remains large within psychology and is genuinely challenging with very few areas developing new research paradigms (Lykken, 1991). Integrating individual and situational factors on a larger scale is often absent (Mischel, 2004). However, rather than simply building new methods that sit as competitors to the status quo, smartphones can build capacity across sub-domains of psychology and other disciplines. Generalisability can remain a long-term goal, but we may have to be realistic in the short-term as this applies to many areas of psychological science. While descriptive research has often not been viewed as fashionable, several chapters hint that we might be witnessing new lines of research that can complement tightly controlled randomised trials or experiments by embracing the ecological validity of the natural world. New technologies provide clear pathways forward, but they will, as before, require a focused effort from researchers themselves. Many of the issues considered are also not new and appear to loop with each new technological development or 'crisis'. Breaking these cycles will also not be straightforward.

Technological Déjà Vu

Narratives surrounding the mass adoption of new technologies are almost always negative across social science. In contrast, these can become overly optimistic within computer science and health research. This dualism of technology being good or bad does not hold up to ecological scrutiny, where the answers fall between these extremes. However, it is quite something to behold how much time psychological science has spent trying to convince itself that smartphones are damaging health, cognition and social communication. The repetitive nature of theorising without considering the quality of evidence or historical precedents in the first instance is equally baffling. An identical web can be woven from research concerning video games and even the internet itself (Davidson and Ellis, 2019b). Designs almost always involve asking people to consider their (often negative) personal experience with technology (Ellis, 2019), and this reflects a general shift away from behavioural measurement in psychology (Doliński, 2018; Sassenberg and Ditrich, 2019). The notion of 'addiction' is therefore woven into multiple narratives when psychologists should, like other areas of social science, really be referring to habitual behaviour, which of course sounds a lot less clinical or dangerous (Pink et al., 2017; Southerton, 2012).

Fear or resistance to technology is also not new, but it has perhaps become increasingly more prevalent as the rate of technological change has increased. The current body of research from psychological science, with few exceptions, follows a pattern where major concerns develop into research pointing towards inherent dangers or harms. This leads to theorisation that attempts to explain the negative impacts of a given technology. However, many of these concerns are then shown to be overinflated or demonstrably false. Research then moves on to a new technology. This pattern has recently looped once more as social media and smartphones no longer appear to be as dangerous as previously suggested (Hall et al., 2019; Heffer et al., 2019; Houghton et al., 2018; Orben and Przybylski, 2019; Orben, Dienlin and Przybylski, 2019; Stronge et al., 2019). Ironically, when new technology or methods are used in a way that benefits research directly, we often find that any negative effects on health and social interaction largely vanish (Johannes et al., 2019).

This cycling of technophobia suggests that no single issue will govern such responses, but, historically, similar factors including social-cultural perspectives, political and philosophical offer some initial insights. Approaches to understanding the impact of new technology vary considerably between disciplines, but this appears to have had little impact on psychology when considering the potential for harm or benefits (e.g., Bogen, 2017; Boyd, 2014). This pathologising of everyday behaviours is not exclusive to *technology use* research but widespread across psychological science. Haslam (2016) initially coined the term of 'concept creep', describing how research interests in negative experience and behaviour have become widespread in psychological science. Hence, there is an increase in pathologising everyday behaviours and experience, which in turn influences research due to our heightened awareness of harm (Haslam, 2016) and, arguably, changing cultural norms. This idea was extended to argue that concept creep can be both positive and negative, where there is potential to uncover meaningful insights into problematic behaviours. However, I would argue that technology research within psychology often falls back onto the 'sloppy overuse of a concept' (Cascardi and Brown, 2016, p. 24) because academics focus on a single negative behaviour, feeling or attitude.

In response, researchers might want to start asking themselves exactly why or how the use of social communication technology would cause harm and develop more suitable programmes of research. Smartphones are certainly not the first technology to be associated with potentially 'addictive' or negative societal impacts (Edgerton, 1995; Parker, 1995), nor will they be the last. Understanding the impact of technology on people and society remains crucial, but clinicians and researchers might also want to consider what drives 'technophobia' in the first place.

Interdisciplinary Research, Speed and Productivity

Research involving new digital technology remains fashionable. I suspect that many authors move into this area because it appears fundable or likely to generate immediate impact. In the United Kingdom, there is a push to develop research that has real-world implications. This is a core part of the Research Excellence Framework, which aims to quantify the quality and quantity of research across different institutions (Martin, 2011). However, it has perhaps encouraged scientists to pitch impact before a complete story has emerged. For example, a large number of scientists provided evidence to a recent UK government enquiry that considered evidence on the negative effects of social media and screen use on young adults. The enquiry concluded that the quality of academic evidence available, much of it from psychology, limited their ability to draw strong conclusions (UK Parliament, 2018). This speaks volumes about the quality and quantity of research that seeks to understand the impact of modern technology on people and society. Premature attempts to derive impact can narrow the focus to such an extent that researchers are unable to see the wood for the trees (Davidson and Ellis, 2019b). Ironically, while psychological science is well positioned to understand, and potentially mitigate, the impacts of new technology, it has perhaps less to contribute when compared to analogous disciplines. World-renowned psychologists are flagging these issues within experimental psychology specifically, but almost every chapter of this book echoes the sentiments of Alan Baddeley perfectly:

In ignoring the history of our field, however, we are in danger not only of rediscovering what is already known but more importantly of repeating costly mistakes. Topics that seem of crucial importance now represent only a thin slice of what has gone before and as such, potentially provide an unduly limited basis for future progress. If, as Newton proposed, we are pygmies standing on the shoulders of giants, it is as well to understand where we stand. (Baddeley, 2018, p. 13)

There is a danger that every new methodological advance or research area is presented as if it will transform the field overnight. While understanding the utility of a new method is important, knowing exactly how this can be applied to specific problems should remain front and centre for the discipline. There is an abundance of applications for smartphones in this regard. As outlined at the start of this book, new methods can tackle long-standing problems provided they appreciate historical perspectives. Only then will we build a coherent body of knowledge instead of continuing to 'reinvent the wheel'.

Some of the problems or issues with research concerning smartphones, and technological innovation in general, could be alleviated by adopting an interdisciplinary approach. Specifically, attempting to understand technology or the impact of a technology on people as a psychologist without bringing in relevant expertise (e.g., computer scientists and software developers) is unlikely to succeed. This can inadvertently make the field difficult to follow; for example, personality research is now scattered across many disciplines and researchers are often unaware of each other. However, if interdisciplinary efforts are prioritised, personality science will advance productively within and beyond its home discipline (Montag and Elhai, 2019). These collaborations will not lessen the contribution of psychological science.

The cognitive revolution and the rise of computational social science have similar origins (Giardino, 2019). The 1950s were a time when different disciplines came together but then drifted apart. One wonders what the ideal relationship between computer science and psychology might look like today. Both communities are interested in understanding personality, improving human–computer interaction and building systems that can help people become safer and happier. Much of this work is complementary, but there may need to be a compromise between (hopefully) slow incremental work from psychologists and the rapid pace of technology development. Cultures are converging to some extent, but three conditions are probably required to further these successful interactions. First, computer scientists often prioritise new insights over rigour and this balance may need to be readdressed somewhat by engaging carefully with experimental design. Second, psychology will have to continue with progress outlined above and re-align its own priorities. Finally, both parties will have to use common terminology to assist with dialogues that includes the needs of specific groups who will benefit from or deliver applied solutions, including interventions (Blandford et al., 2018). Failure to advance this agenda will harm both disciplines.

However, good intentions from researchers are only part of the picture. The pressure to publish and secure a permanent post (referred to as tenure in the United States) actively encourages a pace of progress that can appear impressive on paper but often holds limited value. For example, current expectations placed on researchers in terms of the REF appear to be somewhat incompatible with an interdisciplinary research agenda (REF 2021, n.d.). Researchers who wish to pursue such a line of enquiry are driven to publish across multiple fields by default to ensure long-term success. This places early-career academics under significant pressure. Many perhaps rightly argue that researchers should publish less and focus on high-quality articles (Simmons, Nelson and Simonsohn, 2011). However, while this is valuable for the discipline, it is unlikely to take place at the individual level because a large number of (high-quality) publications are an important criterion when securing tenure. At the other extreme, senior scientists who are publishing several hundred papers a year are, by and large, not adhering to strict guidelines on what determines authorship. This distorts the nature of what is realistic for early-career scientists further (Ioannidis, Klavans and Boyack, 2018). The words of Lazer and colleagues in 2009 are still true for the majority of interdisciplinary researchers in the social sciences:

> Tenure committees and editorial boards need to understand and reward the effort to publish across disciplines. Initially, computational social science needs to be the work of teams of social and computer scientists. In the long run, the question will be whether academia should nurture computational social scientists, or teams of computationally literate social scientists and socially literate computer scientists. (Lazer et al., 2009, p. 722)

It therefore remains essential that institutions enable people and support interdisciplinary research across the board. Senior academics often champion a variety of sensible changes, but this will often require buy-in from research institutes themselves. Others make recommendations that they never apply to their own practices. This is especially pertinent when it comes to adopting open science practices and supporting research staff at every stage of their career (Firth, 2019; Waithira, Mutinda and Cheah, 2019; Wellcome, 2020). Leadership and communication in this domain will be key, otherwise productivity will suffer.

Communication

Beyond the challenges faced when conducting high-quality research, it has become evident while writing this book that, deliberately or otherwise, authors often group themselves according to whether they think technology (including smartphones) is (a) useful for understanding psychological processes, (b) having an impact we do not fully understand or (c) likely to be a significant source of harm that goes beyond genuine issues outlined in Chapter 6. Groups (a) and (b) appear to be guided by the quality of current evidence and are, as a result, willing to change their mind. On the other hand, those who pontificate about the damage this technology can have on our well-being and social interaction continue to push those arguments with variable force. Interdisciplinary divisions struggle to explain these gaps in communication as the majority are based within psychology.

Notwithstanding potential conflicts of interest that are well documented (Chivers, 2019), there is a distinct lack of cross-pollination within psychological science. In fact, it would appear many of those using smartphones to study people and those who want to understand their impact are either unaware of each other's existence or avert their gaze. And here lies a paradox. The very scientists who argue technology is inherently problematic appear to avoid the latest methodological developments that would help support their arguments.

Many studies concerning the impacts of technology and smartphones probably build on existing biases rather than sound science (Bishop, 2019; Protzko and Schooler, 2019). If existing knowledge is built on very weak foundations, an outsider would quickly conclude that our current understanding is poor and start afresh. The harsh reality is that unsubstantiated hype and claims about the impact of technology on people and society continue to be repeated, irrespective of new evidence suggesting the contrary. There is a reluctance from some to engage with sensible debate, which fuels echo chambers (Obradović, 2019). This is sometimes reflected in publication practices, which can shape the discourse and direction of respective fields. For example, several recent editorials and opinion pieces suggest significant progress when it comes to understanding associations between media use and psychological well-being. However, after acknowledging limitations, the portrayal of a successful field becomes less convincing (Elhai, Levine and Hall, 2019; Twenge, 2019a; Wiederhold, 2019). Similarly, a minority of authors, for example Pontes and Griffiths (2019), continue to repeat the mantra that researchers should move to a consensus regarding the existence of gaming disorder despite the fact a majority of academics simply do not agree that the quality of the evidence justified such a diagnostic criterion in the first instance (Aarseth et al., 2017; Van Rooij et al., 2018). While it is challenging for scientists to keep track of the current literature, this almost appears as a form of selective exposure where scientists are avoiding information that would create cognitive dissonance because it is incompatible with current beliefs (Jeong et al., 2019). Some prominent voices have even suggested that the public should not believe scientists who disagree with them (Twenge, 2019b).

One wonders if digital systems that aim to help scientists discover new papers (e.g., *Mendeley*) are also leading scientists down a wormhole that confirms existing biases. For example, if I study 'addictive' smartphone use or how new technology can damage well-being, recommendation systems will provide me with more papers that confirm my suspicions. On the other hand, if I research behaviour change as it applies to physical activity and smartphones, I will be presented with papers from authors who are developing new approaches that aim to make people healthier and happier.

> The best books . . . are those that tell you what you know already. (Orwell, 1949, p. 253)

New techniques will need to go beyond these existing systems. For example, future tools could help point towards missed references. During the review process, authors may correct and improve their papers based on these recommendations, and editors can ensure that the article pays sufficient attention to foregoing theory and alternative arguments. Related tools could also assist with hypothesis development to guide future research (Extance, 2018).

Beyond technological and theoretical advances, how the field engages with some harsh truths is vital in order to evolve and remain relevant (Ellis, 2019). We must ensure that key societal issues – such as the effects of smartphones on children and adults – allow for the spirited exchange of ideas and enthusiastic debate. Discussion is the way forward, not cherry-picking or stonewalling. If we fail, then public funds will be squandered – especially when science is reliant on self-correction over time. Researchers across psychology should therefore strive to pro-actively reflect on critiques at every stage of the research process and respond accordingly. Adversarial collaboration may have to become the norm. Here, people who disagree on a topic work together to examine all the evidence, argue their respective cases, and present a collaborative piece of work.[3]

These realities present new challenges for the British Psychological Society (BPS). Indeed, the BPS and its members have a key role to play when drawing together sufficient resources to ensure key societal issues such as effects of smartphones on children, and individuals of all ages more generally, are fully interrogated both at the empirical level and in dissemination activities. However, while the BPS, the American Psychological Association (APA) and others release statements for those working in policy, these often do not reflect the underlying science and appear more definitive (Elson et al., 2019). Specifically, many statements adopt a specific narrative that does not reflect the spectrum of evidence and opinion. The same issues are prevalent in health-related news more generally, but press releases can mitigate issues by making it clear that correlation does not equate to causality. This does not appear to limit the interest of a piece of news (Adams et al., 2019). Given the methodological issues and inconsistencies reflected throughout this book, future statements going forward should reflect the many unknowns.

Societal dissemination must therefore go beyond binary distinctions. How technology changes people and society is far from clear-cut, and public engagement should reflect that reality. I am in no doubt that there is a well-meaning desire to mitigate and understand problems in society, but there are few certainties in science. Public communication often falls into the trap of providing an easy answer that fails to acknowledge the unknowns. This applies to many areas of behavioural science. Curating broader discussions can instead help reduce and understand the digital divide while simultaneously driving people's curiosity that generates new technological innovations, which continue to change society (often for the better). This will include social historians, scientists, artists and members of the public. We cannot go back to a time before these technologies existed, but we can change the binary nature of what has become an increasingly polarised platform for discussion.

Final Thoughts

The smartphone perfectly reflects the digital age – within and beyond social science. Psychology has a duty to understand how these technologies

---

[3] https://slatestarcodex.com/2019/12/09/2019-adversarial-collaboration-entries/

are changing people and society. This will always be important because people tend to create new technologies first and think about the social ramifications later. On the other hand, most of the technologies present in a modern smartphone already existed in a previous form. These have simply become self-contained and ubiquitous. Established systems like this can therefore provide many researchers with a powerful torch that can shed new light on a variety of psychological phenomena. While challenging, striking a balance between these two somewhat competing demands is achievable.

I am often asked about the future (mostly by journalists). There is more hype than theory to guide my predictions, but three thoughts remain consistent. First, computing power will continue to increase. Second, hyperconnectivity is about to reach a new tier as more digital systems become intertwined. Third, psychological science will have access to even more data about people and society. It is therefore reasonable to assume more of the same, provided people continue to find the technology beneficial, convenient and trouble-free. However, it only takes one new innovation to disrupt everything.

Similar to many 'crises' or debates in psychological science, smartphones will also evolve or be replaced by something new. Unlike new technology, however, psychology's response to mass-adopted technology has remained remarkably consistent. Social scientists might want to remember that these technologies are, in themselves, not a direct threat to society.

They are society: Warts and all. This is what makes them both psychologically interesting and almost irresistible for daily life. The smartphone perfectly reflects so much of what it means to be human in the digital age.

If we want to get closer to the truth, the discipline will have to accept these realities. Psychological science will, in turn, remain relevant in the digital age.

Useful Resources and Further Reading

Zendle, D. & Bowden-Jones, H. (2019). Is excessive use of social media an addiction? *BMJ*, *365*, l2171.
The above letter appeared in the British Medical Journal and concisely considers the many uncertainties around the notion that technology use is inherently harmful.
Yarkoni, T. (2019). The generalizability crisis. *PsyArXiv*.
This paper considers problems encountered when psychologists attempt to generalise knowledge far beyond the confines of existing results. Suggestions on how this situation might be improved in the future are referred to in earlier discussions.

References

Preface

Mehl, M. R. & Conner, T. S. (eds.). (2012). *Handbook of Research Methods for Studying Daily Life*. Guilford Press.

Tajfel, H., Fraser, C., & Jaspars, J. M. F. (eds.). (1984). *The Social Dimension: Volume 1: European Developments in Social Psychology*. Cambridge University Press.

Introduction

Aharony, N., Pan, W., Ip, C., Khayal, I., & Pentland, A. (2011). Social fMRI: Investigating and shaping social mechanisms in the real world. *Pervasive and Mobile Computing*, 7(6), 643–659.

Andrews, S., Ellis, D. A., Shaw, H., & Piwek, L. (2015). Beyond self-report: Tools to compare estimated and real-world smartphone use. *PLOS ONE*, 10(10): e0139004.

Arute, F., Arya, K., Babbush, R., et al. (2019). Quantum supremacy using a programmable superconducting processor. *Nature*, 574(7779), 505–510.

Azrin, N. H., Holz, W., Ulrich, R., & Goldiamond, I. (1961). The control of the content of conversation through reinforcement. *Journal of the Experimental Analysis of Behavior*, 4(1), 25.

Baddeley, A. (2018). *Working Memories: Postmen, Divers and the Cognitive Revolution*. Routledge.

Baumeister, R. F., Vohs, K. D., & Funder, D. C. (2007). Psychology as the science of self- reports and finger movements: Whatever happened to actual behavior? *Perspectives on Psychological Science*, 2(4), 396–403.

Bennett, C. M., Miller, M. B., & Wolford, G. L. (2009). Neural correlates of interspecies perspective taking in the post-mortem Atlantic salmon: An argument for multiple comparisons correction. *Neuroimage*, 47(Suppl. 1), S125.

Bernstein, E. S. & Turban, S. (2018). The impact of the 'open' workspace on human collaboration. *Philosophical Transactions of the Royal Society B: Biological Sciences*, 373(1753), 20170239.

Binet, A. & Simon, T. (1916). *The Development of Intelligence in Children: The Binet-Simon Scale* (vol. 11). Williams & Wilkins.

188 *References*

Boccia, M. L. & Roberts, J. E. (2000). Computer-assisted integration of physiological and behavioural measures. In T. Thompson, D. Felce, & F. J. Symons (eds.), *Behavioral Observation: Technology and Applications in Developmental Disabilities* (pp. 83–97). Brookes.

Buchanan, T. & Smith, J. L. (1999). Using the internet for psychological research: Personality testing on the World Wide Web. *British Journal of Psychology*, *90*(1), 125–144.

Buhrmester, M., Kwang, T., & Gosling, S. D. (2011). Amazon's Mechanical Turk: A new source of inexpensive, yet high-quality, data? *Perspectives on Psychological Science*, *6*(1), 3–5.

Buhrmester, M. D., Talaifar, S., & Gosling, S. D. (2018). An evaluation of Amazon's Mechanical Turk, its rapid rise, and its effective use. *Perspectives on Psychological Science*, *13*(2), 149–154.

Chaffin, D., Heidl, R., Hollenbeck, J. R., et al. (2017). The promise and perils of wearable sensors in organizational research. *Organizational Research Methods*, *20*(1), 3–31.

Chamorro-Premuzic, T., Reimers, S., Hsu, A., & Ahmetoglu, G. (2009). Who art thou? Personality predictors of artistic preferences in a large UK sample: The importance of openness. *British Journal of Psychology*, *100*(3), 501–516.

Chandler, J., Mueller, P., & Paolacci, G. (2014). Nonnaïveté among Amazon Mechanical Turk workers: Consequences and solutions for behavioural researchers. *Behaviour Research Methods*, *46*(1), 112–130.

Choudhury, T. & Pentland, A. (2002, November). The sociometer: A wearable device for understanding human networks. In *CSCW'02 Workshop: Ad Hoc Communications and Collaboration in Ubiquitous Computing Environments*.

Chumbley, J. R. & Friston, K. J. (2009). False discovery rate revisited: FDR and topological inference using Gaussian random fields. *Neuroimage*, *44*(1), 62–70.

Clark, L. A. & Watson, D. (1995). Constructing validity: Basic issues in objective scale development. *Psychological Assessment*, *7*(3), 309.

Clegg, J. W. (2018). *Self-Observation in the Social Sciences*. Routledge.

Cole, P. M., Martin, S. E., & Dennis, T. A. (2004). Emotion regulation as a scientific construct: Methodological challenges and directions for child development research. *Child Development*, *75*, 317–333.

Conner, T. S. & Lehman, B. J. (2012). Getting started: Launching a study in daily life. In M. R. Mehl & T. S. Conner (eds.), *Handbook of Research Methods for Studying Daily Life* (pp. 89–107). Guilford Press.

Davidson, B. I. & Ellis, D. A. (2019). Social media addiction: Technological déjà vu. *BMJ*, *365*, l4277.

Davidson, B. I., Joinson, A., & Jones, S. L. (2018). Technologically enhanced dating: Augmented human relationships, robots and fantasy. In Z. Papacharissi (ed.), *A Networked Self and Love* (pp. 129–155). Routledge.

DeMasi, O., Kording, K., & Recht, B. (2017). Meaningless comparisons lead to false optimism in medical machine learning. *PLOS ONE*, *12*(9), e0184604.

Doliński, D. (2018). Is psychology still a science of behavior? *Social Psychological Bulletin*, *13*, e25025.

Eagle, N., Pentland, A. S., & Lazer, D. (2009). Inferring friendship network structure by using mobile phone data. *Proceedings of the National Academy of Sciences, 106*(36), 15274–15278.

Ellis, D. (2012) Secondary data analysis. *The Psychologist, 25,* 97.

Ellis, D. A. (2019). Are smartphones really that bad? Improving the psychological measurement of technology-related behaviours. *Computers in Human Behavior, 97,* 60–66.

Ellis, D. A. & Jenkins, R. (2012). Weekday affects attendance rate for medical appointments: Large-scale data analysis and implications. *PLOS ONE, 7*(12), e51365.

Ellis, D. A. & Piwek, L. (2016). The future of . . . wearable technology. *CREST Security Review, 1,* 4–5.

Ellis, D. A. & Piwek, L. (2018). Failing to encourage physical activity with wearable technology: What next? *Journal of the Royal Society of Medicine, 111* (9), 310–313.

Ellis, D. A., Wiseman, R., & Jenkins, R. (2015). Mental representations of weekdays. *PLOS ONE, 10*(8), e0134555.

Ellis, D. A., Kaye, L. K., Wilcockson, T. D., & Ryding, F. C. (2018). Digital traces of behaviour within addiction: Response to Griffiths (2017). *International Journal of Mental Health and Addiction, 16*(1), 240–245.

Elmer, T., Chaitanya, K., Purwar, P., & Stadtfeld, C. (2019). The validity of RFID badges measuring face-to-face interactions. *Behavior Research Methods, 51,* 2120–2138.

Emerson, E., Reeves, D., & Felce, D. (2000). Palm-top computer technologies for behavioural observation research. In T. Thompson, D. Felce, & F. J. Symons (eds.), *Behavioral Observation: Technology and Applications in Developmental Disabilities* (pp. 47–59). Brookes.

Farrell, A. D. (1991). Computers and behavioural assessment: Current applications, future possibilities, and obstacles to routine use. *Behavioral Assessment. 13* (2), 159–179.

Festinger, L., Schachter, S., & Back, K. (1950). *Social Pressures in Informal Groups: A Study of Human Factors in Housing.* Harper.

Flake, J. K. & Fried, E. I. (2019). Measurement schmeasurement: Questionable measurement practices and how to avoid them. *PsyArXiv.* DOI:10.31234/osf.io/hs7wm

Fowler, R. D., Seligman, M. E. P., & Koocher, G. P. (1999). The APA 1998 Annual Report. *American Psychologist, 54,* 537–568.

Francis, G. (2012). Publication bias and the failure of replication in experimental psychology. *Psychonomic Bulletin & Review, 19*(6), 975–991.

Freund, K. (1963). A laboratory method for diagnosing predominance of homo and hetero-sexual interest in the male. *Behavior Research and Therapy, 1,* 85–93.

Freund, K. (1965). Diagnosing heterosexual pedophilia by means of a test for sexual interest. *Behavior Research and Therapy, 3,* 229–234.

Geyer, K., Ellis, D. A., & Piwek, L. (2019). A simple location-tracking app for psychological research. *Behavior Research Methods, 51*(6), 2840–2846.

Gladstone, J. J., Matz, S. C., & Lemaire, A. (2019). Can psychological traits be inferred from spending? Evidence from transaction data. *Psychological Science*, 30(7), 1087–1096.

Hanson R. K. & Bussière M. T. (1998). Predicting relapse: A meta-analysis of sexual offender recidivism studies. *Journal of Consulting and Clinical Psychology*, 66(2), 348–362.

Hässler, T., Ullrich, J., Bernardino, M., et al. (2020). A large-scale test of the link between intergroup contact and support for social change. *Nature Human Behavior*, 4(4), 380–386.

Hodson, G., Crisp, R. J., Meleady, R., & Earle, M. (2018). Intergroup contact as an agent of cognitive liberalization. *Perspectives on Psychological Science*, 13(5), 523–548.

Hofmann, B., Haustein, D., & Landeweerd, L. (2017). Smart-glasses: Exposing and elucidating the ethical issues. *Science and Engineering Ethics*, 23(3), 701–721.

Hogg, M. A. & Vaughan, G. (2005). *Introduction to Social Psychology*. Pearson.

Holter, N. J. (1961). New method for heart studies: Continuous electrocardiography of active subjects over long periods is now practical. *Science*, 134(3486), 1214–1220.

Huey, E. (1968). *The Psychology and Pedagogy of Reading (Reprint)*. MIT Press (originally published 1908).

Hung, H., Englebienne, G., & Quiros, L. C. (2014). Detecting conversing groups with a single worn accelerometer. *Proceedings of the 16th International Conference on Multimodal Interaction* (pp. 84–91). ACM Press. https://dl.acm.org/doi/abs/10.1145/2663204.2663228

Ireland, T. & Garnier, S. (2018). Architecture, space and information in constructions built by humans and social insects: A conceptual review. *Philosophical Transactions of the Royal Society B: Biological Sciences*, 373(1753), 20170244.

Jean-Louis, G., Kripke, D. F., Mason, W. J., Elliott, J. A., & Youngstedt, S. D. (2001). Sleep estimation from wrist movement quantified by different actigraphic modalities. *Journal of Neuroscience Methods*, 105(2), 185–191.

Joinson, A. (1999). Social desirability, anonymity, and internet-based questionnaires. *Behavior Research Methods, Instruments, & Computers*, 31(3), 433–438.

Jones, C. (2010). Interdisciplinary approach-advantages, disadvantages, and the future benefits of interdisciplinary studies. *Essai*, 7(1), 26.

Kahng, S. & Iwata, B. A. (1998). Computerized systems for collecting real-time observational data. *Journal of Applied Behavior Analysis*, 31(2), 253–261.

Kalimeri, K., Lepri, B., Kim, T., Pianesi, F., & Pentland, A. (2011). Automatic modeling of dominance effects using granger causality. *Human Behavior Understanding*, 7065, 124–133.

Kahneman, D. (2011). *Thinking, Fast and Slow*. Macmillan.

Keil, T. F., Koschate-Reis, M., & Levine, M. (2020). Contact Logger: Measuring everyday intergroup contact experiences in near-time. *Behavior Research Methods*. https://link.springer.com/article/10.3758/s13428-019-01335-w

Killingsworth, M. A. & Gilbert, D. T. (2010). A wandering mind is an unhappy mind. *Science*, 330(6006), 932.

Kim, T., Chang, A., Holland, L., & Pentland, A. (2008). Meeting mediator: Enhancing group collaboration with sociometric feedback. *Proceedings of the 2008 ACM Conference on Computer Supported Cooperative Work* (pp. 457–466). https://dl.acm.org/doi/abs/10.1145/1460563.1460636

Kim, T., McFee, E., Olguin Olguin, D., Waber, B., & Pentland, A. (2012). Sociometric badges: Using sensor technology to capture new forms of collaboration. *Journal of Organizational Behavior, 33*(3), 412–427.

Kornbrot, D. E., Wiseman, R., & Georgiou, G. J. (2018). Quality science from quality measurement: The role of measurement type with respect to replication and effect size magnitude in psychological research. *PLOS ONE, 13*(2), e0192808.

Kosinski, M., Stillwell, D., & Graepel, T. (2013). Private traits and attributes are predictable from digital records of human behavior. *Proceedings of the National Academy of Sciences, 110*(15), 5802–5805.

Kramer, R. S., Mulgrew, J., Anderson, N. C., et al. (2020). Physically attractive faces attract us physically. *Cognition, 198*, 104193.

Lathia, N., Pejovic, V., Rachuri, K. K., et al. (2013). Smartphones for large-scale behaviour change interventions. *IEEE Pervasive Computing, 12*(3), 66–73.

Lazer, D., Pentland, A., Adamic, L., et al. (2009). Computational social science. *Science, 323*(5915), 721–723.

Levine, M., Taylor, P. J., & Best, R. (2011). Third parties, violence, and conflict resolution: The role of group size and collective action in the microregulation of violence. *Psychological Science, 22*(3), 406–412.

Macdonald, R. G. & Tatler, B. W. (2018). Gaze in a real-world social interaction: A dual eye-tracking study. *Quarterly Journal of Experimental Psychology, 71*(10), 2162–2173.

MacKerron, G. & Mourato, S. (2013). Happiness is greater in natural environments. *Global Environmental Change, 23*(5), 992–1000.

Matusik, J. G., Heidl, R., Hollenbeck, J. R., et al. (2018). Wearable Bluetooth sensors for capturing relational variables and temporal variability in relationships: A construct validation study. *Journal of Applied Psychology, 104*(3), 357–387.

Mazzucato, M. (2013). State of innovation. *New Scientist, 219*(2931), 26–27.

McGrath, M. J., Scanaill, C. N., & Nafus, D. (2014). *Sensor Technologies: Healthcare, Wellness and Environmental Applications*. Apress.

McKeown, S. & Dixon, J. (2017). The 'contact hypothesis': Critical reflections and future directions. *Social and Personality Psychology Compass, 11*(1), e12295.

Mehl, M. R. (2017). The electronically activated recorder (EAR): A method for the naturalistic observation of daily social behavior. *Current Directions in Psychological Science, 26*(2), 184–190.

Mehl, M. R. & Conner, T. S. (eds.). (2012). *Handbook of Research Methods for Studying Daily Life*. Guilford Press.

Mele, M. L. & Federici, S. (2012). Gaze and eye-tracking solutions for psychological research. *Cognitive Processing, 13*(1), 261–265.

Miller, G. (2012). The smartphone psychology manifesto. *Perspectives on Psychological Science, 7*(3), 221–237.

Miller, G. A. (2003). The cognitive revolution: A historical perspective. *Trends in Cognitive Sciences*, *7*(3), 141–144.

Mozos, O. M., Sandulescu, V., Andrews, S., et al. (2017). Stress detection using wearable physiological and sociometric sensors. *International Journal of Neural Systems*, *27*(2), 1650041.

Murakami Wood, D., Ball, K., Graham, S., et al. (2006). *A Report on the Surveillance Society*. Office of the Information Commissioner. https://ico.org.uk/media/abo ut-the-ico/documents/1042390/surveillance-society-full-report-2006.pdf

Musch, J. & Reips, U. D. (2000). A brief history of Web experimenting. In M. Birnbaum (ed.), *Psychological Experiments on the Internet* (pp. 61–88). Academic Press.

Nielson, D. M., Smith, T. A., Sreekumar, V., Dennis, S., & Sederberg, P. B. (2015). Human hippocampus represents space and time during retrieval of real-world memories. *Proceedings of the National Academy of Sciences*, *112*(35), 11078–11083.

OFCOM. (2018). *The Communications Market 2018*. www.ofcom.org.uk/research-and-data/multi-sector-research/cmr/cmr-2018

Open Science Collaboration. (2015). Estimating the reproducibility of psychological science. *Science*, *349* (6251),aac4716.

Orben, A. & Przybylski, A. K. (2019). Screens, teens, and psychological well-being: Evidence from three time-use-diary studies. *Psychological Science*, *30*(5), 682–696.

Paletta, L., Neuschmied, H., Schwarz, M., et al. (2014, March). Smartphone eye tracking toolbox: Accurate gaze recovery on mobile displays. In *Proceedings of the Symposium on Eye Tracking Research and Applications* (pp. 367–368). ACM.

Paolacci, G. & Chandler, J. (2014). Inside the Turk: Understanding Mechanical Turk as a participant pool. *Current Directions in Psychological Science*, *23*(3), 184–188.

Peer, E., Vosgerau, J., & Acquisti, A. (2014). Reputation as a sufficient condition for data quality on Amazon Mechanical Turk. *Behavior Research Methods*, *46*(4), 1023–1031.

Peirce, J. W., Gray, J. R., Simpson, S., et al. (2019). PsychoPy2: Experiments in behaviour made easy. *Behavior Research Methods*.

Pérez-Edgar, K., MacNeill, L. A., & Fu, X. (2020). Navigating through the experienced environment: Insights from mobile eye tracking. *Current Directions in Psychological Science*, 0963721420915880. https://doi.org/10.1177 /0963721420915880

Piwek, L. & Joinson, A. (2017). Automatic tracking of behavior with smartphones: Potential for behavior change interventions. In L. Little, E. Sillence, & A. Joinson (eds.), *Behavior Change Research and Theory* (pp. 137–165). Academic Press.

Piwek, L., Ellis, D. A., & Andrews, S. (2016a). Can programming frameworks bring smartphones into the mainstream of psychological science? *Frontiers in Psychology*, *7*, 1252.

Piwek, L., Ellis, D. A., Andrews, S., & Joinson, A. (2016b). The rise of consumer wearables: Promises and barriers. *PLOS MEDICINE*, *13*(2), e1001953.

Poltavski, D. V. (2015). The use of single-electrode wireless EEG in biobehavioral investigations. In *Mobile Health Technologies* (pp. 375–390). Humana Press.

Poppe, R., Van Der Zee, S., Heylen, D. K., & Taylor, P. J. (2014). AMAB: Automated measurement and analysis of body motion. *Behavior Research Methods*, *46*(3), 625–633.

Pursey, K., Burrows, T. L., Stanwell, P., & Collins, C. E. (2014). How accurate is web-based self-reported height, weight, and body mass index in young adults? *Journal of Medical Internet Research*, *16*(1), e4.

Rachman, S. (1966). Sexual fetishism: An experimental analogue. *The Psychological Record*, *16*(3), 293–296.

Reimers, S. (2007). The BBC internet study: General methodology. *Archives of Sexual Behavior*, *36*(2), 147–161.

Reimers, S. & Stewart, N. (2009). Using SMS text messaging for teaching and data collection in the behavioral sciences. *Behavior Research Methods*, *41*(3), 675–681.

Reimers, S. & Stewart, N. (2015). Presentation and response timing accuracy in Adobe Flash and HTML5/JavaScript Web experiments. *Behavior Research Methods*, *47*(2), 309–327.

Reimers, S. & Stewart, N. (2016). Auditory presentation and synchronization in Adobe Flash and HTML5/JavaScript Web experiments. *Behavior Research Methods*, *48*(3), 897–908.

Roberts, B. W. & Hill, P. L. (2017). Questions and answers about the policy relevance of personality traits. *PsyArXiv*.

Rollason, J. C., Outtrim, J. G., & Mathur, R. S. (2014). A pilot study comparing the DuoFertility® monitor with ultrasound in infertile women. *International Journal of Women's Health*, *6*, 657.

Saguy, T., Tausch, N., Dovidio, J. F., & Pratto, F. (2009). The irony of harmony: Intergroup contact can produce false expectations for equality. *Psychological Science*, *20*(1), 114–121.

Sassenberg, K. & Ditrich, L. (2019). Research in social psychology changed between 2011 and 2016: Larger sample sizes, more self-report measures, and more online studies. *Advances in Methods and Practices in Psychological Science*, *2*(2), 107–114.

Schmidt, E. & Cohen, J. (2013). *The New Digital Age: Reshaping the Future of People, Nations and Business*. Hachette UK.

Shaw, H., Ellis, D. A., Kendrick, L. R., Ziegler, F., & Wiseman, R. (2016). Predicting smartphone operating system from personality and individual differences. *Cyberpsychology, Behavior, and Social Networking*, *19*(12), 727–732.

Shaw, H., Ellis, D. A., & Ziegler, F. (2018). The technology integration model (TIM): A new theory to predict technology adoption and use. *Computers in Human Behavior*, *83*, 204–214.

Simon W. T. & Schouten P. G. (1992). The plethysmograph reconsidered: Comments on Barker and Howell. *Bulletin of the American Academy of Psychiatry and the Law*, *20*, 13–25.

Simmons, J. P., Nelson, L. D., & Simonsohn, U. (2011). False-positive psychology: Undisclosed flexibility in data collection and analysis allows presenting anything as significant. *Psychological Science*, *22*, 1359–1366.

194 *References*

Skinner, B. F. (1971). *Beyond Freedom and Dignity*. Knopf.

Sorokin, P. A. (1950). *Altruistic Love: A Study of American 'Good Neighbors' and Christian Saints*. Beacon Press.

Sun, J. & Vazire, S. (2019). Do people know what they're like in the moment? *Psychological Science*, *30*(3), 405–414.

Tapp, J. & Walden, T. A. (2000). PROCODER: A system for collection and analysis of observational data from videotape. In T. Thompson, D. Felce, & F. J. Symons (eds.) *Behavioural Observation: Technology and Applications in Developmental Disabilities* (pp. 61–70). Brookes.

Thai, S. & Page-Gould, E. (2018). ExperienceSampler: An open-source scaffold for building smartphone apps for experience sampling. *Psychological Methods*, *23* (4), 729.

Tombs, S. & Silverman, I. (2004). Pupillometry: A sexual selection approach. *Evolution and Human Behavior*, *25*(4), 221–228.

Turing, A. M. (1937). On computable numbers, with an application to the Entscheidungsproblem. *Proceedings of the London Mathematical Society*, *2*(1), 230–265.

Uttal, W. R. (2001). *The New Phrenology: The Limits of Localizing Cognitive Processes in the Brain*. The MIT Press.

Watson, J. B. (1913). Psychology as the behaviorist views it. *Psychological Review*, *20* (2), 158.

Weinberg, N. (2019). *Computers in the Information Society*. Routledge.

Weston, S. J., Ritchie, S. J., Rohrer, J. M., & Przybylski, A. K. (2019). Recommendations for increasing the transparency of analysis of preexisting data sets. *Advances in Methods and Practices in Psychological Science*, *2*(3), 214–227.

Wilcockson, T. D. (2017, June). Using eye trackers as indicators of diagnostic markers: Implications from HCI devices. In *International Conference on Intelligent Decision Technologies* (pp. 308–315). Springer.

Wilmer, H. H., Sherman, L. E., & Chein, J. M. (2017). Smartphones and cognition: A review of research exploring the links between mobile technology habits and cognitive functioning. *Frontiers in Psychology*, *8*, 605.

Wiseman, R. (1995). The MegaLab truth test. *Nature*, *373*(6513), 391.

Wiseman, R. (1996). 'MegaLab UK': Participatory science and the mass media. *Public Understanding of Science*, *5*, 167–169.

Wiseman, R. (2007) *Quirkology: The Curious Science of Everyday Lives*. Macmillan.

Wiseman, R. & Watt, C. (2010). Judging a book by its cover: The unconscious influence of pupil size on consumer choice. *Perception*, *39*(10), 1417–1419.

Yarkoni, T. (2019). The generalizability crisis. *PsyArXiv*. DOI:10.31234/osf.io/jqw35

Yang, C. C. & Hsu, Y. L. (2010). A review of accelerometery-based wearable motion detectors for physical activity monitoring. *Sensors*, *10*(8), 7772–7788.

Zhang, Q., Song, X., Shao, X., Shibasaki, R., & Zhao, H. (2013). Unsupervised skeleton extraction and motion capture from 3D deformable matching. *Neurocomputing*, *100*, 170–182.

Chapter 1

Aarseth, E., Bean, A. M., Boonen, H., et al. (2017). Scholars' open debate paper on the World Health Organization ICD-11 Gaming Disorder proposal. *Journal of Behavioral Addictions, 6*(3), 267–270.

Andrews, S., Ellis, D. A., Shaw, H., & Piwek, L. (2015). Beyond self-report: Tools to compare estimated and real-world smartphone use. *PLOS ONE, 10*(10), e0139004.

Baranowski, T. O. M., Masse, L. C., Ragan, B., & Welk, G. (2008). How many days was that? We're still not sure, but we're asking the question better! *Medicine and Science in Sports and Exercise, 40*(7), S544.

Barr, N., Pennycook, G., Stolz, J. A., & Fugelsang, J. A. (2015). The brain in your pocket: Evidence that smartphones are used to supplant thinking. *Computers in Human Behavior, 48*, 473–480.

Baumeister, R. F., Vohs, K. D., & Funder, D. C. (2007). Psychology as the science of self- reports and finger movements: Whatever happened to actual behavior? *Perspectives on Psychological Science, 2*(4), 396–403.

Belk, R. W. (2013). Extended self in a digital world. *Journal of Consumer Research, 40*(3), 477–500.

Bianchi, A. & Phillips, J. G. (2005). Psychological predictors of problem mobile phone use. *CyberPsychology and Behavior, 8*(1), 39–51.

Billieux, J., Van der Linden, M., & Rochat, L. (2008). The role of impulsivity in actual and problematic use of the mobile phone. *Applied Cognitive Psychology, 22* (9), 1195–1210.

Billieux, J., Maurage, P., Lopez-Fernandez, O., Kuss, D. J., & Griffiths, M. D. (2015). Can disordered mobile phone use be considered a behavioural addiction? An update on current evidence and a comprehensive model for future research. *Current Addiction Reports, 2*(2), 156–162.

Bisen, S. S. & Deshpande, Y. M. (2018). Understanding internet addiction: a comprehensive review. *Mental Health Review Journal, 23*(3), 165–184.

Black, A. (2018, February). Take a digital detox. *Sunshine Coast Daily*, p. 22.

Boase, J. & Ling, R. (2013). Measuring mobile phone use: Self-report versus log data. *Journal of Computer-Mediated Communication, 18*(4), 508–519.

Bodford, J. E., Kwan, V. S. Y., & Sobota, D. S. (2017). Fatal attractions: Attachment to smartphones predicts anthropomorphic beliefs and dangerous behaviors. *Cyberpsychology, Behavior, and Social Networking, 20*(5), 320–326.

Buchanan, T., Paine, C., Joinson, A. N., & Reips, U. D. (2007). Development of measures of online privacy concern and protection for use on the internet. *Journal of the American Society for Information Science and Technology, 58*(2), 157–165.

Butt, S. & Phillips, J. G. (2008). Personality and self reported mobile phone use. *Computers in Human Behavior, 24*(2), 346–360.

Chekroud, S. R., Gueorguieva, R., Zheutlin, A. B., et al. (2018). Association between physical exercise and mental health in 1.2 million individuals in the USA between 2011 and 2015: A cross-sectional study. *The Lancet Psychiatry, 5*(9), 739–746.

Chóliz, M. (2012). Mobile-phone addiction in adolescence: The test of mobile phone dependence (TMD). *Progress in Health Science*, *2*(1), 33–44.

Chóliz, M., Pinto, L., Phansalkar, S. S., et al. (2016). Development of a brief multicultural version of the test of mobile phone dependence (TMDbrief) questionnaire. *Frontiers in Psychology*, *7*, 650.

Christensen, M. A., Bettencourt, L., Kaye, L., et al. (2016). Direct measurements of smartphone screen-time: relationships with demographics and sleep. *PLOS ONE*, *11*(11), e0165331.

Clayton, R. B., Leshner, G., & Almond, A. (2015). The extended iSelf: The impact of iPhone separation on cognition, emotion, and physiology. *Journal of Computer-Mediated Communication*, *20*(2), 119–135.

Costigan, S. A., Barnett, L., Plotnikoff, R. C., & Lubans, D. R. (2013). The health indicators associated with screen-based sedentary behavior among adolescent girls: A systematic review. *Journal of Adolescent Health*, *52*(4), 382–392.

Coyne, S. M., Rogers, A. A., Zurcher, J. D., Stockdale, L., & Booth, M. (2020). Does time spent using social media impact mental health? An eight year longitudinal study. *Computers in Human Behavior*, *104*, 106160.

Csibi, S., Griffiths, M. D., Cook, B., Demetrovics, Z., & Szabo, A. (2018). The psychometric properties of the smartphone application-based addiction scale (SABAS). *International Journal of Mental Health and Addiction*, *16*(2), 393–403.

Day, F. R., Ong, K. K., & Perry, J. R. (2018). Elucidating the genetic basis of social interaction and isolation. *Nature Communications*, *9*(1), 2457.

Days, K. T. (2018). *Parents, Media and Panic Through the Years*. Palgrave Pivot.

Doliński, D. (2018). Is psychology still a science of behavior? *Social Psychological Bulletin*, *13*, e25025.

Dozois, D. J. & Rnic, K. (2015). Core beliefs and self-schematic structure in depression. *Current Opinion in Psychology*, *4*, 98–103.

Doughty, M., Rowland, D., & Lawson, S. (2012, July). Who is on your sofa? TV audience communities and second screening social networks. In *Proceedings of the 10th European Conference on Interactive TV and Video* (pp. 79–86). ACM.

Ehrenberg, A., Juckes, S., White, K. M., & Walsh, S. P. (2008). Personality and self-esteem as predictors of young people's technology use. *Cyberpsychology and Behavior*, *11*(6), 739–741.

Elhai, J. D., Levine, J. C., Dvorak, R. D., & Hall, B. J. (2016). Fear of missing out, need for touch, anxiety and depression are related to problematic smartphone use. *Computers in Human Behavior*, *63*, 509–516.

Elhai, J. D., Dvorak, R. D., Levine, J. C., & Hall, B. J. (2017). Problematic smartphone use: A conceptual overview and systematic review of relations with anxiety and depression psychopathology. *Journal of Affective Disorders*, *207*, 251–259.

Elhai, J. D., Tiamiyu, M. F., Weeks, J. W., et al. (2018). Depression and emotion regulation predict objective smartphone use measured over one week. *Personality and Individual Differences*, *133*, 21–28.

Ellis, D. A. & Piwek, L. (2018). Failing to encourage physical activity with wearable technology: What next? *Journal of the Royal Society of Medicine, 111* (9), 310–313.

Ellis, D. A., Kaye, L. K., Wilcockson, T. D., & Ryding, F. C. (2018). Digital traces of behaviour within addiction: Response to Griffiths (2017). *International Journal of Mental Health and Addiction, 16*(1), 240–245.

Ellis, D. A., Davidson, B. I., Shaw, H., & Geyer, K. (2019). Do smartphone usage scales predict behavior? *International Journal of Human-Computer Studies, 130,* 86–92.

Ernala, S. K., Burke, M., Leavitt, A., & Ellison, N. B. (2020). *How Well Do People Report Time Spent on Facebook? An Evaluation of Established Survey Questions with Recommendations.* http://dx.doi.org/10.1145/3313831.3376435.

Foerster, M., Roser, K., Schoeni, A., & Röösli, M. (2015). Problematic mobile phone use in adolescents: Derivation of a short scale MPPUS10. *International Journal of Public Health, 60*(2), 277–286.

Fullwood, C., Quinn, S., Kaye, L. K., & Redding, C. (2017). My virtual friend: A qualitative analysis of the attitudes and experiences of smartphone users: Implications for smartphone attachment. *Computers in Human Behavior, 75,* 347–355.

Ha, J. H., Chin, B., Park, D. H., Ryu, S. H., & Yu, J. (2008). Characteristics of excessive cellular phone use in Korean adolescents. *CyberPsychology and Behavior, 11*(6), 783–784.

Hall, J. A., Xing, C., Ross, E. M., & Johnson, R. M. (2019). Experimentally manipulating social media abstinence: Results of a four-week diary study. *Media Psychology,* 1–17. doi.org/10.1080/15213269.2019.1688171

Haslam, N. (2016). Concept creep: Psychology's expanding concepts of harm and pathology. *Psychological Inquiry, 27*(1), 1–17.

Haslam, S. A., McMahon, C., Cruwys, T., et al. (2018). Social cure, what social cure? The propensity to underestimate the importance of social factors for health. *Social Science & Medicine, 198,* 14–21.

Heffer, T., Good, M., Daly, O., MacDonell, E., & Willoughby, T. (2019). The longitudinal association between social-media use and depressive symptoms among adolescents and young adults: An empirical reply to Twenge et al. (2018). *Clinical Psychological Science, 7*(3), 462–470.

Horwood, S. & Anglim, J. (2018). Personality and problematic smartphone use: A facet-level analysis using the Five Factor Model and HEXACO frameworks. *Computers in Human Behavior, 85,* 349–359.

Houghton, S., Lawrence, D., Hunter, S. C., et al. (2018). Reciprocal relationships between trajectories of depressive symptoms and screen media use during adolescence. *Journal of Youth and Adolescence, 47*(11), 2453–2467.

Hussain, Z., Griffiths, M. D., & Sheffield, D. (2017). An investigation into problematic smartphone use: The role of narcissism, anxiety, and personality factors. *Journal of Behavioral Addictions, 6*(3), 378–386.

Hutton, J. S., Dudley, J., Horowitz-Kraus, T., DeWitt, T., & Holland, S. K. (2020). Associations between screen-based media use and brain white matter integrity in preschool-aged children. *JAMA Pediatrics.* 174(1), e193869–e193869, Published online 4 November.

Ioannidou, F., Hermens, F., & Hodgson, T. L. (2017). Mind your step: The effects of mobile phone use on gaze behavior in stair climbing. *Journal of Technology in Behavioral Science,* 2(3–4), 109–120.

Jankowska, M. M., Schipperijn, J., & Kerr, J. (2015). A framework for using GPS data in physical activity and sedentary behavior studies. *Exercise and Sport Sciences Reviews,* 43(1), 48–56.

Jao, Y. L., Loken, E., MacAndrew, M., Van Haitsma, K., & Kolanowski, A. (2018). Association between social interaction and affect in nursing home residents with dementia. *Ageing & Mental Health,* 22(6), 778–783.

Jenaro, C., Flores, N., Gómez-Vela, M., González-Gil, F., & Caballo, C. (2007). Problematic internet and cell-phone use: Psychological, behavioral, and health correlates. *Addiction Research and Theory,* 15(3), 309–320.

Jensen, M., George, M. J., Russell, M. R., & Odgers, C. L. (2019). Young adolescents' digital technology use and mental health symptoms: Little evidence of longitudinal or daily linkages. *Clinical Psychological Science,* 7(6), 1416–1433, 2167702619859336.

Johannes, N., Meier, A., Reinecke, L., et al. (2020). The relationship between online vigilance and affective well-being in everyday life: Combining smartphone logging with experience sampling. *Media Psychology,* 1–25. https://doi .org/10.1080/15213269.2020.1768122

Jungselius, B. & Weilenmann, A. (2018, July). Conceptualizing 'use' in social media studies. *Proceedings of the 9th International Conference on Social Media and Society* (pp. 325–329). ACM.

Kardos, P., Unoka, Z., Pléh, C., & Soltész, P. (2018). Your mobile phone indeed means your social network: Priming mobile phone activates relationship related concepts. *Computers in Human Behavior,* 88, 84–88.

Katevas, K., Arapakis, I., & Pielot, M. (2018, September). Typical phone use habits: Intense use does not predict negative well-being. In *Proceedings of the 20th International Conference on Human-Computer Interaction with Mobile Devices and Services* (p. 11). ACM.

Katz, E., Blumler, J. G., & Gurevitch, M. (1974). Utilization of mass communication by the individual. In J. G. Blumler & E. Katz (eds.), *The Uses of Mass Communications: Current Perspectives on Gratifications Research* (pp. 19–32). Beverly Hills, CA: SAGE.

Kawasaki, N., Tanei, S., Ogata, F., et al. (2006). Survey on cellular phone usage on students in Thailand. *Journal of Physiological Anthropology,* 25(6), 377–382.

Khouja, J. N., Munafò, M. R., Tilling, K., et al. (2019). Is screen time associated with anxiety or depression in young people? Results from a UK birth cohort. *BMC Public Health,* 19(1), 82.

Kim, D., Lee, Y., Lee, J., Nam, J. K., & Chung, Y. (2014). Development of Korean smartphone addiction proneness scale for youth. *PLOS ONE,* 9(5), e97920.

King, A. L. S., Valença, A. M., Silva, A. C., et al. (2014). 'Nomophobia': Impact of cell phone use interfering with symptoms and emotions of individuals with panic disorder compared with a control group. *Clinical Practice and Epidemiology in Mental Health, 10,* 28–35.

Koo, H. Y. (2009). Development of a cell phone addiction scale for Korean adolescents. *Journal of Korean Academy of Nursing, 39*(6), 818–828.

Kuss, D., Harkin, L., Kanjo, E., & Billieux, J. (2018). Problematic smartphone use: Investigating contemporary experiences using a convergent design. *International Journal of Environmental Research and Public Health, 15*(1), 142.

Kwon, M., Lee, J. Y., Won, W. Y., et al. (2013a). Development and validation of a smartphone addiction scale (SAS). *PLOS ONE, 8*(2), e56936.

Kwon, M., Kim, D. J., Cho, H., & Yang, S. (2013b). The smartphone addiction scale: Development and validation of a short version for adolescents. *PLOS ONE, 8*(12), e83558.

Lally, P., Van Jaarsveld, C. H., Potts, H. W., & Wardle, J. (2010). How are habits formed: Modelling habit formation in the real world. *European Journal of Social Psychology, 40*(6), 998–1009.

Lee, H. K., Kim, J. H., Fava, M., et al. (2017). Development and validation study of the smartphone overuse screening questionnaire. *Psychiatry Research, 257,* 352–357.

Lee, I. M., Shiroma, E. J., Lobelo, F., et al. for Lancet Physical Activity Series Working Group. (2012). Effect of physical inactivity on major non-communicable diseases worldwide: An analysis of burden of disease and life expectancy. *The Lancet, 380*(9838), 219–229.

Lepp, A., Barkley, J. E., & Karpinski, A. C. (2015). The relationship between cell phone use and academic performance in a sample of US college students. *Sage Open, 5*(1), 2158244015573169.

Leung, L. (2008). Linking psychological attributes to addiction and improper use of the mobile phone among adolescents in Hong Kong. *Journal of Children and Media, 2*(2), 93–113.

Lin, Y. H., Chang, L. R., Lee, Y. H., et al. (2014). Development and validation of the smartphone addiction inventory (SPAI). *PLOS ONE, 9*(6), e98312.

Lin, Y. H., Lin, Y. C., Lee, Y. H., et al. (2015). Time distortion associated with smartphone addiction: Identifying smartphone addiction via a mobile application (App). *Journal of Psychiatric Research, 65,* 139–145.

Lin, Y. H., Chiang, C. L., Lin, P. H., et al. (2016). Proposed diagnostic criteria for smartphone addiction. *PLOS ONE, 11*(11), e0163010.

Lin, Y. H., Pan, Y. C., Lin, S. H., & Chen, S. H. (2017). Development of short-form and screening cutoff point of the Smartphone Addiction Inventory (SPAI-SF). *International Journal of Methods in Psychiatric Research, 26*(2), e1525.

Liu, P. T., Ruan, D. B., Yeh, X. Y., et al. (2018). Highly responsive blue light sensor with amorphous indium-zinc-oxide thin-film transistor based architecture. *Scientific Reports, 8*(1), 8153.

Lopez-Fernandez, O., Honrubia-Serrano, L., Freixa-Blanxart, M., & Gibson, W. (2014). Prevalence of problematic mobile phone use in British adolescents. *Cyberpsychology, Behavior, and Social Networking, 17*(2), 91–98.

Lopez-Fernandez, O., Kuss, D. J., Pontes, H. M., et al. (2018). Measurement invariance of the short version of the problematic mobile phone use questionnaire (PMPUQ-SV) across eight languages. *International Journal of Environmental Research and Public Health*, *15*(6), 1213.

Lucero, A. (2018). Living without a mobile phone: An autoethnography. *Proceedings of the 2018 on Designing Interactive Systems Conference 2018 – DIS '18*, 765–776.

Martinotti, G., Villella, C., Di Thiene, D., et al. (2011). Problematic mobile phone use in adolescence: A cross-sectional study. *Journal of Public Health*, *19*(6), 545–551.

Marty-Dugas, J., Ralph, B. C. W., Oakman, J. M., & Smilek, D. (2018). The relation between smartphone use and everyday inattention. *Psychology of Consciousness: Theory, Research, and Practice*, *5*, 46–64.

McGrath, M. J., Scanaill, C. N., & Nafus, D. (2014). *Sensor Technologies: Healthcare, Wellness and Environmental Applications*. Apress.

McKiernan, E. C., Bourne, P. E., Brown, C. T., et al. (2016). How open science helps researchers succeed. *eLife*, *5*, e16800.

Merlo, L. J., Stone, A. M., & Bibbey, A. (2013). Measuring problematic mobile phone use: Development and preliminary psychometric properties of the PUMP Scale. *Journal of Addiction*, *9*, 12807.

Mihajlov, M. & Vejmelka, L. (2017). Internet addiction: A review of the first twenty years. *Psychiatria Danubina*, *29*(3), 260–272.

Miller, G. (2012). The smartphone psychology manifesto. *Perspectives on Psychological Science*, *7*(3), 221–237.

Mou, D. (2016). Battling severe mental illnesses with smartphones: How patients' smartphone data can help improve clinical care. *mHealth*, *2*, 32.

Oliver, E. (2010, June). The challenges in large-scale smartphone user studies. *Proceedings of the 2nd ACM International Workshop on Hot Topics in Planet-Scale Measurement* (p. 5). ACM.

Orben, A. & Przybylski, A. (2019). Screens, teens and psychological well-being: Evidence from three time-use diary studies. *Psychological Science*, *30*(5), 682–696.

Orben, A., Dienlin, T., & Przybylski, A. K. (2019a). Social media's enduring effect on adolescent life satisfaction. *Proceedings of the National Academy of Sciences*, *116*(21), 10226–10228.

Orben, A., Dienlin, T., & Przybylski, A. K. (2019b). Reply to Foster and Jackson: Open scientific practices are the way forward for social media effects research. *Proceedings of the National Academy of Sciences*, *116*(31), 15334–15335.

Oulasvirta, A., Rattenbury, T., Ma, L., & Raita, E. (2012). Habits make smartphone use more pervasive. *Personal and Ubiquitous Computing*, *16*(1), 105–114.

Pachucki, M. C., Ozer, E. J., Barrat, A., & Cattuto, C. (2015). Mental health and social networks in early adolescence: A dynamic study of objectively-measured social interaction behaviors. *Social Science & Medicine*, *125*, 40–50.

Panova, T. & Carbonell, X. (2018). Is smartphone addiction really an addiction? *Journal of Behavioral Addictions*, *7*(2), 252–259.

Piwek, L., Ellis, D. A., & Andrews, S. (2016). Can programming frameworks bring smartphones into the mainstream of psychological science? *Frontiers in Psychology*, *7*, 1252.

Pontes, H. M. & Griffiths, M. D. (2019). A new era for gaming disorder research: Time to shift from consensus to consistency. *Addictive Behaviors*. 106059. https://doi.org/10.1016/j.addbeh.2019.106059

Proctor, R. N. (2012). The history of the discovery of the cigarette–lung cancer link: Evidentiary traditions, corporate denial, global toll. *Tobacco Control*, *21*(2), 87–91.

Przybylski, A. K. & Weinstein, N. (2017). A large-scale test of the goldilocks hypothesis: Quantifying the relations between digital-screen use and the mental well-being of adolescents. *Psychological Science*, *28*(2), 204–215.

Przybylski, A. K. & Weinstein, N. (2019). Investigating the motivational and psychosocial dynamics of dysregulated gaming: Evidence from a preregistered cohort study. *Clinical Psychological Science*, *7*(6), 1257–1265, 2167702619859341.

Richardson, M., Hussain, Z., & Griffiths, M. D. (2018). Problematic smartphone use, nature connectedness, and anxiety. *Journal of Behavioral Addictions*, *7*(1), 109–116.

Rosen, L., Carrier, L. M., Miller, A., Rokkum, J., & Ruiz, A. (2016). Sleeping with technology: Cognitive, affective, and technology usage predictors of sleep problems among college students. *Sleep Health*, *2*(1), 49–56.

Rosen, L. D., Whaling, K., Carrier, L. M., Cheever, N. A., & Rokkum, J. (2013). The media and technology usage and attitudes scale: An empirical investigation. *Computers in Human Behavior*, *29*(6), 2501–2511.

Rosen, L. D., Lim, A. F., Felt, J., et al. (2014). Media and technology use predicts ill-being among children, preteens and teenagers independent of the negative health impacts of exercise and eating habits. *Computers in Human Behavior*, *35*, 364–375.

Rozgonjuk, D., Rosenvald, V., Janno, S., & Täht, K. (2016). Developing a shorter version of the Estonian smartphone addiction proneness scale (E-SAPS18). *Cyberpsychology. Journal of Psychosocial Research on Cyberspace*, *10* (4),article 4.

Rozgonjuk, D., Levine, J. C., Hall, B. J., & Elhai, J. D. (2018). The association between problematic smartphone use, depression and anxiety symptom severity, and objectively measured smartphone use over one week. *Computers in Human Behavior*, *87*, 10–17.

Rutland, J. B., Sheets, T., & Young, T. (2007). Development of a scale to measure problem use of short message service: The SMS Problem Use Diagnostic Questionnaire. *CyberPsychology and Behavior*, *10*(6), 841–844.

Ryding, F. C. & Kaye, L. K. (2018). 'Internet addiction': A conceptual minefield. *International Journal of Mental Health and Addiction*, *16*(1), 225–232.

Sas, C. (2019). Millennials: Digitally connected never unplugged? In *Conference on Human Factors in Computing Systems (CHI'19) Workshop: Designing for Digital Wellbeing: A Research and Practice Agenda*. (pp. 19–22). ACM.

Scharkow, M. (2016). The accuracy of self-reported Internet use – a validation study using client log data. *Communication Methods and Measures*, *10*(1), 13–27.

Shaw, H., Ellis, D. A., Kendrick, L. R., Ziegler, F., & Wiseman, R. (2016). Predicting smartphone operating system from personality and individual differences. *Cyberpsychology, Behavior, and Social Networking*, *19*(12), 727–732.

Shaw, H., Ellis, D. A., & Ziegler, F. V. (2018). The Technology Integration Model (TIM). Predicting the continued use of technology. *Computers in Human Behavior, 83*, 204–214.

Sivadas, E. & Venkatesh, R. (1995). An examination of individual and object-specific influences on the extended self and its relation to attachment and satisfaction. *ACR North American Advances.* www.acrwebsite.org/volumes/777 8/volumes/v22/NA%20-%2022

Stieger, S. & Lewetz, D. (2018). A week without using social media: Results from an ecological momentary intervention study using smartphones. *Cyberpsychology, Behavior, and Social Networking, 21*(10), 618–624.

Stronge, S., Mok, T., Ejova, A., et al. (2019). Social media use is (weakly) related to psychological distress. *Cyberpsychology, Behavior, and Social Networking, 22*(9), 604–609.

Surrat, C. G. (1999). *Netaholics? The Creation of a Pathology.* New York, NY: Nova Science.

Toda, M., Monden, K., Kubo, K., & Morimoto, K. (2004). Cellular phone dependence tendency of female university students. *Japanese Journal of Hygiene, 59*, 383–386.

Takao, M., Takahashi, S., & Kitamura, M. (2009). Addictive personality and problematic mobile phone use. *CyberPsychology & Behavior, 12*(5), 501–507.

Thompson, W. E. & Thompson, M. L. (2017). Smartphones: Addiction, or way of life? *Journal of Ideology, 38* (1),Article 3.

Toda, M., Monden K., Kubo, K., & Morimoto, K. (2004). Cellular phone dependence tendency of female university students. *Nippon Eiseigaku Zasshi (Japanese Journal of Hygiene), 59*(4), 383–386.

Twenge, J. M., Joiner, T. E., Rogers, M. L., & Martin, G. N. (2018). Increases in depressive symptoms, suicide-related outcomes, and suicide rates among US adolescents after 2010 and links to increased new media screen time. *Clinical Psychological Science, 6*(1), 3–17.

UK Parliament (2018). Science and Technology Committee: Impact of social media and screen-use on young people's health inquiry. www.parliament.uk/business/c ommittees/committees-a-z/commons-select/science-and-technology-committee/i nquiries/parliament-2017/impact-of-social-media-young-people-17–19/.

Vanden Abeele, M., Beullens, K., & Roe, K. (2013). Measuring mobile phone use: Gender, age and real usage level in relation to the accuracy and validity of self-reported mobile phone use. *Mobile Media & Communication, 1*(2), 213–236.

Van Rooij, A. J., Ferguson, C. J., Colder Carras, M., et al. (2018). A weak scientific basis for gaming disorder: Let us err on the side of caution. *Journal of Behavioral Addictions, 7*(1), 1–9.

Verduyn, P., Lee, D. S., Park, J., et al. (2015). Passive Facebook usage undermines affective well-being: Experimental and longitudinal evidence. *Journal of Experimental Psychology: General, 144*(2), 480.

Viner, R., Davie, M., & Firth, A. (2019). *The Health Impacts of Screen Time: A Guide for Clinicians and Parents.* Royal College of Paediatrics and Child Health.

Vioque, J., Torres, A., & Quiles, J. (2000). Time spent watching television, sleep duration and obesity in adults living in Valencia, Spain. *International Journal of Obesity*, 24(12), 1683.

Vorderer, P., Krömer, N., & Schneider, F. M. (2016). Permanently online – permanently connected: Explorations into university students' use of social media and mobile smart devices. *Computers in Human Behavior*, 63, 694–703.

Walsh, S. P., White, K. M., & Young, R. M. (2010). Needing to connect: The effect of self and others on young people's involvement with their mobile phones. *Australian Journal of Psychology*, 62(4), 194–203.

Ward, D. M., Dill-Shackleford, K. E., & Mazurek, M. O. (2018). Social media use and happiness in adults with autism spectrum disorder. *Cyberpsychology, Behavior, and Social Networking*, 21(3), 205–209.

Widdicks, K., Ringenson, T., Pargman, D., Kuppusamy, V., & Lago, P. (2018). Undesigning the internet: An exploratory study of reducing everyday internet connectivity. In *5th International Conference on Information and Communication Technology for Sustainability* (pp. 384–369). https://doi.org/10.29007/s221

Wilcockson, T. D. W., Ellis, D. A., & Shaw, H. (2018). Determining typical smartphone usage: What data do we need? *Cyberpsychology, Behavior, and Social Networking*, 21(6), 395–398.

Yen, C. F., Tang, T. C., Yen, J. Y., et al. (2009). Symptoms of problematic cellular phone use, functional impairment and its association with depression among adolescents in Southern Taiwan. *Journal of Adolescence*, 32(4), 863–873.

Yildirim, C. & Correia, A. P. (2015). Exploring the dimensions of nomophobia: Development and validation of a self-reported questionnaire. *Computers in Human Behavior*, 49, 130–137.

Chapter 2

Abraham, C. & Michie, S. (2008). A taxonomy of behavior change techniques used in interventions. *Health Psychology*, 27(3), 379–387.

Ajzen, I. (1991). The theory of planned behavior. *Organizational Behavior and Human Decision Processes*, 50(2), 179–211.

Allen, J. K., Stephens, J., Dennison Himmelfarb, C. R., Stewart, K. J., & Hauck, S. (2013). Randomized controlled pilot study testing use of smartphone technology for obesity treatment. *Journal of Obesity*, 151597. https://doi.org/10.1155/2013/151597

Althoff, T., White, R. W., & Horvitz, E. (2016). Influence of Pokémon Go on physical activity: Study and implications. *Journal of Medical Internet Research*, 18(12), e315.

Andrews, S., Ellis, D. A., Shaw, H., & Piwek, L. (2015). Beyond self-report: Tools to compare estimated and real-world smartphone use. *PLOS ONE*, 10(10), e0139004.

Apple (2017). App Store. www.appstore.com/.

Baas, M., De Dreu, C. K., & Nijstad, B. A. (2008). A meta-analysis of 25 years of mood-creativity research: Hedonic tone, activation, or regulatory focus? *Psychological Bulletin*, 134(6), 779.

Bakker, D., Kazantzis, N., Rickwood, D., & Rickard, N. (2016). Mental health smartphone apps: Review and evidence-based recommendations for future developments. *JMIR Mental Health, 3*(1), e7.

Bandura, A., 1997. *Self-Efficacy: The Exercise of Control.* Freeman.

Barnett, I., Torous, J., Staples, P., et al. (2018). Relapse prediction in schizophrenia through digital phenotyping: A pilot study. *Neuropsychopharmacology, 43*(8), 1660.

Baron, K. G., Abbott, S., Jao, N., Manalo, N., & Mullen, R. (2017). Orthosomnia: Are some patients taking the Quantified Self too far? *Journal of Clinical Sleep Medicine, 13*(2), 351–354.

Baumel, A., Muench, F., Edan, S., & Kane, J. M. (2019). Objective user engagement with mental health apps: Systematic search and panel-based usage analysis. *Journal of Medical Internet Research, 21*(9), e14567.

Biddiss, E. & Irwin, J. (2010). Active video games to promote physical activity in children and youth: A systematic review. *Archives of Pediatrics & Adolescent Medicine, 164*(7), 664–672.

Bielak, A. A., Mogle, J., & Sliwinski, M. J. (2017). What did you do today? Variability in daily activities is related to variability in daily cognitive performance. *The Journals of Gerontology: Series B, 74*(5), 764–771.

Bird, E. L., Baker, G., Mutrie, N., et al. (2013). Behavior change techniques used to promote walking and cycling: A systematic review. *Health Psychology, 32* (8), 829.

Blandford, A., Gibbs, J., Newhouse, N., et al. (2018). Seven lessons for interdisciplinary research on interactive digital health interventions. *Digital Health, 4*, 2055207618770325.

Bloss, C. S., Wineinger, N. E., Peters, M., et al. (2016). A prospective randomized trial examining health care utilization in individuals using multiple smartphone-enabled biosensors. *PeerJ, 4*, e1554.

Bondaronek, P., Slee, A., Hamilton, F. L., & Murray, E. (2019). Relationship between popularity and the likely efficacy: An observational study based on a random selection on top-ranked physical activity apps. *BMJ Open, 9*(11).

Bort-Roig, J., Gilson, N. D., Puig-Ribera, A., Contreras, R. S., & Trost, S. G. (2014). Measuring and influencing physical activity with smartphone technology: A systematic review. *Sports Medicine, 44*, 671–686.

Car, J., Sheikh, A., Wicks, P., & Williams, M. S. (2019). Beyond the hype of big data and artificial intelligence: Building foundations for knowledge and wisdom. *BMC Medicine, 17*(1), 143.

Carlson, J. A., Jankowska, M. M., Meseck, K., et al. (2015). Validity of PALMS GPS scoring of active and passive travel compared to SenseCam. *Medicine and Science in Sports and Exercise, 47*, 662–667.

Carter, M. C., Burley, V. J., Nykjaer, C., & Cade, J. E. (2013). Adherence to a smartphone application for weight loss compared to website and paper diary: Pilot randomized controlled trial. *Journal of Medical Internet Research, 15*(4), e32.

Case, M. A., Burwick, H. A., Volpp, K. G., & Patel, M. S. (2015). Accuracy of smartphone applications and wearable devices for tracking physical activity data. *JAMA, 313*(6), 625–626.

Celis-Morales, C. A., Perez-Bravo, F., Ibanez, L., et al. (2012). Objective vs. self-reported physical activity and sedentary time: Effects of measurement method on relationships with risk biomarkers. *PLOS ONE, 7*(5), e36345.

Chen, F. X., King, A. C., & Hekler, E. B. (2014, April). Healthifying exergames: Improving health outcomes through intentional priming. In *Proceedings of the SIGCHI Conference on Human Factors in Computing Systems* (pp. 1855–1864). ACM.

Cho, C. H., Lee, T., & Kim, M. G. et al. (2019). Mood prediction of patients with mood disorders by machine learning using passive digital phenotypes based on the circadian rhythm: Prospective observational cohort study. *Journal of Medical Internet Research, 21*(4), e11029.

Choi, S., Kim, S., Yang, J. S., et al. (2014). Real-time measurement of human salivary cortisol for the assessment of psychological stress using a smartphone. *Sensing and Bio-Sensing Research, 2*, 8–11.

Chorley, M. J., Whitaker, R. M., & Allen, S. M. (2015). Personality and location-based social networks. *Computers in Human Behavior, 46*, 45–56.

Cohen, S. (2004). Social relationships and health. *American Psychologist, 59*(8), 676.

Conner, T. S. & Silvia, P. J. (2015). Creative days: A daily diary study of emotion, personality, and everyday creativity. *Psychology of Aesthetics, Creativity, and the Arts, 9*(4), 463.

Conner, T. S., DeYoung, C. G., & Silvia, P. J. (2018). Everyday creative activity as a path to flourishing. *The Journal of Positive Psychology, 13*(2), 181–189.

Conroy, D. E., Hojjatinia, S., Lagoa, C. M., et al. (2019). Personalized models of physical activity responses to text message micro-interventions: A proof-of-concept application of control systems engineering methods. *Psychology of Sport and Exercise, 41*, 172–180.

Cresswell, K. M., Blandford, A., & Sheikh, A. (2017). Drawing on human factors engineering to evaluate the effectiveness of health information technology. *Journal of the Royal Society of Medicine, 110*(8), 309–315.

Csikszentmihalyi, M. & Larson, R. (1987). Validity and reliability of the experience-sampling method. *Journal of Nervous and Mental Disease, 175*, 526–536.

DeMasi, O., Kording, K., & Recht, B. (2017). Meaningless comparisons lead to false optimism in medical machine learning. *PLOS ONE, 12*(9), e0184604.

Department of Health and Social Care. (2018). *The Future of Healthcare: Our Vision for Digital, Data and Technology in Health and Care.* www.gov.uk/government/publications/the-future-of-healthcare-our-vision-for-digital-data-and-technology-in-health-and-care.

Donker, T., Petrie, K., Proudfoot, J., et al. (2013). Smartphones for smarter delivery of mental health programs: A systematic review. *Journal of Medical Internet Research, 15*(11), e247.

Dressel, J. & Farid, H. (2018). The accuracy, fairness, and limits of predicting recidivism. *Science Advances, 4*(1), eaao5580.

Du, H. Y., Newton, P. J., Zecchin, R., et al. (2011). An intervention to promote physical activity and self-management in people with stable chronic heart failure The Home-Heart-Walk study: Study protocol for a randomized controlled trial. *Trials, 12*(1), 63.

Dunton, G. F. (2018). Sustaining health-protective behaviors such as physical activity and healthy eating. *JAMA, 320*(7), 639–640.

Dunton, G. F., Huh, J., Leventhal, A. M., et al. (2014). Momentary assessment of affect, physical feeling states, and physical activity in children. *Health Psychology, 33*(3), 255.

Ekman, P. & Friesen, W. V. (1978). *Facial Action Coding Systems*. Consulting Psychologists Press.

Ellis, D. A. & Piwek, L. (2016). The future of . . . wearable technology. *CREST Security Review, 1*, 4–5.

Ellis, D. A. & Piwek, L. (2018). Failing to encourage physical activity with wearable technology: What next? *Journal of the Royal Society of Medicine, 111* (9), 310–313.

Ellis, D. A., Kaye, L. K., Wilcockson, T. D., & Ryding, F. C. (2018). Digital traces of behaviour within addiction: Response to Griffiths (2017). *International Journal of Mental Health and Addiction, 16*(1), 240–245.

Etkin, J. (2016). The hidden cost of personal quantification. *Journal of Consumer Research, 46*(2), 967–984.

Ewell, P. J., Quist, M. C., Øverup, C. S., Watkins, H., & Guadagno, R. E. (2020). Catching more than pocket monsters: Pokémon Go's social and psychological effects on players. *The Journal of Social Psychology, 160*(2), 131–136.

Finkelstein, E. A., Haaland, B. A., Bilger, M., et al. (2016). Effectiveness of activity trackers with and without incentives to increase physical activity (TRIPPA): A randomised controlled trial. *The Lancet Diabetes & Endocrinology, 4*(12), 983–995.

Firth, J., Torous, J., Nicholas, J., et al. (2017a). Can smartphone mental health interventions reduce symptoms of anxiety? A meta-analysis of randomized controlled trials. *Journal of Affective Disorders, 218*, 15–22.

Firth, J., Torous, J., Nicholas, J., et al. (2017b). The efficacy of smartphone-based mental health interventions for depressive symptoms: A meta-analysis of randomized controlled trials. *World Psychiatry, 16*(3), 287–298.

Forshaw, M. (2002). *Essential Health Psychology*. Oxford University Press.

Fukuoka, Y., Haskell, W., Lin, F., & Vittinghoff, E. (2019). Short- and long-term effects of a mobile phone app in conjunction with brief in-person counseling on physical activity among physically inactive women: The mPED randomized clinical trial. *JAMA Network Open, 2*(5), e194281–e194281.

Geyer, K., Ellis, D. A., & Piwek, L. (2019). A simple location-tracking app for psychological research. *Behavior Research Methods, 51*(6), 2840–2846.

Glynn, L. G., Hayes, P. S., Casey, M., et al. (2014). Effectiveness of a smartphone application to promote physical activity in primary care: The SMART MOVE randomised controlled trial. *British Journal of General Practice, 64*(624), e384–e391.

Google. (2017). Play Store. https://play.google.com/store?hl=en.

Gravenhorst, F., Muaremi, A., Bardram, J., et al. (2015). Mobile phones as medical devices in mental disorder treatment: An overview. *Personal and Ubiquitous Computing, 19*(2), 335–353.

Gross, R., Ritz, J., Hughes, M. D., et al. (2019). Two-way mobile phone intervention compared with standard-of-care adherence support after second-line antiretroviral therapy failure: A multinational, randomised controlled trial. *The Lancet Digital Health*, *1*(1), e26–e34.

Grünerbl, A., Oleksy, P., Bahle, G., et al. (2012). Towards smart phone based monitoring of bipolar disorder. In *Proceedings of the Second ACM Workshop on Mobile Systems, Applications, and Services for HealthCare – mHealthSys '12*. ACM Press.

Guy, R., Hocking, J., Wand, H., et al. (2012). How effective are short message service reminders at increasing clinic attendance? A meta-analysis and systematic review. *Health Services Research*, *47*(2), 614–632.

Haedt-Matt, A. A., & Keel, P. K. (2011). Hunger and binge eating: A meta-analysis of studies using ecological momentary assessment. *International Journal of Eating Disorders*, *44*(7), 573–578.

Hamer, M., Batty, G. D., & Kivimaki, M. (2011). Sleep loss due to worry and future risk of cardiovascular disease and all-cause mortality: The Scottish Health Survey. *European Journal of Cardiovascular Prevention and Rehabilitation*, *19*, 1437–1443.

Hammersley, V., Donaghy, E., Parker, R., et al. (2019). Comparing the content and quality of video, telephone, and face-to-face consultations: A non-randomised, quasi-experimental, exploratory study in UK primary care. *British Journal of General Practice*, *69*(686), e595–e604.

Harari, G. M., Müller, S. R., Aung, M. S., & Rentfrow, P. J. (2017). Smartphone sensing methods for studying behavior in everyday life. *Current Opinion in Behavioral Sciences*, *18*, 83–90.

Hekler, E. B., Klasnja, P., Chevance, G., et al. (2019). Why we need a small data paradigm. *BMC Medicine*, *17*(1), 1–9.

Heneghan, C., Howick, J., O'Neill, B., et al. (2012). The evidence underpinning sports performance products: a systematic assessment. *BMJ Open*, *2*(4), e001702.

Henson, P., David, G., Albright, K., & Torous, J. (2019). Deriving a practical framework for the evaluation of health apps. *The Lancet Digital Health*, *1*(2), e52–e54.

Hofmann, W. & Patel, P. V. (2015). SurveySignal: A convenient solution for experience sampling research using participants' own smartphones. *Social Science Computer Review*, *33*, 235–253.

Hofmann, W., Vohs, K. D., & Baumeister, R. F. (2012). What people desire, feel conflicted about, and try to resist in everyday life. *Psychological Science*, *23*(6), 582–588.

Howe, K. B., Suharlim, C., Ueda, P., et al. (2016). Gotta catch 'em all! Pokémon GO and physical activity among young adults: Difference in differences study. *BMJ*, *355*, i6270.

Huang, Y., Xiong, H., Leach, K., et al. (2016). Assessing social anxiety using GPS trajectories and point-of-interest data. In *Proceedings of the 2016 ACM International Joint Conference on Pervasive and Ubiquitous Computing* (pp. 898–903). ACM Press.

Huang, Z., Lum, E., Jimenez, G., et al. (2019). Medication management support in diabetes: A systematic assessment of diabetes self-management apps. *BMC Medicine, 17*(1), 127.

Huffziger, S., Ebner-Priemer, U., Zamoscik, V., et al. (2013). Effects of mood and rumination on cortisol levels in daily life: An ambulatory assessment study in remitted depressed patients and healthy controls. *Psychoneuroendocrinology, 38* (10), 2258–2267.

Iacobucci, G. (2017). Patient data were shared with Google on an 'inappropriate legal basis,' says NHS data guardian. *BMJ, 357*, j2439.

Insel, T. R. (2018). Digital phenotyping: A global tool for psychiatry. *World Psychiatry, 17*(3), 276.

Ioannidis, J. P. (2016). Why most clinical research is not useful. *PLOS MEDICINE, 13*(6), e1002049.

Jacobi, C., Hayward, C., de Zwaan, M., Kraemer, H. C., & Agras, W. S. (2004). Coming to terms with risk factors for eating disorders: Application of risk terminology and suggestions for a general taxonomy. *Psychological Bulletin, 130*(1), 19–65.

Jahng, S., Solhan, M. B., Tomko, R. L., et al. (2011). Affect and alcohol use: An ecological momentary assessment study of outpatients with borderline personality disorder. *Journal of Abnormal Psychology, 120*(3), 572.

Jakicic, J. M., Davis, K. K., Rogers, R. J., et al. (2016). Effect of wearable technology combined with a lifestyle intervention on long-term weight loss: The IDEA randomized clinical trial. *JAMA, 316*(11), 1161–1171.

Jankowska, M. M., Schipperijn, J., & Kerr, J. (2015). A framework for using GPS data in physical activity and sedentary behavior studies. *Exercise and Sport Sciences Reviews, 43*, 48–56.

Jewkes, R. & Dartnall, E. (2019). More research is needed on digital technologies in violence against women. *The Lancet Public Health, 4*(6), e270–e271.

James, P., Jankowska, M., Marx, C., et al. (2016). 'Spatial energetics': Integrating data from GPS, accelerometry, and GIS to address obesity and inactivity. *American Journal of Preventive Medicine, 51*, 792–800.

Juniper Research. (2013). *Smart Wearable Devices. Fitness, Healthcare, Entertainment & Enterprise 2013–2018.* www.juniperresearch.com/reports/Smart_Wearable_Devices.

Kanjo, E., Younis, E. M., & Ang, C. S. (2019). Deep learning analysis of mobile physiological, environmental and location sensor data for emotion detection. *Information Fusion, 49*, 46–56.

Karasouli, E. & Adams, A. (2014). Assessing the evidence for e-resources for mental health self-management: A systematic literature review. *JMIR Mental Health, 1*(1), e3.

Kato, S., Waki, K., Nakamura, S., et al. (2016). Validating the use of photos to measure dietary intake: The method used by DialBetics, a smartphone-based self-management system for diabetes patients. *Diabetology International, 7*(3), 244–251.

Kelly, C. J., Karthikesalingam, A., Suleyman, M., Corrado, G., & King, D. (2019). Key challenges for delivering clinical impact with artificial intelligence. *BMC Medicine*, *17*(1), 195.

Kitsiou, S., Paré, G., & Jaana, M. (2013). Systematic reviews and meta-analyses of home telemonitoring interventions for patients with chronic diseases: A critical assessment of their methodological quality. *Journal of Medical Internet Research*, *15*(7), e150.

Klasnja, P., Hekler, E. B., Shiffman, S., et al. (2015). Microrandomized trials: An experimental design for developing just-in-time adaptive interventions. *Health Psychology*, *34*(S), 1220.

Kluger, A. N. & DeNisi, A. (1996). The effects of feedback interventions on performance: A historical review, a meta-analysis, and a preliminary feedback intervention theory. *Psychological Bulletin*, *119*(2), 254–284.

Kwasnicka, D., Inauen, J., Nieuwenboom, W., et al. (2019). Challenges and solutions for N-of-1 design studies in health psychology. *Health Psychology Review*, *13*(2), 163–178.

Larsen, M. E., Huckvale, K., Nicholas, J., et al. (2019). Using science to sell apps: Evaluation of mental health app store quality claims. *npj Digital Medicine*, *2* (1), 18.

Lathia, N., Pejovic, V., Rachuri, K. K., et al. (2013). Smartphones for large-scale behavior change interventions. *IEEE Pervasive Computing*, *12*(3), 66–73.

Lathia, N., Sandstrom, G. M., Mascolo, C., & Rentfrow, P. J. (2017). Happier people live more active lives: Using smartphones to link happiness and physical activity. *PLOS ONE*, *12*(1), e0160589.

LeBlanc, A. G. & Chaput, J. P. (2017). Pokémon Go: A game changer for the physical inactivity crisis? *Preventive Medicine*, *101*, 235–237.

Lee, I. M., Shiroma, E. J., Lobelo, F., et al. (2012). Effect of physical inactivity on major non-communicable diseases worldwide: An analysis of burden of disease and life expectancy. *Lancet*, *380*, 219–229.

Leigh, S. & Flatt, S. (2015). App-based psychological interventions: Friend or foe? *Evidence-Based Mental Health*, *18*(4), 97–99.

Leventhal, H., Diefenbach, M., & Leventhal, E. A. (1992). Illness cognition: Using common sense to understand treatment adherence and affect cognition interactions. *Cognitive Therapy and Research*, *16*(2), 143–163.

Lichtman, S. W., Pisarska, K., Berman, E. R., et al. (1992). Discrepancy between self-reported and actual caloric intake and exercise in obese subjects. *New England Journal of Medicine*, *327*(27), 1893–1898.

Lieberman, D., Pillsworth, E. G., & Haselton, M. G. (2011). Kin affiliation across the ovulatory cycle: Females avoid fathers when fertile. *Psychological Science*, *22* (1), 13–18.

LiKamWa, R., Liu, Y., Lane, N. D., & Zhong, L. (2013, June). Moodscope: Building a mood sensor from smartphone usage patterns. In *Proceeding of the 11th Annual International Conference on Mobile Systems, Applications, and Services* (pp. 389–402). ACM.

Lui, J. H., Marcus, D. K., & Barry, C. T. (2017). Evidence-based apps? A review of mental health mobile applications in a psychotherapy context. *Professional Psychology: Research and Practice*, *48*(3), 199.

Ly, K. H., Topooco, N., Cederlund, H., et al. (2015). Smartphone-supported versus full behavioural activation for depression: A randomised controlled trial. *PLOS ONE*, *10*(5), e0126559.

Lyons, E. J., Swartz, M. C., Lewis, Z. H., Martinez, E., & Jennings, K. (2017). Feasibility and acceptability of a wearable technology physical activity intervention with telephone counseling for mid-aged and older adults: A randomized controlled pilot trial. *JMIR mHealth and uHealth*, *5*(3), e28.

MacKerron, G. & Mourato, S. (2013). Happiness is greater in natural environments. *Global Environmental Change*, *23*(5), 992–1000.

Marshall, J. & Linehan, C. (2017, May). A scoping review of exertion game research in 2017. In paper presented at the *1st GetAMoveOn Annual Symposium*.

Marsch, L. A. (2018). Opportunities and needs in digital phenotyping. *Neuropsychopharmacology*, *43*(8), 1637.

Martinengo, L., Van Galen, L., Lum, E., et al. (2019). Suicide prevention and depression apps' suicide risk assessment and management: A systematic assessment of adherence to clinical guidelines. *BMC Medicine*, *17*(1), 1–12.

Mateo, G. F., Granado-Font, E., Ferré-Grau, C., & Montaña-Carreras, X. (2015). Mobile phone apps to promote weight loss and increase physical activity: A systematic review and meta-analysis. *Journal of Medical Internet Research*, *17* (11), e253.

McCartney, M. (2016). Margaret McCartney: Game on for Pokémon GO. *BMJ*, *354*, i4306.

Meers, K., Dejonckheere, E., Kalokerinos, E. K., Rummens, K., & Kuppens, P. (2020). mobileQ: A free user-friendly application for collecting experience sampling data. *Behavior Research Methods*, 1–6.

Mercer, K., Li, M., Giangregorio, L., Burns, C., & Grindrod, K. (2016). Behavior change techniques present in wearable activity trackers: A critical analysis. *JMIR mHealth and uHealth*, *4*(2), e40.

Mertz, L. (2016). Are wearables safe? *IEEE Pulse*, *7*(1), 39–43.

Miller, G. (2012). The smartphone psychology manifesto. *Perspectives on Psychological Science*, *7*(3), 221–237.

Mistry, P. (2019). Artificial intelligence in primary care. *British Journal of General Practice*, *69*(686), 422–423.

Mohr, D. C., Schueller, S. M., Montague, E., Burns, M. N., & Rashidi, P. (2014). The behavioral intervention technology model: An integrated conceptual and technological framework for eHealth and mHealth interventions. *Journal of Medical Internet Research*, *16*(6), e146.

Mtema, Z., Changalucha, J., Cleaveland, S., et al. (2016). Mobile phones as surveillance tools: Implementing and evaluating a large-scale intersectoral surveillance system for rabies in Tanzania. *PLOS MEDICINE*, *13*(4), e1002002.

Müller, S. R., Harari, G. M., Mehrotra, A., et al. (2017). Using human raters to characterize the psychological characteristics of GPS-based places. In Lee, S.,

Takayama, L., & Truong, K. (eds.), *UbiComp '17: Proceedings of the 2017 ACM International Joint Conference on Pervasive and Ubiquitous Computing and Proceedings of the 2017 ACM International Symposium on Wearable Computers* (pp. 157–160). ACM Press.

Muse, E. D., Barrett, P. M., Steinhubl, S. R., & Topol, E. J. (2017). Towards a smart medical home. *The Lancet, 389*(10067), 358.

Naslund, J. A., Aschbrenner, K. A., Scherer, E. A., et al. (2016). Wearable devices and mobile technologies for supporting behavioral weight loss among people with serious mental illness. *Psychiatry Research, 244*, 139–144.

Nebeker, C., Torous, J., & Ellis, R. J. B. (2019). Building the case for actionable ethics in digital health research supported by artificial intelligence. *BMC Medicine, 17*(1), 137.

Newman, M. G., Jacobson, N. C., Zainal, N. H., et al. (2019). The effects of worry in daily life: An ecological momentary assessment study supporting the tenets of the contrast avoidance model. *Clinical Psychological Science, 7*(4), 794–810, 2167702619827019.

Obermeyer, Z., Powers, B., Vogeli, C., & Mullainathan, S. (2019). Dissecting racial bias in an algorithm used to manage the health of populations. *Science, 366* (6464), 447–453.

O'Donnell, R., Richardson, B., Fuller-Tyszkiewicz, M., et al. (2019). Ecological momentary assessment of drinking in young adults: An investigation into social context, affect and motives. *Addictive Behaviors, 98*, 106019.

OFCOM (2018). *Children and Parents: Media Use and Attitudes Report*. Available from www.ofcom.org.uk/__data/assets/pdf_file/0024/134907/children-and-parents-media-use-and-attitudes-2018.pdf.

Ogilvie, D., Foster, C. E., Rothnie, H., et al. (2007). Interventions to promote walking: Systematic review. *BMJ, 334*(7605), 1204.

Oikonomidi, T., Vivot, A., Tran, V. T., et al. (2019). A methodologic systematic review of mobile health behavior change randomized trials. *American Journal of Preventive Medicine, 57*(6), 836–843.

O'Kane, M. J., Bunting, B., Copeland, M., & Coates, V. E. (2008). Efficacy of self monitoring of blood glucose in patients with newly diagnosed type 2 diabetes (ESMON study): Randomised controlled trial. *BMJ, 336*(7654), 1174–1177.

Oliveira, J. S., Sherrington, C., Zheng, E. R., Franco, M. R., & Tiedemann, A. (2019). Effect of interventions using physical activity trackers on physical activity in people aged 60 years and over: A systematic review and meta-analysis. *British Journal of Sports Medicine*, 1–8. DOI:10.1136/bjsports-2018-100324

Palmius, N., Tsanas, A., Saunders, K. E. A., et al. (2017). Detecting bipolar depression from geographic location data. *IEEE Transactions on Biomedical Engineering, 64*, 1761–1771.

Patel, M. S., Asch, D. A., & Volpp, K. G. (2015). Wearable devices as facilitators, not drivers, of health behavior change. *JAMA, 313*(5), 459–460.

Phillips, C. B., Edwards, J. D., Andel, R., & Kilpatrick, M. (2016). Daily physical activity and cognitive function variability in older adults. *Journal of Aging and Physical Activity, 24*, 256–267.

Piwek, L. & Joinson, A. (2017). Automatic tracking of behavior with smartphones: Potential for behavior change interventions. In L. Little, E. Sillence, & A. Joinson (eds.), *Behavior Change Research and Theory* (pp. 137–165). Academic Press.

Piwek, L., Ellis, D. A., & Andrews, S. (2016a). Can programming frameworks bring smartphones into the mainstream of psychological science? *Frontiers in Psychology*, 7, 1252.

Piwek, L., Ellis, D. A., Andrews, S. & Joinson, A. (2016b). The rise of consumer wearables: Promises and barriers. *PLOS MEDICINE*, 13(2): e1001953.

Portio Research. (2011). *Portio Research Mobile Factbook 2011*. Available from www .telecomsmarketresearch.com/Free_Telecoms_Market_Research/Portio_Resea rch_Mobile_Factbook_2011_DownloadQ.pdf.

Puiatti, A., Mudda, S., Giordano, S., & Mayora, O. (2011). Smartphone-centred wearable sensors network for monitoring patients with bipolar disorder. In 2011 *Annual International Conference of the IEEE Engineering in Medicine and Biology Society*. IEEE.

Rachuri, K. K., Musolesi, M., Mascolo, C., et al. (2010, September). EmotionSense: A mobile phones based adaptive platform for experimental social psychology research. In *Proceedings of the 12th ACM International Conference on Ubiquitous Computing* (pp. 281–290). ACM.

Reinertsen, E. & Clifford, G. D. (2018). A review of physiological and behavioral monitoring with digital sensors for neuropsychiatric illnesses. *Physiological Measurement*, 39(5), 05TR01.

Roda, A., Michelini, E., Zangheri, M., et al. (2016). Smartphone-based biosensors: A critical review and perspectives. *TrAC Trends in Analytical Chemistry*, 79, 317–325.

Rodriguez-Villa, E. & Torous, J. (2019). Regulating digital health technologies with transparency: The case for dynamic and multi-stakeholder evaluation. *BMC Medicine*, 17(1), 1–5.

Ryan, M. (2019). Insights into undertaking research using apps. *PsyPAG Quarterly*, 109, 4–6.

Saeb, S., Lattie, E. G., Schueller, S. M., Kording, K. P., & Mohr, D. C. (2016). The relationship between mobile phone location sensor data and depressive symptom severity. *PeerJ*, 4, e2537.

Sandstrom, G. M., Lathia, N., Mascolo, C., & Rentfrow, P. J. (2017). Putting mood in context: Using smartphones to examine how people feel in different locations. *Journal of Research in Personality*, 69, 96–101.

Sandulescu, V., Andrews, S., Ellis, D., Dobrescu, R. & Mozos, O. M. (2015). Mobile app for stress monitoring using voice features. *Proceedings of the IEEE E-health and Bioengineering Conference (EHB)*. IEEE.

Schueller, S. M., Aguilera, A., & Mohr, D. C. (2017). Ecological momentary interventions for depression and anxiety. *Depression and Anxiety*, 34(6), 540–545.

Segui, F. L., Bufill, C. P., Gimenez, N. A., Roldan, J. M., & Cuyas, F. G. (2018). The prescription of mobile apps by primary care teams: A pilot project in Catalonia. *JMIR mHealth and uHealth*, 6(6), e10701.

Simpson, C. C. & Mazzeo, S. E. (2017). Calorie counting and fitness tracking technology: Associations with eating disorder symptomatology. *Eating Behaviors, 26*, 89–92.

Shankar, A., McMunn, A., Banks, J., & Steptoe, A. (2011). Loneliness, social isolation, and behavioral and biological health indicators in older adults. *Health Psychology, 30*(4), 377.

Shiffman, S., Stone, A. A., & Hufford, M. R. (2008). Ecological momentary assessment. *Annual Review of Clinical Psychology, 4*, 1–32.

Steinmo, S., Hagger-Johnson, G., & Shahab, L. (2014). Bidirectional association between mental health and physical activity in older adults: Whitehall II prospective cohort study. *Preventive Medicine, 66*, 74–79.

Stone, A. A. & Shiffman, S. (1994). Ecological momentary assessment (EMA) in behavioral medicine. *Annals of Behavioral Medicine, 16*(3), 199–202.

Stone, A. A. & Shiffman, S. (2002). Capturing momentary, self-report data: A proposal for reporting guidelines. *Guidelines for Momentary Research, 24*, 236–243.

Suk, M. & Prabhakaran, B. (2014). Real-time mobile facial expression recognition system – a case study. In *Proceedings of the IEEE Conference on Computer Vision and Pattern Recognition Workshops* (pp. 132–137). IEEE.

Sullivan, A. N. & Lachman, M. E. (2016). Behavior change with fitness technology in sedentary adults: A review of the evidence for increasing physical activity. *Frontiers in Public Health, 4*, 289.

Thai, S. & Page-Gould, E. (2018). ExperienceSampler: An open-source scaffold for building smartphone apps for experience sampling. *Psychological Methods, 23*(4), 729.

Tomlinson, M., Rotheram-Borus, M. J., Swartz, L., & Tsai, A. C. (2013). Scaling up mHealth: Where is the evidence? *PLOS MEDICINE, 10*(2), e1001382.

Torous, J., Larsen, M. E., Depp, C., et al. (2018). Smartphones, sensors, and machine learning to advance real-time prediction and interventions for suicide prevention: A review of current progress and next steps. *Current Psychiatry Reports, 20*(7), 51.

Torous, J., Lipschitz, J., Ng, M., & Firth, J. (2020). Dropout rates in clinical trials of smartphone apps for depressive symptoms: A systematic review and meta-analysis. *Journal of Affective Disorders, 263*(15), 413–419.

Trull, T. J. & Ebner-Priemer, U. (2014). The role of ambulatory assessment in psychological science. *Current Directions in Psychological Science, 23*(6), 466–470.

Vaidyam, A. N., Wisniewski, H., Halamka, J. D., Kashavan, M. S., & Torous, J. B. (2019). Chatbots and conversational agents in mental health: A review of the psychiatric landscape. *The Canadian Journal of Psychiatry, 64*(7), 456–464.

van Berkel, N., Luo, C., Ferreira, D., Goncalves, J., & Kostakos, V. (2015). The curse of quantified-self: An endless quest for answers. In *Adjunct Proceedings of the 2015 ACM 30 International Joint Conference on Pervasive and Ubiquitous Computing and Proceedings of the 2015 ACM International Symposium on Wearable Computers* (pp. 973–978). ACM.

van Berkel, N., Goncalves, J., Hosio, S., et al. (2020). Overcoming compliance bias in self-report studies: A cross-study analysis. *International Journal of Human-Computer Studies, 134*, 1–12.

Versluis, A., Verkuil, B., Spinhoven, P., van der Ploeg, M. M., & Brosschot, J. F. (2016). Changing mental health and positive psychological well-being using ecological momentary interventions: A systematic review and meta-analysis. *Journal of Medical Internet Research, 18*(6), e152.

Weise, S., Ong, J., Tesler, N. A., Kim, S., & Roth, W. T. (2013). Worried sleep: 24-h monitoring in high and low worriers. *Biological Psychology, 94*, 61–70.

Weisel, K. K., Fuhrmann, L. M., Berking, M., et al. (2019). Standalone smartphone apps for mental health – a systematic review and meta-analysis. *npj Digital Medicine, 2*(1), 1–10.

White, M. P., Alcock, I., Grellier, J., et al. (2019). Spending at least 120 minutes a week in nature is associated with good health and wellbeing. *Scientific Reports, 9*(1), 7730.

Wiederhold, B. K. (2015). Behavioral health apps abundant, but evidence-based research nearly nonexistent. *Cyberpsychology, Behavior, and Social Networking, 18*(6), 309–310.

Wilbur, J., Michaels Miller, A., Chandler, P., & McDevitt, J. (2003). Determinants of physical activity and adherence to a 24-week home-based walking program in African American and Caucasian women. *Research in Nursing & Health, 26*(3), 213–224.

Wilcockson, T. D. W., Ellis, D. A., & Shaw, H. (2018). Determining typical smartphone usage: What data do we need? *Cyberpsychology, Behavior, and Social Networking, 21*(6), 395–398.

Wilhelm, P. & Schoebi, D. (2007). Assessing mood in daily life. *European Journal of Psychological Assessment, 23*(4), 258–267.

Williamson, A. E., McQueenie, R., Ellis, D. A., McConnachie, A., & Wilson, P. (2020). General practice recording of Adverse Childhood Experiences. *BJGP Open 4*(1), 20X101011.

Williamson, V., Darby, J., & Fear, N. T. (2019). Identifying probable post-traumatic stress disorder: Applying supervised machine learning to data from a UK military cohort AU – Leightley, Daniel. *Journal of Mental Health, 28*(1), 34–41.

Wolf, J. A., Moreau, J. F., Akilov, O., et al. (2013). Diagnostic inaccuracy of smartphone applications for melanoma detection. *JAMA Dermatology, 149*(4), 422–426.

Womble, L. G., Wadden, T. A., McGuckin, B. G., et al. (2004). A randomized controlled trial of a commercial internet weight loss program. *Obesity Research, 12*(6), 1011–1018.

Wykes, T. (2019). Racing towards a digital paradise or a digital hell? *Journal of Mental Health, 28*(1), 1–3.

Zangheri, M., Cevenini, L., Anfossi, L., et al. (2015). A simple and compact smartphone accessory for quantitative chemiluminescence-based lateral flow immunoassay for salivary cortisol detection. *Biosensors and Bioelectronics, 64*, 63–68.

Chapter 3

Abeele, M. M. V., Antheunis, M. L., & Schouten, A. P. (2016). The effect of mobile messaging during a conversation on impression formation and interaction quality. *Computers in Human Behavior, 62,* 562–569.

Abels, M., Abeele, M. V., Van Telgen, T., et al. (2018). Nod, nod, ignore: An exploratory observational study on the relation between parental mobile media use and parental responsiveness towards young children. *The Talking Species: Perspectives on the Evolutionary, Neuronal, and Cultural Foundations of Language,* 195–228. https://thetalkingspecies.luef.eu/chapter/chapter_07.pdf

Aharony, N., Pan, W., Ip, C., Khayal, I., & Pentland, A. (2011). Social fMRI: Investigating and shaping social mechanisms in the real world. *Pervasive and Mobile Computing, 7*(6), 643–659.

Allen, T. D. & Shockley, K. (2009). Flexible work arrangements: Help or hype. In D. Russell Crane & Jeffrey E. Hill (eds.), *Handbook of Families and Work: Interdisciplinary Perspectives,* (pp. 265–284).

Al-Saggaf, Y., MacCulloch, R., & Wiener, K. (2019). Trait boredom is a predictor of phubbing frequency. *Journal of Technology in Behavioral Science, 4*(3), 245–252.

Altman, I. (1975). *The Environment and Social Behavior.* Brooks/Cole.

Altman, I. (1993). Dialectics, physical environments, and personal relationships. *Communications Monographs, 60*(1), 26–34.

Baumeister, R. F., Vohs, K. D., & Funder, D. C. (2007). Psychology as the science of self- reports and finger movements: Whatever happened to actual behavior? *Perspectives on Psychological Science, 2*(4), 396–403.

Baxter, L. A. (1982). Strategies for ending relationships: Two studies. *Western Journal of Communication (includes Communication Reports), 46*(3), 223–241.

Berkman, L. F., Glass, T., Brissette, I., & Seeman, T. E. (2000). From social integration to health: Durkheim in the new millennium. *Social Science & Medicine, 51*(6), 843–857.

Bielak, A. A., Mogle, J., & Sliwinski, M. J. (2017). What did you do today? Variability in daily activities is related to variability in daily cognitive performance. *The Journals of Gerontology: Series B, 74*(5), 764–771.

Brownell, K. D., & Horgen, K. B. (2004). *Food Fight: The Inside Story of the Food Industry, America's Obesity Crisis, and What We Can Do about It.* Contemporary Books.

Burt, R. S. (2003). The social structure of competition. In Rob Cross, Andrew Parker, & Lisa Sasson (eds.), *Networks in the Knowledge Economy,* 13–56.

Cheek, J. M. & Buss, A. H. (1981). Shyness and sociability. *Journal of Personality and Social Psychology, 41*(2), 330.

Chen, H. T. & Li, X. (2017). The contribution of mobile social media to social capital and psychological well-being: Examining the role of communicative use, friending and self-disclosure. *Computers in Human Behavior, 75,* 958–965.

Chotpitayasunondh, V. & Douglas, K. M. (2016). How 'phubbing' becomes the norm: The antecedents and consequences of snubbing via smartphone. *Computers in Human Behavior, 63,* 9–18.

Choudhury, T. & Pentland, A. (2002, November). The sociometer: A wearable device for understanding human networks. In *CSCW'02 Workshop: Ad Hoc Communications and Collaboration in Ubiquitous Computing Environments.*

Cohen, S. (2004). Social relationships and health. *American Psychologist, 59*(8), 676.

Connolly, J. (2015). UK nightclubs closing at 'alarming rate', industry figures suggest. BBC newsbeat. www.bbc.co.uk/newsbeat/article/33713015/uk-nightclubs-closing-at-alarming-rate-industry-figures-suggest.

Davidson, B. I. & Ellis, D. A. (2019). Social media addiction: Technological déjà vu. *BMJ, 365*, l4277.

Davidson, B. I, Joinson, A., & Jones, S. L. (2018). Technologically enhanced dating: Augmented human relationships, robots and fantasy (pp. 145–171). In Z. Papacharissi (ed.), *A Networked Self and Love*. Routledge.

Davidson, B. I., Jones, S. L., Joinson, A. N., & Hinds, J. (2019). The evolution of online ideological communities. *PloS one, 14*(5), e0216932.

DeMaris, A. (2018). Marriage advantage in subjective well-being: Causal effect or unmeasured heterogeneity? *Marriage & Family Review, 54*(4), 335–350.

de Montjoye, Y. A., Hidalgo, C. A., Verleysen, M., & Blondel, V. D. (2013). Unique in the crowd: The privacy bounds of human mobility. *Scientific Reports, 3*, 1376.

Derks, D., Bakker, A. B., Peters, P., & van Wingerden, P. (2016). Work-related smartphone use, work–family conflict and family role performance: The role of segmentation preference. *Human Relations, 69*(5), 1045–1068.

Ditchfield, H. (2019). Behind the screen of Facebook: Identity construction in the rehearsal stage of online interaction. *New Media & Society, 22*(6), 927–943, https://doi.org/10.1177/1461444819873644.

Do, T. M. T. & Gatica-Perez, D. (2014). Where and what: Using smartphones to predict next locations and applications in daily life. *Pervasive and Mobile Computing, 12*, 79–91.

Dwyer, R. J., Kushlev, K., & Dunn, E. W. (2018). Smartphone use undermines enjoyment of face-to-face social interactions. *Journal of Experimental Social Psychology, 78*, 233–239.

Eagle, N., de Montjoye, Y. A., & Bettencourt, L. M. (2009, August). Community computing: Comparisons between rural and urban societies using mobile phone data. In *2009 International Conference on Computational Science and Engineering* (vol. 4, pp. 144–150). IEEE.

Eagle, N., Pentland, A. S., & Lazer, D. (2009). Inferring friendship network structure by using mobile phone data. *Proceedings of the National Academy of Sciences, 106*(36), 15274–15278.

Eagle, N., Macy, M., & Claxton, R. (2010). Network diversity and economic development. *Science, 328*(5981), 1029–1031.

Eisenberger, N. I., Lieberman, M. D., & Williams, K. D. (2003). Does rejection hurt? An fMRI study of social exclusion. *Science, 302*(5643), 290–292.

Elmer, T., Chaitanya, K., Purwar, P., & Stadtfeld, C. (2019). The validity of RFID badges measuring face-to-face interactions. *Behavior Research Methods, 51*, 2120–2138.

Emanuel, R., Bell, R., Cotton, C., et al. (2015). The truth about smartphone addiction. *College Student Journal, 49*(2), 291–299.

Farrell, A. K. & Stanton, S. C. (2019). Toward a mechanistic understanding of links between close relationships and physical health. *Current Directions in Psychological Science, 28*(5), 483–489.

Finkel, E. J., Eastwick, P. W., Karney, B. R., Reis, H. T., & Sprecher, S. (2012). Online dating: A critical analysis from the perspective of psychological science. *Psychological Science in the Public Interest, 13*(1), 3–66.

Finkel, E. J., Norton, M. I., Reis, H. T., et al. (2015). When does familiarity promote versus undermine interpersonal attraction? A proposed integrative model from erstwhile adversaries. *Perspectives on Psychological Science, 10* (1), 3-19.

Fiore, A. T. & Donath, J. S. (2005, April). Homophily in online dating: When do you like someone like yourself? In *CHI'05 Extended Abstracts on Human Factors in Computing Systems* (pp. 1371–1374). ACM.

Fiore, A. T., Taylor, L. S., Mendelsohn, G. A., & Hearst, M. (2008, April). Assessing attractiveness in online dating profiles. In *Proceedings of the SIGCHI Conference on Human Factors in Computing Systems* (pp. 797–806). ACM.

Fiore, A. T., Taylor, L. S., Zhong, X., Mendelsohn, G. A., & Cheshire, C. (2010, January). Who's right and who writes: People, profiles, contacts, and replies in online dating. In *2010 43rd Hawaii International Conference on System Sciences* (pp. 1–10). IEEE.

Fischer, C. S. (1994). *America Calling: A Social History of the Telephone to 1940.* University of California Press.

Funder, D. C. (ed.). (1999). *Personality Judgment: A Realistic Approach to Person Perception.* Elsevier.

Funder, D. C. (2012). Accurate personality judgement. *Current Directions in Psychological Science, 21,* 177–182.

Gershon, I. (2010). *The Breakup 2.0: Disconnecting Over New Media.* Cornell University Press.

González, M. C., Hidalgo, C. A., & Barabási, A. L. (2008). Understanding individual human mobility patterns. *Nature, 453*(7196), 779–782.

Granovetter, M. (1973). The strength of weak ties. *The American Journal of Sociology, 78* (6), 1360.

Haigh, A. (2015). *Stop Phubbing.* http://stopphubbing.com.

Hancock, J. T., Toma, C., & Ellison, N. (2007, April). The truth about lying in online dating profiles. In *Proceedings of the SIGCHI Conference on Human Factors in Computing Systems* (pp. 449–452). ACM.

Harari, G. M., Müller, S. R., Aung, M. S., & Rentfrow, P. J. (2017a). Smartphone sensing methods for studying behavior in everyday life. *Current Opinion in Behavioral Sciences, 18,* 83–90.

Harari, G. M., Gosling, S. D., Wang, R., et al. (2017b). Patterns of behaviour change in students over an academic term: A preliminary study of activity and sociability behaviours using smartphone sensing methods. *Computers in Human Behavior, 67,* 129–138.

Harari, G. M., Müller, S. R., Stachl, C., et al. (2019). Sensing sociability: Individual differences in young adults' conversation, calling, texting, and app use behaviours in daily life. *Journal of Personality and Social Psychology.* https://doi.org/10.1037/pspp0000245

Hawkley, L. C., Wroblewski, K., Kaiser, T., Luhmann, M., & Schumm, L. P. (2019). Are US older adults getting lonelier? Age, period, and cohort differences. *Psychology and Aging, 34*(8), 1144.

Heller, A. S., Shi, T. C., Ezie, C. E. C., et al. (2020). Association between real-world experiential diversity and positive affect relates to hippocampal–striatal functional connectivity.*Nat Neurosci.* https://doi.org/10.1038/s41593-020-0636-4

Herbst, K. C., Gaertner, L., & Insko, C. A. (2003). My head says yes but my heart says no: Cognitive and affective attraction as a function of similarity to the ideal self. *Journal of Personality and Social Psychology, 84*(6), 1206

Hodson, G., Crisp, R. J., Meleady, R., & Earle, M. (2018). Intergroup contact as an agent of cognitive liberalization. *Perspectives on Psychological Science, 13*(5), 523–548.

Hogan, B. (2018). Break-ups and the limits of encoding love. In Z. Papacharissi (ed.), *A Networked Self and Love* (pp. 113–128). Routledge.

Hogg, M. A. & Vaughan, G. (2005). *Introduction to Social Psychology.* Pearson.

Holt-Lunstad, J., Smith, T. B., Baker, M., Harris, T., & Stephenson, D. (2015). Loneliness and social isolation as risk factors for mortality: A meta-analytic review. *Perspectives on Psychological Science, 10*(2), 227–237.

Hunter, J. F., Hooker, E. D., Rohleder, N., & Pressman, S. D. (2018). The use of smartphones as a digital security blanket: The influence of phone use and availability on psychological and physiological responses to social exclusion. *Psychosomatic Medicine, 80*(4), 345–352.

Ireland, M. E., Slatcher, R. B., Eastwick, P. W., et al. (2011). Language style matching predicts relationship initiation and stability. *Psychological Science, 22*(1), 39–44.

Joinson, A. N. (2004). Self-esteem, interpersonal risk, and preference for e-mail to face-to-face communication. *CyberPsychology & Behavior, 7*(4), 472–478.

Juniper Research. (2014). *Mobile Messaging Markets. Technical Report.* http://www.juniperresearch.com/press-release/mobile-messaging-pr1.

Katz, J. E. (1997). The social side of information networking. *Society, 34*(3), 9–12.

Kazdin, A. E. (2007). Mediators and mechanisms of change in psychotherapy research. *Annual Review of Clinical Psychology, 3*, 1–27.

Keil, T. F., Koschate-Reis, M., & Levine, M. (2020). Contact Logger: Measuring everyday intergroup contact experiences in near-time. *Behavior Research Methods.* https://link.springer.com/article/10.3758/s13428-019-01335-w

Kreager, D. A., Cavanagh, S. E., Yen, J., & Yu, M. (2014). 'Where have all the good men gone?' Gendered interactions in online dating. *Journal of Marriage and Family, 76*(2), 387–410.

Kushlev, K. & Dunn, E. W. (2019). Smartphones distract parents from cultivating feelings of connection when spending time with their children. *Journal of Social and Personal Relationships, 36*(6), 1619–1639.

References 219

Kushlev, K. & Heintzelman, S. J. (2018). Put the phone down: Testing a complement-interfere model of computer-mediated communication in the context of face-to-face interactions. *Social Psychological and Personality Science*, 9(6), 702–710.

Kushlev, K., Dwyer, R., & Dunn, E. W. (2019a). The social price of constant connectivity: Smartphones impose subtle costs on well-being. *Current Directions in Psychological Science*, 28(4), 347–352. 0963721419847200.

Kushlev, K., Hunter, J. F., Proulx, J., Pressman, S. D., & Dunn, E. (2019b). Smartphones reduce smiles between strangers. *Computers in Human Behavior*, 91, 12–16.

Lazarević, L. B., Bjekić, J., Živanović, M., & Knežević, G. (2020). Ambulatory assessment of language use: Evidence on the temporal stability of Electronically Activated Recorder and stream of consciousness data. *Behavior Research Methods*, 1–19. DOI:10.3758/s13428-020-01361-z

Letzring, T. D., Wells, S. M., & Funder, D. C. (2006). Information quantity and quality affect the realistic accuracy of personality judgment. *Journal of Personality and Social Psychology*, 91(1), 111.

Li-Barber, K. T. (2012). Self-disclosure and student satisfaction with Facebook. *Computers in Human Behavior*, 28(2), 624–630.

Lieberman, D., Pillsworth, E. G., & Haselton, M. G. (2011). Kin affiliation across the ovulatory cycle: Females avoid fathers when fertile. *Psychological Science*, 22(1), 13–18.

Liu, J. (2017). Mobile phones, social ties and collective action mobilization in China. *Acta Sociologica*, 60(3), 213–227.

Markey, P. M. & Wells, S. M. (2002). Interpersonal perception in internet chat rooms. *Journal of Research in Personality*, 36(2), 134–146.

Mazmanian, M., Orlikowski, W. J., & Yates, J. (2013). The autonomy paradox: The implications of mobile email devices for knowledge professionals. *Organization Science*, 24(5), 1337–1357.

McEwan, B. & Zanolla, D. (2013). When online meets offline: A field investigation of modality switching. *Computers in Human Behavior*, 29(4), 1565–1571.

McKeown, S. & Dixon, J. (2017). The 'contact hypothesis': Critical reflections and future directions. *Social and Personality Psychology Compass*, 11(1), e12295.

Mehl, M. R. & Pennebaker, J. W. (2003). The social dynamics of a cultural upheaval: Social interactions surrounding September 11, 2001. *Psychological Science*, 14(6), 579–585.

Mikkola, H., Oinas, M. M., & Kumpulainen, K. (2008, March). Net-based identity and body image among young IRC-gallery users. In *Society for Information Technology & Teacher Education International Conference* (pp. 3080–3085). Association for the Advancement of Computing in Education (AACE).

Misra, S., Cheng, L., Genevie, J., & Yuan, M. (2016). The iPhone effect: The quality of in-person social interactions in the presence of mobile devices. *Environment and Behavior*, 48(2), 275–298.

Montoya, M. R., Horton, R. S., & Kirchner, J. (2008). Is actual similarity necessary for attraction? A meta-analysis of actual and perceived similarity. *Journal of Social and Personal Relationships*, 25(6), 889–922.

Murray, S. (2019). How broadband and cell phone access have impacted marriage and divorce in the US. *Review of Economics of the Household*, 1–29.

Nadkarni, A. & Hofmann, S. G. (2012). Why do people use Facebook? *Personality and Individual Differences*, 52(3), 243–249.

O'Connor, S. C. & Rosenblood, L. K. (1996). Affiliation motivation in everyday experience: A theoretical comparison. *Journal of Personality and Social Psychology*, 70(3), 513–522

Onnela, J. P., Saramäki, J., Hyvönen, J., et al. (2007). Structure and tie strengths in mobile communication networks. *Proceedings of the National Academy of Sciences*, 104(18), 7332–7336.

Osmani, V., Carreras, I., Matic, A., & Saar, P. (2014). An analysis of distance estimation to detect proximity in social interactions. *Journal of Ambient Intelligence and Humanized Computing*, 5(3), 297–306.

Page, S. E. (2008). *The Difference: How the Power of Diversity Creates Better Groups, Firms, Schools, and Societies-New Edition*. Princeton University Press.

Paul, A. (2014). Is online better than offline for meeting partners? Depends: Are you looking to marry or to date? *Cyberpsychology, Behavior, and Social Networking*, 17(10), 664–667.

Pettigrew, T. F. & Tropp, L. R. (2006). A meta-analytic test of intergroup contact theory. *Journal of Personality and Social Psychology*, 90(5), 751.

Pittman, M. & Reich, B. (2016). Social media and loneliness: Why an Instagram picture may be worth more than a thousand Twitter words. *Computers in Human Behavior*, 62, 155–167.

Piwek, L. & Joinson, A. (2016). 'What do they snapchat about?' Patterns of use in time-limited instant messaging service. *Computers in Human Behavior*, 54, 358–367.

Piwek, L., Ellis, D. A., & Andrews, S. (2016). Can programming frameworks bring smartphones into the mainstream of psychological science? *Frontiers in Psychology*, 7, 1252.

Przybylski, A. K. & Weinstein, N. (2013). Can you connect with me now? How the presence of mobile communication technology influences face-to-face conversation quality. *Journal of Social and Personal Relationships*, 30(3), 237–246.

Ramirez Jr, A. & Zhang, S. (2007). When online meets offline: The effect of modality switching on relational communication. *Communication Monographs*, 74(3), 287–310.

Ramirez, A., Sumner, E. M., Fleuriet, C., & Cole, M. (2014). When online dating partners meet offline: The effect of modality switching on relational communication between online daters. *Journal of Computer-Mediated Communication*, 20(1), 99–114.

Rheingold, H. (1993). *The Virtual Community*. Addison-Wesley Longman Publishing Co.

Roberts, J. A. & David, M. E. (2016). My life has become a major distraction from my cell phone: Partner phubbing and relationship satisfaction among romantic partners. *Computers in Human Behavior*, 54, 134–141.

Roesner, F., Gill, B. T., & Kohno, T. (2014, March). Sex, lies, or kittens? Investigating the use of Snapchat's self-destructing messages. In *International Conference on Financial Cryptography and Data Security* (pp. 64–76). Springer.

Rohrer, J. M. (2018). Thinking clearly about correlations and causation: Graphical causal models for observational data. *Advances in Methods and Practices in Psychological Science*, *1*(1), 27–42.

Rosenfeld, M. J. (2017). Marriage, choice, and couplehood in the age of the internet. *Sociological Science*, *4*, 490–510.

Rosenfeld, M. J. & Thomas, R. J. (2012). Searching for a mate: The rise of the internet as a social intermediary. *American Sociological Review*, *77*(4), 523–547.

Rosenfeld, M. J., Thomas, R. J., & Hausen, S. (2019). Disintermediating your friends: How online dating in the United States displaces other ways of meeting. *Proceedings of the National Academy of Sciences*, *116*(36), 17753–17758.

Rotondi, V., Stanca, L., & Tomasuolo, M. (2017). Connecting alone: Smartphone use, quality of social interactions and well-being. *Journal of Economic Psychology*, *63*, 17–26.

Satchell, L. P. (2019). From photograph to face-to-face: Brief interactions change person and personality judgments. *Journal of Experimental Social Psychology*, *82*, 266-276.

Sbarra, D. A., Briskin, J. L., & Slatcher, R. B. (2019). Smartphones and close relationships: The case for an evolutionary mismatch. *Perspectives on Psychological Science*, *14*(4), 596–618. 1745691619826535.

Scharlott, B. W. & Christ, W. G. (1995). Overcoming relationship-initiation barriers: The impact of a computer-dating system on sex role, shyness, and appearance inhibitions. *Computers in Human Behavior*, *11*(2), 191–204.

Schöendienst, V. & Dang-Xuan, L. (2011, July). The role of linguistic properties in online dating communication – a large-scale study of contact initiation messages. In *PACIS* (p. 169).

Selwyn, N. (2011). Making sense of young people, education and digital technology: The role of sociological theory. *Oxford Review of Education*, *38*(1), 81–96.

Shaw, H., Taylor, P., Conchie, S., & Ellis, D. A. (2019). Language style matching: A comprehensive list of articles and tools. *PsyArXiv*.

Shepard, C., Rahmati, A., Tossell, C., Zhong, L., & Kortum, P. (2011). LiveLab: Measuring wireless networks and smartphone users in the field. *ACM SIGMETRICS Performance Evaluation Review*, *38*(3), 15–20.

Smith, A. & Anderson, M. (2016). *5 Facts about Online Dating. Fact Tank*. www.pewresearch.org/fact-tank/2016/02/29/5-facts-about-online-dating/.

Stroebe, M., Gregem, M. M., Gergen, K. J., & Stroebe, W. (1992). Broken hearts or broken bonds. *American Psychologist*, *47*(10), 1205–1212.

Stopczynski, A., Sekara, V., Sapiezynski, P., et al. (2014). Measuring large-scale social networks with high resolution. *PLOS ONE*, *9*(4), e95978.

Sun, J. & Vazire, S. (2019). Do people know what they're like in the moment? *Psychological Science*, *30*(3), 405–414.

Sunnafrank, M. (1986). Predicted outcome value during initial interactions a reformulation of uncertainty reduction theory. *Human Communication Research, 13*(1), 3–33

Tausczik, Y. R. & Pennebaker, J. W. (2010). The psychological meaning of words: LIWC and computerized text analysis methods. *Journal of Language and Social Psychology, 29*(1), 24–54.

Tidwell, L. C. & Walther, J. B. (2002). Computer-mediated communication effects on disclosure, impressions, and interpersonal evaluations: Getting to know one another a bit at a time. *Human Communication Research, 28*(3), 317–348.

Trzesniewski, K. H. & Donnellan, M. B. (2010). Rethinking 'Generation Me': A study of cohort effects from 1976–2006. *Perspectives on Psychological Science, 5* (1), 58–75.

Tyson, G., Perta, V. C., Haddadi, H., & Seto, M. C. (2016, August). A first look at user activity on Tinder. In *Proceedings of the 2016 IEEE/ACM International Conference on Advances in Social Networks Analysis and Mining* (pp. 461–466). IEEE Press.

Van Praag, H., Kempermann, G., & Gage, F. H. (2000). Neural consequences of enviromental enrichment. *Nature Reviews Neuroscience, 1*(3), 191–198.

Verduyn, P., Ybarra, O., Résibois, M., Jonides, J., & Kross, E. (2017). Do social network sites enhance or undermine subjective well-being? A critical review. *Social Issues and Policy Review, 11*(1), 274–302.

Wall, H. J., Taylor, P. J., Dixon, J., Conchie, S. M., & Ellis, D. A. (2013). Rich contexts do not always enrich the accuracy of personality judgments. *Journal of Experimental Social Psychology, 49*(6), 1190–1195.

Wang, R., Chen, F., Chen, Z., et al. (2014, September). StudentLife: Assessing mental health, academic performance and behavioural trends of college students using smartphones. In *Proceedings of the 2014 ACM International Joint Conference on Pervasive and Ubiquitous Computing* (pp. 3–14). ACM.

Wei, R. & Lo, V. H. (2006). Staying connected while on the move: Cell phone use and social connectedness. *New Media & Society, 8*(1), 53–72.

Wetzel, C. G. & Insko, C. A. (1982). The similarity-attraction relationship: Is there an ideal one? *Journal of Experimental Social Psychology, 18*(3), 253–276.

Whitty, M. T. (2007). The art of selling one's 'self' on an online dating site: The BAR approach. In *Online Matchmaking* (pp. 57–69). Palgrave Macmillan.

Whitty, M. T. (2011). E-dating: The five phases on online dating. In *Electronic Services: Concepts, Methodologies, Tools and Applications* (pp. 1376–1389). IGI Global.

World Bank Group. (2015). *Mobile Cellular Subscriptions (per 100 people)*. https:// data.worldbank.org/indicator/IT.CEL.SETS.P2.

Wilcockson, T. D. W., Ellis, D. A., & Shaw, H. (2018) Determining typical smartphone usage: What data do we need? *Cyberpsychology, Behavior, and Social Networking, 21*(6), 395–398.

Yang, C. C. (2016). Instagram use, loneliness, and social comparison orientation: Interact and browse on social media, but don't compare. *Cyberpsychology, Behavior, and Social Networking, 19*(12), 703–708.

Chapter 4

Aaker, J. L. (1997). Dimensions of brand personality. *Journal of Marketing Research*, *34*(3), 347–356.

Adam, H. & Galinsky, A. D. (2012). Enclothed cognition. *Journal of Experimental Social Psychology*, *48*(4), 918–925.

Adam, H. & Galinsky, A. D. (2019). Reflections on enclothed cognition: Commentary on Burns et al. *Journal of Experimental Social Psychology*, *83*, 157–159.

Andrews, S., Ellis, D. A., Shaw, H., & Piwek, L. (2015). Beyond self-report: Tools to compare estimates and real world smartphone use. *PLOS ONE*, *10*(10), e0139004.

Ashton, M. C. & Lee, K. (2009). The HEXACO–60: A short measure of the major dimensions of personality. *Journal of Personality Assessment*, *91*(4), 340–345.

Ashton, M. C., Lee, K., & De Vries, R. E. (2014). The HEXACO Honesty-Humility, Agreeableness, and Emotionality factors: A review of research and theory. *Personality and Social Psychology Review*, *18*(2), 139–152.

Back, M. D., Stopfer, J. M., Vazire, S., et al. (2010). Facebook profiles reflect actual personality, not self-idealization. *Psychological Science*, *21*(3), 372–374.

Barry, C. T., McDougall, K. H., Anderson, A. C., et al. (2019). 'Check your selfie before you wreck your selfie': Personality ratings of Instagram users as a function of self-image posts. *Journal of Research in Personality*, *82*, 103843.

Baumert, A., Schmitt, M., Perugini, M., et al. (2017). Integrating personality structure, personality process, and personality development. *European Journal of Personality*, *31*(5), 503–528.

Belk, R. W. (1988). Possessions and the extended self. *Journal of Consumer Research*, *15*(2), 139–168.

Belk, R. W. (2013). Extended self in a digital world. *Journal of Consumer Research*, *40*(3), 477–500.

Bevan, C. & Fraser, D. S. (2016). Different strokes for different folks? Revealing the physical characteristics of smartphone users from their swipe gestures. *International Journal of Human-Computer Studies*, *88*, 51–61.

Bleidorn, W. & Hopwood, C. J. (2019). Using machine learning to advance personality assessment and theory. *Personality and Social Psychology Review*, *23*(2), 190–203.

Bleidorn, W., Hopwood, C. J., & Lucas, R. E. (2018). Life events and personality change. *Journal of Personality*, *86*, 83–96.

Boyce, J., Wood, A. M. and Powdthavee, N. (2012). Is personality fixed? Personality changes as much as 'variable' economic factors and more strongly predicts changes to life satisfaction. *Social Indicators Research*, *22*, 1–19.

Boyd, R. L. & Pennebaker, J. W. (2017). Language-based personality: A new approach to personality in a digital world. *Current Opinion in Behavioral Sciences*, *18*, 63–68.

Brady, R. R., Verran, J., Damani, N. N., & Gibb, A. P. (2009). Review of mobile communication devices as potential reservoirs of nosocomial pathogens. *Journal of Hospital Infection*, *71*(4), 295–300.

Brady, R. R., Hunt, A. C., Visvanathan, A., et al. (2011). Mobile phone technology and hospitalized patients: A cross-sectional surveillance study of bacterial colonization, and patient opinions and behaviours. *Clinical Microbiology and Infection, 17*(6), 830–835.

Brunswik, E. (1956). *Perception and the Representative Design of Psychological Experiments.* University of California Press.

Burns, D. M., Fox, E. L., Greenstein, M., Olbright, G., & Montgomery, D. (2019). An old task in new clothes: A preregistered direct replication attempt of enclothed cognition effects on Stroop performance. *Journal of Experimental Social Psychology, 83*, 150–156.

Burtăverde, V., Vlăsceanu, S., & Avram, E. (2019). Exploring the relationship between personality structure and smartphone usage. *Current Psychology*, 1–13.

Canossa, A., Badler, J. B., El-Nasr, M. S., Tignor, S., & Colvin, R. C. (2015). In your face (t) impact of personality and context on gameplay behavior. In *FDG.*

Cattell, R. B. (1958). What is 'objective' in 'objective personality tests'? *Journal of Counseling Psychology, 5*(4), 285.

Chittaranjan, G., Blom, J., & Gatica-Perez, D. (2011, June). Who's who with big-five: Analyzing and classifying personality traits with smartphones. In *2011 15th Annual International Symposium on Wearable Computers* (pp. 29–36). IEEE.

Chittaranjan, G., Blom, J., & Gatica-Perez, D. (2013). Mining large-scale smartphone data for personality studies. *Personal and Ubiquitous Computing, 17*(3), 433–450.

Christensen, M. A., Bettencourt, L., Kaye, L., et al. (2016). Direct measurements of smartphone screen-time: relationships with demographics and sleep. *PLOS ONE, 11*(11), e0165331.

Clegg, J. W. (2018). *Self-observation in the Social Sciences.* Routledge.

Connolly, J. J., Kavanagh, E. J., & Viswesvaran, C. (2007). The convergent validity between self and observer ratings of personality: A meta-analytic review. *International Journal of Selection and Assessment, 15*(1), 110–117.

Davis, J. L., Love, T. P., & Fares, P. (2019). Collective social identity: Synthesizing identity theory and social identity theory using digital data. *Social Psychology Quarterly, 82*(3), 254–273.

Deary, I. J., Weiss, A., & Batty, G. D. (2010). Intelligence and personality as predictors of illness and death: How researchers in differential psychology and chronic disease epidemiology are collaborating to understand and address health inequalities. *Psychological Science in the Public Interest, 11*(2), 53–79.

DeMasi, O., Kording, K., & Recht, B. (2017). Meaningless comparisons lead to false optimism in medical machine learning. *PLOS ONE, 12*(9), e0184604.

de Montjoye, Y. A., Quoidbach, J., Robic, F., & Pentland, A. S. (2013, April). Predicting personality using novel mobile phone-based metrics. In *International Conference on Social Computing, Behavioural-Cultural Modeling, and Prediction* (pp. 48–55). Springer.

Edmonds, G. W., Jackson, J. J., Fayard, J. V., & Roberts, B. W. (2008). Is character fate, or is there hope to change my personality yet? *Social and Personality Psychology Compass, 2*(1), 399–413.

Ellis, D. A. (2013) *Everyday Time Processing*. PhD thesis, University of Glasgow.

Ellis, D. A. (2019). Are smartphones really that bad? Improving the psychological measurement of technology-related behaviours. *Computers in Human Behavior*, *97*, 60–66.

Ellis, D. A. & Jenkins, R. (2015). Watch-wearing as a marker of conscientiousness. *PeerJ*, *3*, e1210.

Ferrer-i-Carbonell, A. & Frijters, P. (2004). How important is methodology for the estimates of the determinants of happiness? *The Economic Journal*, *114*(497), 641–659.

Forbes. (2014). What kind of person prefers an iPhone? http://www.forbes.com /sites/toddhixon/2014/04/10/what-kind-ofperson-an-iphone /#d65d9533e5a6.

Funder, D. C. (1995). On the accuracy of personality judgment: A realistic approach. *Psychological Review*, *102*(4), 652.

Funder, D. C. (2012). Accurate personality judgement. *Current Directions in Psychological Science*, *21*, 177–182.

Gao, N., Shao, W., & Salim, F. D. (2019). Predicting personality traits from physical activity intensity. *Computer*, *52*(7), 47–56.

Gladstone, J. J., Matz, S. C., & Lemaire, A. (2019). Can psychological traits be inferred from spending? Evidence from transaction data. *Psychological Science*, 0956797619849435.

Gosling, S. D., Ko, S. J., Mannarelli, T., & Morris, M. E. (2002). A room with a cue: Personality judgments based on offices and bedrooms. *Journal of Personality and Social Psychology*, *82*(3), 379.

Gosling, S. D., Rentfrow, P. J., & Swann Jr, W. B. (2003). A very brief measure of the Big-Five personality domains. *Journal of Research in Personality*, *37*(6), 504–528.

Götz, F. M., Stieger, S., & Reips, U. D. (2017). Users of the main smartphone operating systems (iOS, Android) differ only little in personality. *PLOS ONE*, *12*(5), e0176921.

Harari, G. M., Müller, S. R., Aung, M. S., & Rentfrow, P. J. (2017). Smartphone sensing methods for studying behavior in everyday life. *Current Opinion in Behavioral Sciences*, *18*, 83–90.

Harari, G. M., Müller, S. R., Stachl, C., et al. (2019). Sensing sociability: Individual differences in young adults' conversation, calling, texting, and app use behaviours in daily life. *Journal of Personality and Social Psychology*. https://doi.org/10.1037 /pspp0000245

Hinds, J. & Joinson, A. (2019). Human and computer personality prediction from digital footprints. *Current Directions in Psychological Science*, *28*(2), 204–211.

Horne, J. A. & Östberg, O. (1976). A self-assessment questionnaire to determine morningness-eveningness in human circadian rhythms. *International Journal of Chronobiology*, *4*, 97–110.

Hu, H., Bezemer, C. P., & Hassan, A. E. (2018). Studying the consistency of star ratings and the complaints in 1 & 2-star user reviews for top free cross-platform Android and iOS apps. *Empirical Software Engineering*, *23*(6), 3442–3475.

IDC. (2016). *Smartphone OS Market Share. Q2.* www.idc.com/prodserv/smart phone-os-market-share.jsp.

Joiner, R., Stewart, C., & Beaney, C. (2015). Gender digital divide. In D. L. Rosen, N. Cheever, & C. Mark (eds.), *The Wiley Handbook of Psychology, Technology, and Society* (pp. 74–88). John Wiley & Sons.

Kagan, J. (2001). The need for new constructs. *Psychological Inquiry, 12*(2), 84–103.

Kaye, L. K., Malone, S. A., & Wall, H. J. (2017). Emojis: Insights, affordances, and possibilities for psychological science. *Trends in Cognitive Sciences, 21*(2), 66–68.

Kern, M. L. & Friedman, H. S. (2008). Do conscientious individuals live longer? A quantitative review. *Health Psychology, 27*(5), 505.

Kneidinger-Müller, B. (2019). When the smartphone goes offline: A factorial survey of smartphone users' experiences of mobile unavailability. *Computers in Human Behavior, 98,* 1–10.

Kosinski, M., Stillwell, D., & Graepel, T. (2013). Private traits and attributes are predictable from digital records of human behavior. *Proceedings of the National Academy of Sciences, 110*(15), 5802–5805.

Laajaj, R., Macours, K., Hernandez, D. A. P., et al. (2019). Challenges to capture the big five personality traits in non-WEIRD populations. *Science Advances, 5* (7),eaaw5226.

Lee, K. & Ashton, M. C. (2012). Getting mad and getting even: Agreeableness and Honesty-Humility as predictors of revenge intentions. *Personality and Individual Differences, 52*(5), 596–600.

Lewis, M. (2001). Issues in the study of personality development. *Psychological Inquiry, 12*(2), 67–83.

Malhotra, N. K. (1988). Self concept and product choice: An integrated perspective. *Journal of Economic Psychology, 9*(1), 1–28.

Matthews, G., Deary, I. J. & Whiteman, M. C. (2009). *Personality Traits* (3rd ed.). Cambridge University Press.

McCord, J. L., Harman, J. L., & Purl, J. (2019). Game-like personality testing: An emerging mode of personality assessment. *Personality and Individual Differences, 143,* 95–102.

Meadow, J. F., Altrichter, A. E., & Green, J. L. (2014). Mobile phones carry the personal microbiome of their owners. *PeerJ, 2,* e447.

Mickalowski, K., Mickelson, M., & Keltgen, J. (2008). Apple's iPhone launch: A case study in effective marketing. *The Business Review, 9*(2), 283–288.

Mischel, W. (2004). Toward an integrative science of the person. *Annual Review of Psychology, 55*(1), 1–22.

Mischel, W. & Shoda, Y. (1995). A cognitive-affective system theory of personality: Reconceptualizing situations, dispositions, dynamics, and invariance in personality structure. *Psychological Review, 102*(2), 246.

Mønsted, B., Mollgaard, A., & Mathiesen, J. (2018). Phonebased metric as a predictor for basic personality traits. *Journal of Research in Personality, 74,* 16–22.

Montag, C. & Elhai, J. D. (2019). A new agenda for personality psychology in the digital age? *Personality and Individual Differences, 147,* 128–134.

Ozer, D. J. & Benet-Martinez, V. (2006). Personality and the prediction of consequential outcomes. *Annual Review of Psychology, 57*, 401–421.

Pal, P., Roy, A., Moore, G., et al. (2013). Keypad mobile phones are associated with a significant increased risk of microbial contamination compared to touch screen phones. *Journal of Infection Prevention, 14*(2), 65–68.

Paunonen, S. V. & Ashton, M. C. (2001). Big Five factors and facets and the prediction of behavior. *Journal of Personality and Social Psychology, 81*, 524–539.

Paxton, A. & Griffiths, T. L. (2017). Finding the traces of behavioral and cognitive processes in big data and naturally occurring datasets. *Behavior Research Methods, 49*(5), 1630–1638.

Pedrero-Pérez, E. J., Morales-Alonso, S., Rodríguez-Rives, E., et al. (2019). Smartphone nonusers: Associated sociodemographic and health variables. *Cyberpsychology, Behavior, and Social Networking, 22*(9), 597–603. DOI:10.1089/cyber.2019.0130

Piwek, L., Ellis, D. A. & Andrews, S. (2016a). Can programming frameworks bring smartphones into the mainstream of psychological science? *Frontiers in Psychology, 7*, 1704.

Piwek, L., Ellis, D. A., Andrews, S., & Joinson, A. (2016b). The rise of consumer wearables: Promises and barriers. *PLOS MEDICINE, 13*(2), e1001953.

Quercia, D., Kosinski, M., Stillwell, D., & Crowcroft, J. (2011, October). Our Twitter profiles, our selves: Predicting personality with Twitter. In *2011 IEEE Third International Conference on Privacy, Security, Risk and Trust and 2011 IEEE Third International Conference on Social Computing* (pp. 180–185). IEEE.

Roberts, B. W. & Hill, P. L. (2017). Questions and answers about the policy relevance of personality traits. *PsyArXiv.* DOI:10.31234/osf.io/8cf7h

Roberts, B. W., Walton, K. E., & Bogg, T. (2005). Conscientiousness and health across the life course. *Review of General Psychology, 9*, 156–168.

Roberts, B. W., Kuncel, N. R., Shiner, R., Caspi, A., & Goldberg, L. R. (2007). The power of personality: The comparative validity of personality traits, socio-economic status, and cognitive ability for predicting important life outcomes. *Perspectives on Psychological Science, 2*(4), 313–345.

Sassenberg, K. & Ditrich, L. (2019). Research in social psychology changed between 2011 and 2016: Larger sample sizes, more self-report measures, and more online studies. *Advances in Methods and Practices in Psychological Science, 2* (2), 107–114.

Seneviratne, S., Seneviratne, A., Mohapatra, P., & Mahanti, A. (2014). Predicting user traits from a snapshot of apps installed on a smartphone. *ACM SIGMOBILE Mobile Computing and Communications Review, 18*(2), 1–8.

Shaw, H., Ellis, D. A., Kendrick, L., Ziegler, F., & Wiseman, R. (2016). Predicting smartphone operating system from personality and individual differences. *Cyberpsychology, Behavior, and Social Networking, 19*(12), 727–732

Soto, C. J. & John, O. P. (2017). The next big five inventory (BFI-2): Developing and assessing a hierarchical model with 15 facets to enhance bandwidth, fidelity, and predictive power. *Journal of Personality and Social Psychology, 113*(1), 117–143.

Srivastave, S. S., John, O. P., Gosling, S. D., & Potter, J. (2003). Development of personality in early and middle adulthood: Set like plaster or persistent change. *Journal of Personality and Social Research, 84*(5), 1041–1053.

Stachl, C., Au, Q., Schoedel, R., et al. (2019a, June 12). Behavioral patterns in smartphone usage predict Big Five personality traits. *PsyArXiv*. DOI:10.31234/osf.io/ks4vd

Stachl, C., Pargent, F., Hilbert, S., et al. (2019b). Personality research and assessment in the era of machine learning. *PsyArxiv*. DOI:10.31234/osf.io/efnj8

Sun, J. & Vazire, S. (2019). Do people know what they're like in the moment? *Psychological Science, 30*(3), 405–414.

Sundar, A. & Noseworthy, T. J. (2016). Too exciting to fail, too sincere to succeed: The effects of brand personality on sensory disconfirmation. *Journal of Consumer Research, 43*(1), 44–67.

Tolea, M. I., Terracciano, A., Simonsick, E. M., et al. (2012). Associations between personality traits, physical activity level, and muscle strength. *Journal of Research in Personality, 46*(3), 264–270.

Tsapeli, F. & Musolesi, M. (2015). Investigating causality in human behaviour from smartphone sensor data: A quasi-experimental approach. *EPJ Data Science, 4*(1), 24.

Tuzcuiglu, A., Fayda, S. N., Tuniyazi, Y., & Zübeyde, Ö. Z. (2018). Do the effects of brand personality dimensions on brand loyalty change according to customers' personalities? *Turkish Journal of Marketing, 3*(2), 84–107.

Vazire, S. & Gosling, S. D. (2004). e-Perceptions: Personality impressions based on personal websites. *Journal of Personality and Social Psychology, 87*(1), 123.

Vazire, S. & Mehl, M. R. (2008). Knowing me, knowing you: The accuracy and unique predictive validity of self-ratings and other-ratings of daily behavior. *Journal of Personality and Social Psychology, 95*(5), 1202.

Wang, W., Harari, G. M., Wang, R., et al. (2018). Sensing behavioural change over time: Using within-person variability features from mobile sensing to predict personality traits. *Proceedings of the ACM on Interactive, Mobile, Wearable and Ubiquitous Technologies, 2*(3), 141.

Wilcockson, T. D. W., Ellis, D. A., & Shaw, H. (2018). Determining typical smartphone usage: What data do we need? *Cyberpsychology, Behavior, and Social Networking, 21*(6), 395–398.

Xu, R., Frey, R. M., Fleisch, E., & Ilic, A. (2016). Understanding the impact of personality traits on mobile app adoption – Insights from a large-scale field study. *Computers in Human Behavior, 62*, 244–256.

Yakoub, F., Zein, M., Yasser, K., Adl, A., & Hassanien, A. E. (2015). Predicting personality traits and social context based on mining the smartphones SMS data. In *Intelligent Data Analysis and Applications* (pp. 511–521). Springer.

Ziegler, M., Horstmann, K. T., & Ziegler, J. (2019). Personality in situations: Going beyond the OCEAN and introducing the Situation Five. *Psychological Assessment, 31*(4), 567.

Chapter 5

Albert, G. & Lotan, T. (2018). How many times do young drivers actually touch their smartphone screens while driving? *IET Intelligent Transport Systems*, *12*(6), 414–419.

Andrews, S., Ellis, D. A., Shaw, H., & Piwek, L. (2015). Beyond self-report: Tools to compare estimates and real world smartphone use. *PLOS ONE*, *10* (10), e0139004

Apple (2016). *Apple ResearchKit*. Available from http://researchkit.org.

Barr, N., Pennycook, G., Stolz, J. A., & Fugelsang, J. A. (2015). The brain in your pocket: Evidence that smartphones are used to supplant thinking. *Computers in Human Behavior*, *48*, 473–480.

Baumeister, R. F., Muraven, M., & Tice, D. M. (2000). Ego depletion: A resource model of volition, self-regulation, and controlled processing. *Social Cognition*, *18*, 130–150.

Baumgartner, S. E., Lemmens, J. S., Weeda, W. D., & Huizinga, M. (2016). Measuring media multitasking. *Journal of Media Psychology*, *29*, 1–10

Bauerlein, M. (2011). Too dumb for complex texts? *Educational Leadership*, *68*(5), 28–33.

Benson, L., English, T., Conroy, D. E., et al. (2019). Age differences in emotion regulation strategy use, variability, and flexibility: An experience sampling approach. *Developmental Psychology*, *55*(9), 1951.

Beyens, I., Valkenburg, P. M., & Piotrowski, J. T. (2018). Screen media use and ADHD-related behaviours: Four decades of research. *Proceedings of the National Academy of Sciences*, *115*(40), 9875–9881.

Bielak, A. A., Mogle, J., & Sliwinski, M. J. (2017). What did you do today? Variability in daily activities is related to variability in daily cognitive performance. *The Journals of Gerontology: Series B*, *74*(5), 764–771.

Birnbaum, M. H. (2004). Human research and data collection via the internet. *Annual Review of Psychology*, *55*, 803–832.

Boari, D., Fraser, M., Stanton Fraser, D., & Cater, K. (2012, May). Augmenting spatial skills with mobile devices. In *Proceedings of the SIGCHI Conference on Human Factors in Computing Systems* (pp. 1611–1620). ACM.

Bolt, D. B. & Crawford, R. A. (2000). *Digital Divide: Computers and Our Children's Future*. TV Books Incorporated.

Bright Horizons. (2020). *Modern Families Index 2020*. Available from https://sol utions.brighthorizons.co.uk/resources/research/modern-families-index-2020?g clid=CjwKCAiA6vXwBRBKEiwAYE7iS6BDDOAYPwulu9wb8MptsgK13zen oxgmYLNzDekkvRHw7FvPWPWDERoCJicQAvD_BwE.

Brown, H. R., Zeidman, P., Smittenaar, P., et al. (2014). Crowdsourcing for cognitive science – the utility of smartphones. *PLOS ONE*, *9*(7), e100662.

Brunet, J. F., Dagenais, D., Therrien, M., Gartenberg, D., & Forest, G. (2017). Validation of sleep-2-Peak: A smartphone application that can detect fatigue-related changes in reaction times during sleep deprivation. *Behavior Research Methods*, *49*(4), 1460–1469.

Buchanan, A. E. (2011). Cognitive enhancement and education. *School Field, 9*(2), 145–162.

Burnett, G. E. & Lee, K. (2005). The effect of vehicle navigation systems on the formation of cognitive maps. In *International Conference of Traffic and Transport Psychology*. https://trid.trb.org/view/762956

Cain, N. & Gradisar, M. (2010). Electronic media use and sleep in school-aged children and adolescents: A review. *Sleep Medicine, 11*(8), 735–742.

Carpenter, S. (2018). Ten steps in scale development and reporting: A guide for researchers. *Communication Methods and Measures, 12*(1), 25–44.

Carr, N. (2008). Is Google making us stupid? *Yearbook of the National Society for the Study of Education, 107*(2), 89–94.

Carr, N. (2010). *What the Internet Is Doing To Our Brains*. Roadshow.

Chassiakos, Y. L. R., Radesky, J., Christakis, D., Moreno, M. A., & Cross, C. (2016). Children and adolescents and digital media. *Pediatrics, 138*(5), e20162593.

Christensen, M. A., Bettencourt, L., Kaye, L., et al. (2016). Direct measurements of smartphone screen-time: Relationships with demographics and sleep. *PLOS ONE, 11*(11), e0165331.

Clayton, R. B., Leshner, G., & Almond, A. (2015). The extended iSelf: The impact of iPhone separation on cognition, emotion, and physiology. *Journal of Computer-Mediated Communication, 20*(2), 119–135.

Cole, P. M., Martin, S. E., & Dennis, T. A. (2004). Emotion regulation as a scientific construct: Methodological challenges and directions for child development research. *Child Development, 75*, 317–333.

Costigan, S. A., Barnett, L., Plotnikoff, R. C., & Lubans, D. R. (2013). The health indicators associated with screen-based sedentary behaviour among adolescent girls: A systematic review. *Journal of Adolescent Health, 52*(4), 382–392.

Coughlan, G., Coutrot, A., Khondoker, M., et al. (2019). Toward personalized cognitive diagnostics of at-genetic-risk Alzheimer's disease. *Proceedings of the National Academy of Sciences, 116*(19), 9285–9292.

Courage, M. L. (2017). Screen media and the youngest viewers: Implications for attention and learning. In *Cognitive Development in Digital Contexts* (pp. 3–28). Academic Press.

Coutrot, A., Silva, R., Manley, E., et al. (2018). Global determinants of navigation ability. *Current Biology, 28*(17), 2861–2866.

Coutrot, A., Schmidt, S., Coutrot, L., et al. (2019). Virtual navigation tested on a mobile app is predictive of real-world wayfinding navigation performance. *PLOS ONE, 14*(3), e0213272.

Crone, E. A. & Konijn, E. A. (2018). Media use and brain development during adolescence. *Nature Communications, 9*(1), 1–10.

Dennis, S. J., Yim, H., Sreekumar, V., et al. (2017). A hierarchical Bayesian model of 'memory for when' based on experience sampling data. In P. Bello, M. Guarini, M. McShane, & B. Scassellati (eds.), *Proceedings of the 39th Annual Conference of the Cognitive Science Society* (pp. 295–300). Cognitive Science Society.

Dora, J., van Hooff, M., Geurts, S., Kompier, M. A. J., & Bijleveld, E. (2020). Fatigue, boredom, and objectively-measured smartphone use at work. *PsyArXiv*. DOI:10.31234/osf.io/uy8rs

Downey, D. B. & Gibbs, B. G. (2020). Kids these days: are face-to-face social skills among American children declining? *American Journal of Sociology*, 125(4), 1030–1083.

Dunbar, R. I. (1992). Neocortex size as a constraint on group size in primates. *Journal of Human Evolution*, 22(6), 469–493.

Ellis, D. A. (2019). Are smartphones really that bad? Improving the psychological measurement of technology-related behaviours. *Computers in Human Behavior*, 97, 60–66.

Engelberg, J. K., Hill, L. L., Rybar, J., & Styer, T. (2015). Distracted driving behaviours related to cell phone use among middle-aged adults. *Journal of Transport & Health*, 2(3), 434–440.

Engström, J., Johansson, E., & Östlund, J. (2005). Effects of visual and cognitive load in real and simulated motorway driving. *Transportation Research Part F: Traffic Psychology and Behaviour*, 8(2), 97–120.

Felisoni, D. D. & Godoi, A. S. (2018). Cell phone usage and academic performance: An experiment. *Computers & Education*, 117, 175–187.

Fikkers, K. M., Piotrowski, J. T., & Valkenburg, P. M. (2019). Child's play? Assessing the bidirectional longitudinal relationship between gaming and intelligence in early childhood. *Journal of Communication*, 69(2), 124–143.

Fiske, S. T. & Taylor, S. E. (2013). *Social Cognition: From Brains to Culture*. Sage.

Fleischhauer, M., Enge, S., Brocke, B., et al. (2010). Same or different? Clarifying the relationship of need for cognition to personality and intelligence. *Personality and Social Psychology Bulletin*, 36(1), 82–96.

Frith, J. & Kalin, J. (2016). Here, I used to be: Mobile media and practices of place-based digital memory. *Space and Culture*, 19(1), 43–55.

Frost, P., Donahue, P., Goeben, K., et al. (2019). An examination of the potential lingering effects of smartphone use on cognition. *Applied Cognitive Psychology*, 33(6), 1055–1067.

Geyer, K., Ellis, D. A., & Piwek, L. (2019). A simple location-tracking app for psychological research. *Behavior Research Methods*, 51(6), 2840–2846.

Giang, W. C., Hoekstra-Atwood, L., & Donmez, B. (2014, September). Driver engagement in notifications: A comparison of visual-manual interaction between smartwatches and smartphones. In *Proceedings of the Human Factors and Ergonomics Society Annual Meeting* (vol. 58, no. 1, pp. 2161–2165). Sage Publications.

Gielis, K. (2019, October). Screening for mild cognitive impairment through digital biomarkers of cognitive performance in games. In *Extended Abstracts of the Annual Symposium on Computer-Human Interaction in Play Companion Extended Abstracts* (pp. 7–13). ACM.

Gindrat, A. D., Chytiris, M., Balerna, M., Rouiller, E. M., & Ghosh, A. (2015). Use-dependent cortical processing from fingertips in touchscreen phone users. *Current Biology*, 25(1), 109–116.

Giunchiglia, F., Zeni, M., Gobbi, E., Bignotti, E., & Bison, I. (2018). Mobile social media usage and academic performance. *Computers in Human Behavior*, *82*, 177–185.

Grant, D. A., Honn, K. A., Layton, M. E., Riedy, S. M., & Van Dongen, H. P. (2017). 3-minute smartphone-based and tablet-based psychomotor vigilance tests for the assessment of reduced alertness due to sleep deprivation. *Behavior Research Methods*, *49*(3), 1020–1029.

Greenfield, S. (2015). *Mind Change: How Digital Technologies Are Leaving Their Mark On Our Brains*. Random House Incorporated.

Hadar, A. A., Eliraz, D., Lazarovits, A., Alyagon, U., & Zangen, A. (2015). Using longitudinal exposure to causally link smartphone usage to changes in behaviour, cognition and right prefrontal neural activity. *Brain Stimulation: Basic, Translational, and Clinical Research in Neuromodulation*, *8*(2), 318.

Haigh, A. (2015). *Stop Phubbing*. http://stopphubbing.com.

Haslam, N. (2016). Concept creep: Psychology's expanding concepts of harm and pathology. *Psychological Inquiry*, *27*(1), 1–17.

Hawi, N. S., Samaha, M., & Griffiths, M. D. (2019). The Digital Addiction Scale for Children: Development and validation. *Cyberpsychology, Behavior, and Social Networking*.

Henkel, L. A. (2014). Point-and-shoot memories: The influence of taking photos on memory for a museum tour. *Psychological Science*, *25*(2), 396–402.

Horberry, T., Osborne, R., & Young, K. (2019). Pedestrian smartphone distraction: Prevalence and potential severity. *Transportation Research Part F: Traffic Psychology and Behaviour*, *60*, 515–523.

Houghton, S., Hunter, S. C., Rosenberg, M., et al. (2015). Virtually impossible: Limiting Australian children and adolescents daily screen based media use. *BMC Public Health*, *15*(1), 5.

Hudson, J. (2019). Spatial navigation: A behavioural biomarker for improved dementia diagnosis. *Journal of Geriatric Care and Research*, *6*(1), 20–22.

Hutton, J. S., Dudley, J., Horowitz-Kraus, T., DeWitt, T., & Holland, S. K. (2020). Associations between screen-based media use and brain white matter integrity in preschool-aged children. *JAMA Paediatrics*, 174(1), e193869–e193869, Published online 4 November.

Hyman Jr, I. E., Boss, S. M., Wise, B. M., McKenzie, K. E., & Caggiano, J. M. (2010). Did you see the unicycling clown? Inattentional blindness while walking and talking on a cell phone. *Applied Cognitive Psychology*, *24*(5), 597–607.

Inzlicht, M., Schmeichel, B. J., & Macrae, C. N. (2014). Why self-control seems (but may not be) limited. *Trends in Cognitive Sciences*, *18*(3), 127–133.

Ioannidou, F., Hermens, F., & Hodgson, T. L. (2017). Mind your step: The effects of mobile phone use on gaze behaviour in stair climbing. *Journal of Technology in Behavioral Science*, *2*(3–4), 109–120.

Johannes, N., Dora, J., & Rusz, D. (2019). Social smartphone apps do not capture attention despite their perceived high reward value. *Collabra: Psychology*, *5*(1), 14.

Kahneman, D. (2011). *Thinking, Fast and Slow*. Macmillan.

Kaye, L. K., Monk, R. L., & Hamlin, I. (2018). 'Feeling appy?': Using app-based methodology to explore contextual effects on real-time cognitions, affect and behaviours. In *Doing Research In and On the Digital* (pp. 10–29). Routledge.

Kieslich, P. J., Schoemann, M., Grage, T., Hepp, J., & Scherbaum, S. (2020). Design factors in mouse-tracking: What makes a difference?. *Behavior Research Methods*, 52(1), 317–341.

Konstantopoulos, P., Chapman, P., & Crundall, D. (2010). Driver's visual attention as a function of driving experience and visibility. Using a driving simulator to explore drivers' eye movements in day, night and rain driving. *Accident Analysis & Prevention*, 42(3), 827–834.

Lamble, D., Kauranen, T., Laakso, M., & Summala, H. (1999). Cognitive load and detection thresholds in car following situations: Safety implications for using mobile (cellular) telephones while driving. *Accident Analysis & Prevention*, 31(6), 617–623.

Lepp, A., Barkley, J. E., & Karpinski, A. C. (2015). The relationship between cell phone use and academic performance in a sample of US college students. *Sage Open*, 5(1), 2158244015573169.

Linkenauger, S. A., Weser, V., & Proffitt, D. R. (2019). Choosing efficient actions: Deciding where to walk. *PLOS ONE*, 14(9), e0219729.

Lui, K. F. & Wong, A. C. N. (2012). Does media multitasking always hurt? A positive correlation between multitasking and multisensory integration. *Psychonomic Bulletin & Review*, 19(4), 647–653.

Lumsden, J., Edwards, E. A., Lawrence, N. S., Coyle, D., & Munafò, M. R. (2016). Gamification of cognitive assessment and cognitive training: A systematic review of applications and efficacy. *JMIR Serious Games*, 4(2), e11.

Mack, C. C., Harding, M., Davies, N., & Ward, G. (2019). RECAPP-XPR: A smartphone application for presenting and recalling experimentally controlled stimuli over longer timescales. *Behavior Research Methods*, 51(4), 1804–1823.

Mackes, N. K., Golm, D., Sarkar, S., et al. (2020). Early childhood deprivation is associated with alterations in adult brain structure despite subsequent environmental enrichment. *Proceedings of the National Academy of Sciences*, 117(1), 641–649.

Mandryk, R. L. & Birk, M. V. (2019). The potential of game-based digital biomarkers for modeling mental health. *JMIR Mental Health*, 6(4), e13485.

Marsh, E. J. & Rajaram, S. (2019). The digital expansion of the mind: Implications of internet usage for memory and cognition. *Journal of Applied Research in Memory and Cognition*, 8, 1–14.

Marty-Dugas, J., Ralph, B. C., Oakman, J. M., & Smilek, D. (2018). The relation between smartphone use and everyday inattention. *Psychology of Consciousness: Theory, Research, and Practice*, 5(1), 46.

Matsumura, K. & Yamakoshi, T. (2013). iPhysioMeter: A new approach for measuring heart rate and normalized pulse volume using only a smartphone. *Behavior Research Methods*, 45(4), 1272–1278.

Mavoa, J., Carter, M., & Gibbs, M. (2018). Children and Minecraft: A survey of children's digital play. *New Media & Society, 20*(9), 3283–3303.

McNab, F., Zeidman, P., Rutledge, R. B., et al. (2015). Age-related changes in working memory and the ability to ignore distraction. *Proceedings of the National Academy of Sciences, 112*(20), 6515–6518.

McQueenie, R., Ellis, D. A., McConnachie, A., Wilson, P., & Williamson, A. E. (2019). Morbidity, mortality and missed appointments in healthcare: A national retrospective data linkage study. *BMC Medicine, 17*(1), 2.

Miyasike-daSilva, V., Allard, F., & McIlroy, W. E. (2011). Where do we look when we walk on stairs? Gaze behaviour on stairs, transitions, and handrails. *Experimental Brain Research, 209*(1), 73–83.

Moisala, M., Salmela, V., Hietajärvi, L., et al. (2016). Media multitasking is associated with distractibility and increased prefrontal activity in adolescents and young adults. *NeuroImage, 134*, 113–121.

Monaghan, P., Sio, U. N., Lau, S. W., et al. (2015). Sleep promotes analogical transfer in problem solving. *Cognition, 143*, 25–30.

Nasar, J., Hecht, P., & Wener, R. (2008). Mobile telephones, distracted attention, and pedestrian safety. *Accident Analysis & Prevention, 40*(1), 69–75.

Nasar, J. L. & Troyer, D. (2013). Pedestrian injuries due to mobile phone use in public places. *Accident Analysis & Prevention, 57*, 91–95.

Neisser, U. (1985). The role of theory in the ecological study of memory. *Journal of Experimental Psychology: General, 114*, 272–276.

Nielson, D. M., Smith, T. A., Sreekumar, V., Dennis, S., & Sederberg, P. B. (2015). Human hippocampus represents space and time during retrieval of real-world memories. *Proceedings of the National Academy of Sciences, 112*(35), 11078–11083.

Nikkelen, S. W., Valkenburg, P. M., Huizinga, M., & Bushman, B. J. (2014). Media use and ADHD-related behaviours in children and adolescents: A meta-analysis. *Developmental Psychology, 50*(9), 2228.

Ophir, E., Nass, C., & Wagner, A. D. (2009). Cognitive control in media multitaskers. *Proceedings of the National Academy of Sciences, 106*(37), 15583–15587.

Owens, J. M., Tefft, B. C., Guo, F., et al. (2018). *Crash Risk of Cell Phone Use While Driving: Case-Crossover Study of SHRP 2 Naturalistic Driving Data* (No. 18–03148). https://trid.trb.org/view/1495640

Özkul, D. & Humphreys, L. (2015). Record and remember: Memory and meaning-making practices through mobile media. *Mobile Media & Communication, 3*(3), 351–365.

Paletta, L., Neuschmied, H., Schwarz, M., et al. (2014, March). Smartphone eye tracking toolbox: Accurate gaze recovery on mobile displays. In *Proceedings of the Symposium on Eye Tracking Research and Applications* (pp. 367–368). ACM.

Peirce, J., Gray, J. R., Simpson, S., et al. (2019). PsychoPy2: Experiments in behavior made easy. *Behavior Research Methods, 51*(1), 195–203.

Pindek, S., Krajcevska, A., & Spector, P. E. (2018). Cyberloafing as a coping mechanism: Dealing with workplace boredom. *Computers in Human Behavior, 86*, 147–152.

Piwek, L. & Joinson, A. (2016). 'What do they snapchat about?' Patterns of use in time-limited instant messaging service. *Computers in Human Behavior, 54*, 358–367.

Protzko, J. & Schooler, J. W. (2019). Kids these days: Why the youth of today seem lacking. *Science Advances, 5* (10),eaav5916.

Przybylski, A. K. & Weinstein, N. (2019). Digital screen time limits and young children's psychological well-being: Evidence from a population-based study. *Child Development, 90*(1), e56–e65.

Ra, C. K., Cho, J., Stone, M. D., et al. (2018). Association of digital media use with subsequent symptoms of attention-deficit/hyperactivity disorder among adolescents. *JAMA, 320*(3), 255–263.

Redelmeier, D. A. & Tibshirani, R. J. (1997). Association between cellular-telephone calls and motor vehicle collisions. *New England Journal of Medicine, 336*(7), 453–458.

Rosenbaum, D. A. (2009). Walking down memory lane: Where walkers look as they descend stairs provides hints about how they control their walking behaviour. *The American Journal of Psychology, 122*(4), 425–430. www.jstor.org/stab le/27784419

Russell, G., Rodgers, L. R., Ukoumunne, O. C., & Ford, T. (2014). Prevalence of parent-reported ASD and ADHD in the UK: Findings from the Millennium Cohort Study. *Journal of Autism and Developmental Disorders, 44*(1), 31–40.

Sanbonmatsu, D. M., Strayer, D. L., Medeiros-Ward, N., & Watson, J. M. (2013). Who multi-tasks and why? Multi-tasking ability, perceived multi-tasking ability, impulsivity, and sensation seeking. *PLOS ONE, 8*(1), e54402.

Schwebel, D. C., Stavrinos, D., Byington, K. W., et al. (2012). Distraction and pedestrian safety: How talking on the phone, texting, and listening to music impact crossing the street. *Accident Analysis & Prevention, 45*, 266–271.

Sherman, L. E., Payton, A. A., Hernandez, L. M., Greenfield, P. M., & Dapretto, M. (2016). The power of the like in adolescence: Effects of peer influence on neural and behavioural responses to social media. *Psychological Science, 27*(7), 1027–1035.

Seo, D. G., Park, Y., Kim, M. K., & Park, J. (2016). Mobile phone dependency and its impacts on adolescents' social and academic behaviors. *Computers in Human Behavior, 63*, 282–292.

Silk, J. S. (2019). Context and dynamics: The new frontier for developmental research on emotion regulation. *Developmental Psychology, 55*(9), 2009–2014.

Spanakis, P., Jones, A., Field, M., & Christiansen, P. (2019). A Stroop in the hand is worth two on the laptop: Superior reliability of a smartphone based alcohol Stroop in the real world. *Substance Use & Misuse, 54*(4), 692–698.

Sparrow, B., Liu, J., & Wegner, D. M. (2011). Google effects on memory: Cognitive consequences of having information at our fingertips. *Science, 333* (6043), 776–778.

Stavrinos, D., Byington, K. W., & Schwebel, D. C. (2009). Effect of cell phone distraction on pediatric pedestrian injury risk. *Pediatrics, 123*(2), e179–e185.

Stevens, A. & Minton, R. (2001). In-vehicle distraction and fatal accidents in England and Wales. *Accident Analysis & Prevention, 33*(4), 539–545.

Stieger, S., Lewetz, D., & Reips, U. D. (2018). Can smartphones be used to bring computer-based tasks from the lab to the field? A mobile experience-sampling method study about the pace of life. *Behavior Research Methods*, *50*(6), 2267–2275.

Stiglic, N. & Viner, R. M. (2019). Effects of screentime on the health and well-being of children and adolescents: A systematic review of reviews. *BMJ Open*, *9*(1), e023191.

Stothart, C., Mitchum, A., & Yehnert, C. (2015). The attentional cost of receiving a cell phone notification. *Journal of Experimental Psychology: Human Perception and Performance*, *41*(4), 893.

Strayer, D. L., Drews, F. A., & Crouch, D. J. (2006). A comparison of the cell phone driver and the drunk driver. *Human Factors*, *48*(2), 381–391.

Taylor, G., Monaghan, P., & Westermann, G. (2018). Investigating the association between children's screen media exposure and vocabulary size in the UK. *Journal of Children and Media*, *12*(1), 51–65.

Teki, S., Kumar, S., & Griffiths, T. D. (2016). Large-scale analysis of auditory segregation behavior crowdsourced via a smartphone app. *PLOS ONE*, *11*(4), e0153916.

Thornton, B., Faires, A., Robbins, M., & Rollins, E. (2014). The mere presence of a cell phone may be distracting. *Social Psychology*, *45*, 479–488.

Tamir, D. I., Templeton, E. M., Ward, A. F., & Zaki, J. (2018). Media usage diminishes memory for experiences. *Journal of Experimental Social Psychology*, *76*, 161–168.

Törnros, J. E., & Bolling, A. K. (2005). Mobile phone use – effects of handheld and handsfree phones on driving performance. *Accident Analysis & Prevention*, *37*(5), 902–909.

Turner, A., Topor, M., Stewart, A., et al. (2019). *Open Code and Software: A Primer from UK Reproducibility Network (UKRN)*. www.bristol.ac.uk/media-library/sites/expsych/documents/ukrn/UKRN_Primer_Open_Code_Software.pdf.

Twenge, J. M. (2017). *iGen: Why Today's Super-Connected Kids Are Growing Up Less Rebellious, More Tolerant, Less Happy – And Completely Unprepared For Adulthood – And What That Means For The Rest Of Us*. Simon and Schuster.

Uncapher, M. R., Thieu, M. K., & Wagner, A. D. (2016). Media multitasking and memory: Differences in working memory and long-term memory. *Psychonomic Bulletin & Review*, *23*(2), 483–490.

Vadillo, M. A., Gold, N., & Osman, M. (2018). Searching for the bottom of the ego well: Failure to uncover ego depletion in Many Labs 3. *Royal Society Open Science*, *5*(8), 180390.

Voinea, C., Vică, C., Mihailov, E., & Savulescu, J. (2020). The internet as cognitive enhancement. *Science and Engineering Ethics*.

Wagner, D. T., Barnes, C. M., Lim, V. K., & Ferris, D. L. (2012). Lost sleep and cyberloafing: Evidence from the laboratory and a daylight saving time quasi-experiment. *Journal of Applied Psychology*, *97*(5), 1068.

Waller, J. M., Silk, J. S., Stone, L. B., & Dahl, R. E. (2014). Co-rumination and co-problem solving in the daily lives of adolescents with major depressive disorder. *Journal of the American Academy of Child & Adolescent Psychiatry, 53*, 869–878.

Wang, R., Harari, G., Hao, P., Zhou, X., & Campbell, A. T. (2015, September). SmartGPA: How smartphones can assess and predict academic performance of college students. In *Proceedings of the 2015 ACM International Joint Conference on Pervasive and Ubiquitous Computing* (pp. 295–306). ACM.

Ward, A. F., Duke, K., Gneezy, A., & Bos, M. W. (2017). Brain drain: The mere presence of one's own smartphone reduces available cognitive capacity. *Journal of the Association for Consumer Research, 2*(2), 140–154.

Westgate, E. C. & Wilson, T. D. (2018). Boring thoughts and bored minds: The MAC model of boredom and cognitive engagement. *Psychological Review, 125* (5), 689.

White, K. M., Hyde, M. K., Walsh, S. P., & Watson, B. (2010). Mobile phone use while driving: An investigation of the beliefs influencing drivers' hands-free and hand-held mobile phone use. *Transportation Research Part F: Traffic Psychology and Behaviour, 13*(1), 9–20.

Wilmer, H. H. & Chein, J. M. (2016). Mobile technology habits: Patterns of association among device usage, intertemporal preference, impulse control, and reward sensitivity. *Psychonomic Bulletin & Review, 23*(5), 1607–1614.

Wilmer, H. H., Sherman, L. E., & Chein, J. M. (2017). Smartphones and cognition: A review of research exploring the links between mobile technology habits and cognitive functioning. *Frontiers in Psychology, 8*, 605.

Wilcockson, T. D. W., Ellis, D. A., & Shaw, H. (2018). Determining typical smartphone usage: What data do we need? *Cyberpsychology, Behavior, and Social Networking, 21*(6), 395–398.

Yeykelis, L., Cummings, J. J., & Reeves, B. (2014). Multitasking on a single device: Arousal and the frequency, anticipation, and prediction of switching between media content on a computer. *Journal of Communication, 64*(1), 167–192.

Zimmerman, F., Shalom, D., Gonzalez, P. A., et al. (2016). Arithmetic on your phone: A large scale investigation of simple additions and multiplications. *PLOS ONE, 11*(12), e0168431.

Chapter 6

Acquisti, A., Brandimarte, L., & Loewenstein, G. (2015). Privacy and human behavior in the age of information. *Science, 347*(6221), 509–514.

Adams, D. A., Nelson, R. R., & Todd, P. A. (1992). Perceived usefulness, ease of use, and usage of information technology: A replication. *MIS Quarterly*, 227–247. DOI:10.2307/249577

Ajzen, I. (1991). The theory of planned behavior. *Organizational Behavior and Human Decision Processes, 50*(2), 179–211.

Alsaleh, M., Alomar, N., & Alarifi, A. (2017). Smartphone users: Understanding how security mechanisms are perceived and new persuasive methods. *PLOS ONE, 12*(3), e0173284.

Aly, A., Macdonald, S., Jarvis, L., & Chen, T. M. (2017). Introduction to the special issue: Terrorist online propaganda and radicalization. *Studies in Conflict & Terrorism*, *40*, 1–9.

Android. (2018). *Services Overview*. https://developer.android.com/guide/compo nents/services.

Annansingh, F. & Veli, T. (2016). An investigation into risks awareness and e-safety needs of children on the internet: A study of Devon, UK. *Interactive Technology and Smart Education*, *13*(2), 147–165.

Aviv, A. J., Gibson, K. L., Mossop, E., Blaze, M., & Smith, J. M. (2010). Smudge attacks on smartphone touch screens. *Woot*, *10*, 1–7.

Balebako, R., Marsh, A., Lin, J., Hong, J. I., & Cranor, L. (2014). *The Privacy and Security Behaviors of Smartphone App Developers*. Available from https://kilthub .cmu.edu/articles/The_Privacy_and_Security_Behaviors_of_Smartphone_Ap p_Developers/6470528.

Bandura, A. (1986). *Social Foundations of Thought and Action*. Prentice-Hall.

Bansal, G. (2017). Distinguishing between privacy and security concerns: An empirical examination and scale validation. *Journal of Computer Information Systems*, *57*(4), 330–343.

Barbaro, M., Zeller, T., & Hansell, S. (2006). A face is exposed for AOL searcher no. 4417749. *New York Times*, *9*(2008), 8.

Barnes, S. B. (2006). A privacy paradox: Social networking in the United States. *First Monday*, *11*(9).

Baruh, L., Secinti, E., & Cemalcilar, Z. (2017). Online privacy concerns and privacy management: A meta-analytical review. *Journal of Communication*, *67*(1), 26–53.

BBC (2000). *The Shipman Tapes*. Available from http://news.bbc.co.uk/1/hi/in_ depth/uk/2000/the_shipman_murders/the_shipman_files/613286.stm.

BBC (2019a). *Samsung: Anyone's Thumbprint Can Unlock Galaxy S10 Phone*. Available from www.bbc.co.uk/news/technology-50080586.

BBC (2019b). *Google Pixel 4 Face Unlock Works If Eyes Are Shut*. Available from www.bbc.co.uk/news/technology-50085630.

Boyd, D. & Hargittai, E. (2013). Connected and concerned: Variation in parents' online safety concerns. *Policy & Internet*, *5*(3), 245–269.

British Psychological Society (2013). *Ethics Guidelines for Internet-Mediated Research*. Available from www.bps.org.uk/system/files/Public.

Brownell, K. D. & Horgen, K. B. (2004). *Food Fight: The Inside Story of the Food Industry, America's Obesity Crisis, and What We Can Do about It*. Contemporary Books.

Brostoff, S. & Sasse, M. A. (2000). Are passfaces more usable than passwords? A field trial investigation. In *People and Computers XIV – Usability or Else!* (pp. 405–424). Springer.

Burton, A. M., Wilson, S., Cowan, M., & Bruce, V. (1999). Face recognition in poor-quality video: Evidence from security surveillance. *Psychological Science*, *10* (3), 243–248.

Burton, A. M., Jenkins, R., & Schweinberger, S. R. (2011). Mental representations of familiar faces. *British Journal of Psychology*, *102*(4), 943–958.

Chen, H., Chung, W., Qin, J., et al. (2008). Uncovering the dark Web: A case study of Jihad on the Web. *Journal of the American Society for Information Science and Technology*, *59*(8), 1347–1359.

Chin, E., Felt, A. P., Sekar, V., & Wagner, D. (2012, July). Measuring user confidence in smartphone security and privacy. In *Proceedings of the Eighth Symposium on Usable Privacy and Security* (pp. 1–16).

Crawford, H. & Renaud, K. (2014). Understanding user perceptions of transparent authentication on a mobile device. *Journal of Trust Management*, *1*(1), 7.

Crawford, H., Renaud, K., & Storer, T. (2013). A framework for continuous, transparent mobile device authentication. *Computers & Security*, *39*, 127–136.

Creese, S., Hodges, D., Jamison-Powell, S., & Whitty, M. (2013, July). Relationships between password choices, perceptions of risk and security expertise. In *International Conference on Human Aspects of Information Security, Privacy, and Trust* (pp. 80–89). Springer, Berlin, Heidelberg.

Daley, J. (2014). *Spare Us the Small Print*. Available from www.fairerfinance.com /business/blog/spare-us-the-small-print.

De Montjoye, Y. A., Hidalgo, C. A., Verleysen, M., & Blondel, V. D. (2013). Unique in the crowd: The privacy bounds of human mobility. *Scientific Reports*, *3*, 1376.

Dennis, S., Garrett, P., Yim, H., et al. (2019a). Privacy versus open science. *Behavior Research Methods*, *51*(4), 1839–1848.

Dennis, S., Yim, H., Garrett, P., Sreekumar, V., & Stone, B. (2019b). A system for collecting and analyzing experience-sampling data. *Behavior Research Methods*, *51*(4), 1824–1838.

Dienlin, T. & Metzger, M. J. (2016). An extended privacy calculus model for SNSs: Analyzing self-disclosure and self-withdrawal in a representative US sample. *Journal of Computer-Mediated Communication*, *21*(5), 368–383.

Dienlin, T. & Trepte, S. (2015). Is the privacy paradox a relic of the past? An in-depth analysis of privacy attitudes and privacy behaviors. *European Journal of Social Psychology*, *45*(3), 285–297.

Dienlin, T., Masur, P., & Trepte, S. (2019). A longitudinal analysis of the privacy paradox. *SocArXiv*. DOI:10.31235/osf.io/fm4h7

Dwork, C. & Roth, A. (2014). The algorithmic foundations of differential privacy. *Foundations and Trends in Theoretical Computer Science*, *9*(3–4), 211–407.

Ellis, D. A. & Piwek, L. (2016). The future of . . . wearable technology. *CREST Security Review*, *1*, 4–5.

Enck, W., Octeau, D., McDaniel, P. D., & Chaudhuri, S. (2011, August). A study of Android application security. *USENIX Security Symposium*, *2*, 2.

Felt, A. P., Chin, E., Hanna, S., Song, D., & Wagner, D. (2011, October). Android permissions demystified. In *Proceedings of the 18th ACM Conference on Computer and Communications Security* (pp. 627–638). ACM.

Felt, A. P., Egelman, S., & Wagner, D. (2012, October). I've got 99 problems, but vibration ain't one: A survey of smartphone users' concerns. In *Proceedings of the Second ACM Workshop on Security and Privacy in Smartphones and Mobile Devices* (pp. 33–44). ACM.

Festinger, L. (1962). *A Theory of Cognitive Dissonance*. Stanford University Press.

Flynn, L. & Klieber, W. (2015). Smartphone security. *IEEE Pervasive Computing*, *14*(4), 16–21.

Geyer, K., Ellis, D. A. & Piwek, L. (2019). A simple location-tracking app for psychological research. *Behavior Research Methods*, *51*(6), 2840–2846.

George, M. J. & Odgers, C. L. (2015). Seven fears and the science of how mobile technologies may be influencing adolescents in the digital age. *Perspectives on Psychological Science*, *10*(6), 832–851.

Glisson, W. B., Storer, T., Mayall, G., Moug, I., & Grispos, G. (2011). Electronic retention: What does your mobile phone reveal about you? *International Journal of Information Security*, *10*(6), 337.

Gluck, J. P. (1997). Harry F. Harlow and animal research: Reflection on the ethical paradox. *Ethics & Behavior*, *7*(2), 149–161.

Grinberg, N., Joseph, K., Friedland, L., Swire-Thompson, B., & Lazer, D. (2019). Fake news on Twitter during the 2016 US presidential election. *Science*, *363* (6425), 374–378.

Grispos, G., Glisson, W. B., & Storer, T. (2015). Recovering residual forensic data from smartphone interactions with cloud storage providers. *arXiv*. DOI:10.1016/B978-0-12-801595-7.00016-1

Gross, E. F. (2004). Adolescent internet use: What we expect, what teens report. *Journal of Applied Developmental Psychology*, *25*(6), 633–649.

Harari, G. M., Müller, S. R., Aung, M. S., & Rentfrow, P. J. (2017). Smartphone sensing methods for studying behavior in everyday life. *Current Opinion in Behavioral Sciences*, *18*, 83–90.

Hinds, J. & Joinson, A. (2019). Human and computer personality prediction from digital footprints. *Current Directions in Psychological Science*, *28*(2), 204–211.

Holman, E. A., Garfin, D. R., Lubens, P., & Silver, R. C. (2020). Media exposure to collective trauma, mental health, and functioning: Does it matter what you see? *Clinical Psychological Science*, 8(1), 111–124. 2167702619858300.

Houghton, D. J. & Joinson, A. N. (2010). Privacy, social network sites, and social relations. *Journal of Technology in Human Services*, *28*(1–2), 74–94.

Hviid, A., Hansen, J. V., Frisch, M., & Melbye, M. (2019). Measles, mumps, rubella vaccination and autism: A nationwide cohort study. *Annals of Internal Medicine*, *170*(8), 513–520.

Isaak, J. & Hanna, M. J. (2018). User data privacy: Facebook, Cambridge Analytica, and privacy protection. *Computer*, *51*(8), 56–59.

James, P., Jankowska, M., Marx, C., et al. (2016). 'Spatial energetics': Integrating data from GPS, accelerometry, and GIS to address obesity and inactivity. *American Journal of Preventive Medicine*, *51*(5), 792–800.

Jenkins, R. & Burton, A. M. (2008). 100% accuracy in automatic face recognition. *Science*, *319*(5862), 435.

Jenkins, R. & Burton, A. M. (2011). Stable face representations. *Philosophical Transactions of the Royal Society B: Biological Sciences*, *366*(1571), 1671–1683.

Jenkins, R., White, D., Van Montfort, X., & Burton, A. M. (2011). Variability in photos of the same face. *Cognition*, *121*(3), 313–323.

Jenkins, R., McLachlan, J. L., & Renaud, K. (2014). Facelock: Familiarity-based graphical authentication. *PeerJ*, 2, e444.

Jeon, W., Kim, J., Lee, Y., & Won, D. (2011, July). A practical analysis of smartphone security. In *Symposium on Human Interface* (pp. 311–320). Springer.

John, N. A. & Nissenbaum, A. (2019). An agnotological analysis of APIs: Or, disconnectivity and the ideological limits of our knowledge of social media. *The Information Society*, 35(1), 1–12.

Jones, C. M., McCarthy, R. V., Halawi, L., & Mujtaba, B. (2010). Utilizing the technology acceptance model to assess the employee adoption of information systems security measures. *Issues in Information Systems*, 11(1), 9.

Jones, H. S., Towse, J. N., & Race, N. (2015). Susceptibility to email fraud: A review of psychological perspectives, data-collection methods, and ethical considerations. *International Journal of Cyber Behavior, Psychology and Learning (IJCBPL)*, 5(3), 13–29.

Jones, H. S., Towse, J. N., Race, N., & Harrison, T. (2019). Email fraud: The search for psychological predictors of susceptibility. *PLOS ONE*, 14(1), e0209684.

Kearns, G. S. (2016). Countering mobile device threats: A mobile device security model. *Journal of Forensic & Investigative Accounting*, 8(1), 36–48.

Khan, S., Nauman, M., Othman, A. T., & Musa, S. (2012, June). How secure is your smartphone: An analysis of smartphone security mechanisms. In *Proceedings Title: 2012 International Conference on Cyber Security, Cyber Warfare and Digital Forensic (CyberSec)* (pp. 76–81). IEEE.

Klettke, B., Hallford, D. J., Clancy, E., Mellor, D. J., & Toumbourou, J. W. (2019). Sexting and psychological distress: The role of unwanted and coerced sexts. *Cyberpsychology, Behavior, and Social Networking*, 22(4), 237–242.

Korshunov, P. & Marcel, S. (2018). Deepfakes: A new threat to face recognition? Assessment and detection. *arXiv Preprint:1812.08685*. https://arxiv.org/abs/1812.08685

Krasnova, H., Spiekermann, S., Koroleva, K., & Hildebrand, T. (2010). Online social networks: Why we disclose. *Journal of Information Technology*, 25(2), 109–125.

Lazer, D. M., Baum, M. A., Benkler, Y., et al. (2018). The science of fake news. *Science*, 359(6380), 1094–1096.

Leavitt, N. (2011). Mobile security: Finally a serious problem? *Computer*, 44(6), 11–14.

Liang, H. & Xue, Y. (2009). Avoidance of information technology threats: A theoretical perspective. *MIS Quarterly*, 71–90.

Liang, H. & Xue, Y. (2010). Understanding security behaviours in personal computer usage: A threat avoidance perspective. *Journal of the Association for Information Systems*, 11(7), 394–413.

Lopez, T., Sharp, H., Tun, T., et al. (2019, May). Talking about security with professional developers. In *Proceedings of the Joint 7th International Workshop on Conducting Empirical Studies in Industry and 6th International Workshop on Software Engineering Research and Industrial Practice* (pp. 34–40). IEEE Press.

Lowry, P. B., Zhang, J., Wang, C., & Siponen, M. (2016). Why do adults engage in cyberbullying on social media? An integration of online disinhibition and deindividuation effects with the social structure and social learning model. *Information Systems Research, 27*(4), 962–986.

Maarek, M., McGregor, L., Louchart, S., & McMenemy, R. (2019, June). How could serious games support secure programming? Designing a study replication and intervention. In *2019 IEEE European Symposium on Security and Privacy Workshops (EuroS&PW)* (pp. 139–148). IEEE.

Macaulay, P. J., Boulton, M. J., Betts, L. R., et al. (2019). Subjective versus objective knowledge of online safety/dangers as predictors of children's perceived online safety and attitudes towards e-safety education in the United Kingdom. *Journal of Children and Media*, 1–20. DOI:10.1080/17482798.2019.1697716

Marks, D. F. (2018). American psychologists, the Central Intelligence Agency, and enhanced interrogation. *Health Psychology Open, 5*(2), 2055102918796610.

McKenna, P. (2007). The rise of cyberbullying. *New Scientist, 195*(2613), 26–27.

Metz, C. & Satariono, A. (2019). Facebook restricts live streaming after New Zealand shooting. *The New York Times, 15*.

Miller, G. (2012). The smartphone psychology manifesto. *Perspectives on Psychological Science, 7*(3), 221–237.

Mylonas, A., Kastania, A., & Gritzalis, D. (2013). Delegate the smartphone user? Security awareness in smartphone platforms. *Computers & Security, 34*, 47–66.

Newman, L. H. (2019). An iPhone app that protects your privacy – for real this time. *Wired*. Available from www.wired.com/story/guardian-firewall-ios-app/.

Ng, B. Y. & Rahim, M. (2005). A socio-behavioural study of home computer users' intention to practice security. *PACIS 2005 Proceedings, 20*.

Ng, B. Y., Kankanhalli, A., & Xu, Y. C. (2009). Studying users' computer security behaviour: A health belief perspective. *Decision Support Systems, 46*(4), 815–825.

Nguyen, T., McDonald, J. T., & Glisson, W. B. (2017, January). Exploitation and detection of a malicious mobile application. In *Proceedings of the 50th Hawaii International Conference on System Sciences*.

Ojeda, M., Del Rey, R., & Hunter, S. C. (2019). Longitudinal relationships between sexting and involvement in both bullying and cyberbullying. *Journal of Adolescence, 77*, 81–89.

Orben, A., Dienlin, T., & Przybylski, A. K. (2019). Social media's enduring effect on adolescent life satisfaction. *Proceedings of the National Academy of Sciences, 116*(21), 10226–10228.

Osmani, V., Carreras, I., Matic, A., & Saar, P. (2014). An analysis of distance estimation to detect proximity in social interactions. *Journal of Ambient Intelligence and Humanized Computing, 5*(3), 297–306.

Pieterse, H., Olivier, M., & van Heerden, R. (2019). Evaluation framework for detecting manipulated smartphone data. *SAIEE Africa Research Journal, 110*(2), 67–76.

Piwek, L., Ellis, D. A., & Andrews, S. (2016). Can programming frameworks bring smartphones into the mainstream of psychological science? *Frontiers in Psychology, 7*, 1252.

Ponemon Institute Research. (2015). *Report on the State of Mobile Application Insecurity.* Sponsored by IBM Independently conducted by Ponemon Institute LLC. Publication Date: 2015 Feb.

Povolotskiy R., Gupta N., Leverant, A. B., Kandinov, A. & Paskhover, B. (2019). Head and neck injuries associated with cell phone use. *JAMA Otolaryngol Head Neck Surg.*

Powell, R. A., Digdon, N., Harris, B., & Smithson, C. (2014). Correcting the record on Watson, Rayner, and Little Albert: Albert Barger as 'Psychology's lost boy'. *American Psychologist, 69*(6), 600.

Prabhakar, S., Pankanti, S., & Jain, A. K. (2003). Biometric recognition: Security and privacy concerns. *IEEE Security & Privacy* (2), 33–42.

Quintana, D. S. (2020). A synthetic dataset primer for the biobehavioural sciences to promote reproducibility and hypothesis generation. *Elife, 9*, e53275.

Ramachandran, R., Oh, T., & Stackpole, W. (2012, June). Android anti-virus analysis. In *Annual Symposium on Information Assurance & Secure Knowledge Management* (pp. 35–40). http://citeseerx.ist.psu.edu/viewdoc/download?doi=10.1.1.295.7508&rep=rep1&type=pdf

Rice, E., Rhoades, H., Winetrobe, H., et al. (2012). Sexually explicit cell phone messaging associated with sexual risk among adolescents. *Pediatrics, 130*(4), 667–673.

Robertson, D. J., Kramer, R. S., & Burton, A. M. (2015). Face averages enhance user recognition for smartphone security. *PLOS ONE, 10*(3), e0119460.

Rogers, R. W. (1975). A protection motivation theory of fear appeals and attitude change. *The Journal of Psychology, 91*(1), 93–114.

Schäfer, M. S. (2012). Online communication on climate change and climate politics: A literature review. *Wiley Interdisciplinary Reviews: Climate Change, 3* (6), 527–543.

Scharkowa, M., Mangoldb, F., Stierc, S. and Breuerc, J. (2020). How social network sites and other online intermediaries increase exposure to news. *Proceedings of the National Academy of Sciences*, https://doi.org/10.1073/pnas.1918279117.

Scully, R. P. (2019). Hidden surveillance. *New Scientist, 243*(3247), 20–21.

Seneviratne, S., Seneviratne, A., Mohapatra, P., & Mahanti, A. (2014). Predicting user traits from a snapshot of apps installed on a smartphone. *ACM SIGMOBILE Mobile Computing and Communications Review, 18*(2), 1–8.

Song, C., Qu, Z., Blumm, N., & Barabási, A. L. (2010). Limits of predictability in human mobility. *Science, 327*(5968), 1018–1021.

Stuart, A., Bandara, A. K., & Levine, M. (2019). The psychology of privacy in the digital age. *Social and Personality Psychology Compass, 13*(11), e12507.

Szot, T., Specht, C., Specht, M., & Dabrowski, P. S. (2019). Comparative analysis of positioning accuracy of Samsung Galaxy smartphones in stationary measurements. *PLOS ONE, 14*(4), e0215562.

Symantec (2014). *How Safe Is Your Quantified Self?* Available from www.symantec.com/content/en/us/enterprise/media/security_response/whitepapers/how-safe-is-your-quantified-self.pdf.

Talbot, C. V., Gavin, J., Van Steen, T., & Morey, Y. (2017). A content analysis of thinspiration, fitspiration, and bonespiration imagery on social media. *Journal of Eating Disorders, 5*(1), 40.

Thompson, N., McGill, T. J., & Wang, X. (2017). 'Security begins at home': Determinants of home computer and mobile device security behaviour. *Computers & Security, 70*, 376–391.

Tiggemann, M. & McGill, B. (2004). The role of social comparison in the effect of magazine advertisements on women's mood and body dissatisfaction. *Journal of Social and Clinical Psychology, 23*(1), 23–44.

Trepte, S., Scharkow, M., & Dienlin, T. (2020). The privacy calculus contextualized: The influence of affordances. *Computers in Human Behavior, 104*, 106115.

Tsai, H. Y. S., Jiang, M., Alhabash, S., et al. (2016). Understanding online safety behaviours: A protection motivation theory perspective. *Computers & Security, 59*, 138–150.

Van der Linden, D., Rashid, A., Williams, E., & Warinschi, B. (2018, May). Safe cryptography for all: Toward visual metaphor driven cryptography building blocks. In *2018 IEEE/ACM 1st International Workshop on Security Awareness from Design to Deployment (SEAD)* (pp. 41–44). IEEE.

Van Kleek, M., Liccardi, I., Binns, R., et al. (2017, May). Better the devil you know: Exposing the data sharing practices of smartphone apps. In *Proceedings of the 2017 CHI Conference on Human Factors in Computing Systems* (pp. 5208–5220). ACM.

Vishwanath, A., Herath, T., Chen, R., Wang, J., & Rao, H. R. (2011). Why do people get phished? Testing individual differences in phishing vulnerability within an integrated, information processing model. *Decision Support Systems, 51*(3), 576–586.

Vishwanath, A., Harrison, B., & Ng, Y. J. (2018). Suspicion, cognition, and automaticity model of phishing susceptibility. *Communication Research, 45*(8), 1146–1166.

Wachter, S. (2018). Normative challenges of identification in the Internet of Things: Privacy, profiling, discrimination, and the GDPR. *Computer Law & Security Review, 34*(3), 436–449.

Wang, Y. & Kosinski, M. (2018). Deep neural networks are more accurate than humans at detecting sexual orientation from facial images. *Journal of Personality and Social Psychology, 114*(2), 246.

Weir, C., Rashid, A., & Noble, J. (2016a). How to improve the security skills of mobile app developers? Comparing and contrasting expert views. In *Twelfth Symposium on Usable Privacy and Security ({SOUPS} 2016)*. www.usenix.org/conference/soups2016/workshop-program/wsiw16/presentation/weir

Weir, C., Rashid, A., & Noble, J. (2016b, November). Reaching the masses: A new subdiscipline of app programmer education. In *Proceedings of the 2016 24th ACM SIGSOFT International Symposium on Foundations of Software Engineering* (pp. 936–939). ACM.

Whitty, M. T. (2018). Do you love me? Psychological characteristics of romance scam victims. *Cyberpsychology, Behavior, and Social Networking, 21*(2), 105–109.

Whitty, M. T. & Buchanan, T. (2016). The online dating romance scam: The psychological impact on victims – both financial and non-financial. *Criminology & Criminal Justice, 16*(2), 176–194.

Williams, E. J., Beardmore, A., & Joinson, A. N. (2017). Individual differences in susceptibility to online influence: A theoretical review. *Computers in Human Behavior, 72*, 412–421.

Williams, E. J., Hinds, J., & Joinson, A. N. (2018). Exploring susceptibility to phishing in the workplace. *International Journal of Human-Computer Studies, 120*, 1–13.

Williamson, A. E., McQueenie, R., Ellis, D. A., McConnachie, A., & Wilson, P. (2020). General practice recording of Adverse Childhood Experiences. *BJGP Open, 4*(1), 20X101011.

Woodlock, D. (2017). The abuse of technology in domestic violence and stalking. *Violence Against Women, 23*(5), 584–602.

Yang, C. C., Holden, S. M., & Carter, M. D. (2018). Social media social comparison of ability (but not opinion) predicts lower identity clarity: Identity processing style as a mediator. *Journal of Youth and Adolescence, 47* (10), 2114–2128.

Yang, X., Li, Y., & Lyu, S. (2019, May). Exposing deep fakes using inconsistent head poses. In *ICASSP 2019 – 2019 IEEE International Conference on Acoustics, Speech and Signal Processing (ICASSP)* (pp. 8261–8265). IEEE.

Zimmer, M. (2018). Addressing conceptual gaps in big data research ethics: An application of contextual integrity. *Social Media & Society, 4*(2), 2056305118768300.

Conclusion

Aarseth, E., Bean, A. M., Boonen, H., et al. (2017). Scholars' open debate paper on the World Health Organization ICD-11 Gaming Disorder proposal. *Journal of Behavioral Addictions, 6*(3), 267–270.

Adams, R. C., Challenger, A., Bratton, L., et al. (2019). Claims of causality in health news: A randomised trial. *BMC Medicine, 17*(1), 91.

Andrews, S., Ellis, D. A., Shaw, H., & Piwek, L. (2015). Beyond self-report: Tools to compare estimates and real world smartphone use. *PLOS ONE, 10* (10), e0139004.

Apple (2016). *Apple ResearchKit*. Available from http://researchkit.org.

Baddeley, A. (2018). *Working Memories: Postmen, Divers and the Cognitive Revolution*. Routledge.

Belk, R. W. (1988). Possessions and the extended self. *Journal of Consumer Research, 15*(2), 139–168.

Belk, R. W. (2013). Extended self in a digital world. *Journal of Consumer Research, 40*(3), 477–500.

Billieux, J., Philippot, P., Schmid, C., et al. (2015). Is dysfunctional use of the mobile phone a behavioural addiction? Confronting symptom-based versus process-based approaches. *Clinical Psychology & Psychotherapy, 22*(5), 460–468.

Bishop, D. V. (2020). The psychology of experimental psychologists: Overcoming cognitive constraints to improve research: The 47th Sir Frederic Bartlett Lecture. *Quarterly Journal of Experimental Psychology, 73*(1), 1–19, 1747021819886519.

Blandford, A., Gibbs, J., Newhouse, N., et al. (2018). Seven lessons for interdisciplinary research on interactive digital health interventions. *Digital Health, 4,* 2055207618770325.

Blank, G., Dutton, W. H., & Lefkowitz, J. (2019) *Perceived Threats to Privacy Online: The Internet in Britain. Oxford Internet Survey 2019.* Oxford Internet Institute, University of Oxford.

Bogen, J. (2017). Theory and observation in science. In E. N. Zalt (ed.), *Stanford Encyclopedia of Philosophy.* https://plato.stanford.edu/archives/sum2017/entries/science-theory-observation/.

Box, G. E. (1976). Science and statistics. *Journal of the American Statistical Association, 71*(356), 791–799.

Boyd, D. (2014). *It's Complicated: The Social Lives of Networked Teens.* Yale University Press.

Brainard, D. H. (1997). The psychophysics toolbox. *Spatial Vision, 10*(4), 433–436.

Brand, M., Rumpf, H. J., King, D. L., Potenza, M. N., & Wegmann, E. (2020). Clarifying terminologies in research on gaming disorder and other addictive behaviors: Distinctions between core symptoms and underlying psychological processes. *Current Opinion in Psychology.*

Buhrmester, M., Kwang, T., & Gosling, S. D. (2011). Amazon's Mechanical Turk: A new source of inexpensive, yet high-quality, data? *Perspectives on Psychological Science, 6*(1), 3–5.

Cahalan, S. (2019). Stanford professor who changed America with just one study was a liar. *New York Post.* Available from https://nypost.com/2019/11/02/stanford-professor-who-changed-america-with-just-one-study-was-also-a-liar/.

Cascardi, M. & Brown, C. (2016). Concept creep or meaningful expansion? Response to Haslam. *Psychological Inquiry, 27*(1), 24–28.

Chabris, C. F., Hebert, B. M., Benjamin, D. J., et al. (2012). Most reported genetic associations with general intelligence are probably false positives. *Psychological Science, 23*(11), 1314–1323.

Chivers, T. (2019). Does psychology have a conflict-of-interest problem? *Nature, 571,* 20–23.

Cohen, J. (2016). The earth is round (p<. 05). In L. L. Harlow, S. A. Mulaik, & J. H. Steiger (eds.), *What If There Were No Significance Tests?* (pp. 69–82). Routledge.

Dang, J., King, K. M., & Inzlicht, M. (2020). Why are self-report and behavioral measures weakly correlated?. *Trends in Cognitive Sciences, 24*(4), 267–269.

Davidson, B. I., Ellis, D. A., Bowman, N. D., et al. (2019a). Avoiding irrelevance: The manifestation and impacts of technophobia in psychological science. *PsyArXiv* DOI:10.31234/osf.io/b9f4p

Davidson, B. I. & Ellis, D. A. (2019b). Social media addiction: Technological déjà vu. *BMJ, 365,* l4277.

Davis, F. D., Bagozzie, R. P., & Warshaw, P. R. (1989). User acceptance of computer technology: A comparison of two theoretical models authors. *INFORMS*, *35*(8), 982e1003.

Deng, T., Kanthawala, S., Meng, J., et al. (2019). Measuring smartphone usage and task switching with log tracking and self-reports. *Mobile Media & Communication*, *7*(1), 3–23.

Dennis, S., Yim, H., Garrett, P., Sreekumar, V., & Stone, B. (2019a). A system for collecting and analyzing experience-sampling data. *Behavior Research Methods*, *51*(4), 1824–1838.

Dennis, S., Garrett, P., Yim, H., et al. (2019b). Privacy versus open science. *Behavior Research Methods*, 51(4), 1839–1848.

Doliński, D. (2018). Is psychology still a science of behaviour? *Social Psychological Bulletin*. *13*, e25025.

Edgerton, D. (1995). Technophobia then and now. *Nature*, *376*(6542), 653–654.

Extance, A. (2018). How AI technology can tame the scientific literature. *Nature*, *561*(7722), 273.

Ellis, D. A. (2019). Are smartphones really that bad? Improving the psychological measurement of technology-related behaviours. *Computers in Human Behavior*, *97*, 60–66.

Ellis, D. A. & Merdian, H. L. (2015). Thinking outside the box: Developing dynamic data visualizations for psychology with Shiny. *Frontiers in Psychology*, *6*, 1782.

Ellis, D. A., Davidson, B. I., Shaw, H., & Geyer, K. (2019). Do smartphone usage scales predict behaviour? *International Journal of Human-Computer Studies*, *130*, 86–92.

Elmer, T., Chaitanya, K., Purwar, P., & Stadtfeld, C. (2019). The validity of RFID badges measuring face-to-face interactions. *Behavior Research Methods*, *51*, 2120–2138.

Elhai, J. D., Levine, J. C., & Hall, B. J. (2019). Problematic smartphone use and mental health problems: Current state of research and future directions. *Dusunen Adam*, *32*(1), 1–3.

Elson, M., Ferguson, C. J., Gregerson, M., et al. (2019). Do policy statements on media effects faithfully represent the science? *Advances in Methods and Practices in Psychological Science*, *2*(1), 12–25.

Epskamp, S. (2019). Reproducibility and replicability in a fast-paced methodological world. *Advances in Methods and Practices in Psychological Science*, *2*(2), 145–155.

Ferreira, D., Kostakos, V., & Schweizer, I. (2017). Human sensors on the move. In *Participatory Sensing, Opinions and Collective Awareness* (pp. 9–19). Springer.

Firth, U. (*online first*, 2019). Fast lane to slow science. *Trends in Cognitive Science*.

Flake, J. K. & Fried, E. I. (2019). Measurement schmeasurement: Questionable measurement practices and how to avoid them. *PsyArXiv*. DOI:10.31234/osf.io/hs7wm

Francis, G. (2012). Publication bias and the failure of replication in experimental psychology. *Psychonomic Bulletin & Review*, *19*(6), 975–991.

Formotus (2016). *Figuring the Costs of Custom Mobile Business App Development.* Available from www.formotus.com/14018/blog-mobility/figuring-the-costs-of-custom-mobile-business-app-development.

Geyer, K., Ellis, D. A., & Piwek, L. (2019). A simple location-tracking app for psychological research. *Behavior Research Methods, 51*(6), 2840–2846.

Giardino, V. (2019). Philosophy and psychological science: Let's revive the cognitive revolution! *APS Observer, 32*(4).

Gonzalez, R. (2018). The research behind Google's new tools for digital well-being. *Wired.* www.wired.com/story/the-research-behind-googles-new-tools-for-digital-well-being/.

Griffiths, M. (2005). A 'components' model of addiction within a biopsychosocial framework. *Journal of Substance Use, 10*(4), 191–197.

Hall, J. A., Xing, C., Ross, E. M., & Johnson, R. M. (2019). Experimentally manipulating social media abstinence: Results of a four-week diary study. *Media Psychology,* 1–17.

Hand, D. J. (2014). Wonderful examples, but let's not close our eyes. *Statistical Science, 29*(1), 98–100.

Haslam, N. (2016). Concepts of harm and pathology. *Psychological Inquiry, 27* (1), 1–17.

Hässler, T., Ullrich, J., Bernardino, M., et al. (2020). A large-scale test of the link between intergroup contact and support for social change. *Nature Human Behaviour,* 1–7.

Haxby, J. V., Parasuraman, R., Lalonde, F., & Abboud, H. (1993). SuperLab: General-purpose Macintosh software for human experimental psychology and psychological testing. *Behavior Research Methods, Instruments, & Computers, 25* (3), 400–405.

Hedge, C., Powell, G., & Sumner, P. (2018). The reliability paradox: Why robust cognitive tasks do not produce reliable individual differences. *Behavior Research Methods, 50*(3), 1166–1186.

Heffer, T., Good, M., Daly, O., MacDonell, E., & Willoughby, T. (2019). The longitudinal association between social-media use and depressive symptoms among adolescents and young adults: An empirical reply to Twenge et al. (2018). *Clinical Psychological Science, 7*(3), 462–470.

Houghton, S., Lawrence, D., Hunter, S. C., et al. (2018). Reciprocal relationships between trajectories of depressive symptoms and screen media use during adolescence. *Journal of Youth and Adolescence, 47*(11), 2453–2467.

Hutson, M. (2018). Missing data hinder replication of artificial intelligence studies. Available from www.sciencemag.org/news/2018/02/missing-data-hinder-replication-artificial-intelligence-studies.

Hutton, J. S., Dudley, J., Horowitz-Kraus, T., DeWitt, T., & Holland, S. K. (2019). Associations between screen-based media use and brain white matter integrity in preschool-aged children. *JAMA Pediatrics.* Published online 4 November.

Ioannidis, J. P. A., Klavans, R. & Boyack, K. W. (2018). Thousands of scientists publish a paper every five days. *Nature, 561,* 167–169.

Jacobucci, R., & Grimm, K. J. (2020). Machine learning and psychological research: The unexplored effect of measurement. *Perspectives on Psychological Science*, 1745691620902467.

Jeong, M., Zo, H., Lee, C. H., & Ceran, Y. (2019). Feeling displeasure from online social media postings: A study using cognitive dissonance theory. *Computers in Human Behavior, 97*, 231–240.

Johannes, N., Meier, A., Reinecke, L., et al. (2019). The relationship between online vigilance and affective well-being in everyday life: Combining smart-phone logging with experience sampling. *PsyArXiv*. DOI:10.31234/osf.io/t3wc2

Keil, T. F., Koschate-Reis, M., & Levine, M. (2020). Contact Logger: Measuring everyday intergroup contact experiences in near-time. *Behavior Research Methods*. https://link.springer.com/article/10.3758/s13428-019-01335-w

Kerr, N. L. (1998). HARKing: Hypothesizing after the results are known. *Personality and Social Psychology Review, 2*(3), 196–217.

Kim, P. H., Ployhart, R. E., & Gibson, C. B. (2018). Editors' comments: Is organizational behavior overtheorized?. *Academy of Management Review, 43* (4), 541–545.

King, W. R. & He, J. (2006). A meta-analysis of the technology acceptance model. *Information & Management, 43*(6), 740–755.

Klein, S. B. (2014). What can recent replication failures tell us about the theoretical commitments of psychology? *Theory & Psychology, 24*(3), 326–338.

Kubovy, M. (2020). Lives as collections of strands: An essay in descriptive psychology. *Perspectives on Psychological Science*, 15(2), 497–515. 1745691619887145.

Kuss, D. J. & Griffiths, M. D. (2017). Social networking sites and addiction: Ten lessons learned. *International Journal of Environmental Research and Public Health, 14*(3), 311.

Lakens, D. (2015). Comment: What p-hacking really looks like: A comment on Masicampo and LaLande (2012). *Quarterly Journal of Experimental Psychology, 68*(4), 829–832.

Lazer, D., Pentland, A., Adamic, L., et al. (2009). Computational social science. *Science, 323*(5915), 721–723.

Lykken, D. T. (1991). What's wrong with psychology anyway? In D. Cicchetti & W. Grove (eds.), *Thinking Clearly about Psychology*. University of Minnesota Press.

Li, Y., & Baron, J. (2012). *Behavioral Research Data Analysis with R*. Springer.

Luijken, K., Groenwold, R. H., Van Calster, B., Steyerberg, E. W., & van Smeden, M. (2019). Impact of predictor measurement heterogeneity across settings on the performance of prediction models: A measurement error perspective. *Statistics in Medicine, 38*(18), 3444–3459.

Martin, B. R. (2011). The Research Excellence Framework and the 'impact agenda': Are we creating a Frankenstein monster? *Research Evaluation, 20*(3), 247–254.

Maxwell, S. E. (2004). The persistence of underpowered studies in psychological research: Causes, consequences, and remedies. *Psychological Methods, 9*(2), 147.

Miller, G. (2012). The smartphone psychology manifesto. *Perspectives on Psychological Science, 7*(3), 221–237.

Mischel, W. (2004). Toward an integrative science of the person. *Annual Review of Psychology, 55*(1), 1–22.

Mondol, A. S., Ra, H. K., Salekin, A., et al. (2016). LifeMaps: An automated diary system based on the structure of lives. In *Proceedings of the 14th ACM Conference on Embedded Network Sensor Systems CD-ROM, SenSys'16* (pp. 348–349).

Montag, C. & Elhai, J. D. (2019). A new agenda for personality psychology in the digital age? *Personality and Individual Differences, 147*, 128–134.

Muthukrishna, M. & Henrich, J. (2019). A problem in theory. *Nature Human Behavior, 3*(3), 221–229.

Nagel, M., Jansen, P. R., Stringer, S., et al. (2018). Meta-analysis of genome-wide association studies for neuroticism in 449,484 individuals identifies novel genetic loci and pathways. *Nature Genetics, 50*(7), 920.

Oberauer, K. & Lewandowsky, S. (2019). Addressing the theory crisis in psychology. *Psychonomic Bulletin & Review, 26*(5), 1596–1618.

Obradović, S. (2019). Publication pressures create knowledge silos. *Nature Human Behavior, 3*, 1028.

Open Science Collaboration. (2015). Estimating the reproducibility of psychological science. *Science, 349* (6251),aac4716.

Orben, A. & Przybylski, A. (2019). Screens, teens and psychological well-being: Evidence from three time-use diary studies. *Psychological Science, 30*(5), 682–696.

Orben, A., Dienlin, T., & Przybylski, A. K. (2019). Social media's enduring effect on adolescent life satisfaction. *Proceedings of the National Academy of Sciences, 116*(21), 10226–10228.

Orwell, G. (1949). *Nineteen Eighty-Four.* Secker & Warburg.

Oulasvirta, A., Rattenbury, T., Ma, L., & Raita, E. (2012). Habits make smartphone use more pervasive. *Personal and Ubiquitous Computing, 16*(1), 105–114.

Parker, S. (1995). *Science Discoveries: Alexander Graham Bell.* Chelsea House Publishers.

Parsons, S., Kruijt, A. W., & Fox, E. (2019). Psychological science needs a standard practice of reporting the reliability of cognitive-behavioral measurements. *Advances in Methods and Practices in Psychological Science, 2*(4), 378–395.

Peer, E., Vosgerau, J., & Acquisti, A. (2014). Reputation as a sufficient condition for data quality on Amazon Mechanical Turk. *Behavior Research Methods, 46*(4), 1023–1031.

Peirce, J. W. (2007). PsychoPy – psychophysics software in Python. *Journal of Neuroscience Methods, 162*(1–2), 8–13.

Pelosi, A. J. (2019). Personality and fatal diseases: Revisiting a scientific scandal. *Journal of Health Psychology, 24*(4), 421–439.

Peng, R. D. (2011). Reproducible research in computational science. *Science, 334* (6060), 1226–1227.

Pentland, A. (2008). *Honest Signals: How They Shape Our World.* MIT Press.

Phaf, R. H. (2020). Publish less, read more. *Theory & Psychology,* 0959354319898250.

Pink, S., Sumartojo, S., Lupton, D., & Heyes La Bond, C. (2017). Mundane data: The routines, contingencies and accomplishments of digital living. *Big Data & Society, 4*(1), 2053951717700924.

Piwek, L., Petrini, K., & Pollick, F. (2016). A dyadic stimulus set of audiovisual affective displays for the study of multisensory, emotional, social interactions. *Behavior Research Methods, 48*(4), 1285–1295.

Poldrack, R. A. (2019). The costs of reproducibility. *Neuron, 101*(1), 11–14.

Pontes, H. M. & Griffiths, M. D. (2019). A new era for gaming disorder research: Time to shift from consensus to consistency. *Addictive Behaviors.* https://doi .org/10.1016/j.addbeh.2019.106059

Protzko, J., & Schooler, J. W. (2019). Kids these days: Why the youth of today seem lacking.*Science Advances, 5* (10),eaav5916.

Reeves, B., Ram, N., Robinson, T. N., et al. (2019). Screenomics: A framework to capture and analyze personal life experiences and the ways that technology shapes them. *Human–Computer Interaction*, 1–52. DOI:10.1080/07370024.2019.1578652

REF 2021 (n.d.). Guidance pages that list key documents providing guidance on REF 2021. Available from www.ref.ac.uk/guidance/.

Reicher, S., & Haslam, S. A. (2006). Rethinking the psychology of tyranny: The BBC prison study. *British Journal of Social Psychology, 45*(1), 1–40.

Rhemtulla, M., van Bork, R., & Borsboom, D. (2019). Worse than measurement error: Consequences of inappropriate latent variable measurement models. *Psychological Methods, 25*(1), 30–45.

Rohrer, J. M. (2018). Thinking clearly about correlations and causation: Graphical causal models for observational data. *Advances in Methods and Practices in Psychological Science, 1*(1), 27–42.

Runyan, J. D. & Steinke, E. G. (2015). Virtues, ecological momentary assessment/ intervention and smartphone technology. *Frontiers in Psychology, 6*, 481.

Ryding, F. C. & Kaye, L. K. (2018). 'Internet addiction': A conceptual minefield. *International Journal of Mental Health and Addiction, 16*(1), 225–232.

Sassenberg, K. & Ditrich, L. (2019). Research in social psychology changed between 2011 and 2016: Larger sample sizes, more self-report measures, and more online studies. *Advances in Methods and Practices in Psychological Science, 2* (2), 107–114.

Simmons, J. P., Nelson, L. D., & Simonsohn, U. (2011). False-positive psychology: Undisclosed flexibility in data collection and analysis allows presenting anything as significant. *Psychological Science, 22*, 1359–1366.

Sochat, V. V., Eisenberg, I. W., Enkavi, A. Z., et al. (2016). The experiment factory: Standardizing behavioural experiments. *Frontiers in Psychology, 7*, 610.

Southerton, D. (2013). Habits, routines and temporalities of consumption: From individual behaviours to the reproduction of everyday practices. *Time & Society, 22*(3), 335–355.

Starns, J. J., Cataldo, A. M., Rotello, C. M., et al. (2019). Assessing theoretical conclusions with blinded inference to investigate a potential inference crisis. *Advances in Methods and Practices in Psychological Science, 2*(4), 335–349.

Stronge, S., Mok, T., Ejova, A., et al. (2019). Social media use is (weakly) related to psychological distress. *Cyberpsychology, Behavior, and Social Networking, 22*(9), 604–609.

Szot, T., Specht, C., Specht, M., & Dabrowski, P. S. (2019). Comparative analysis of positioning accuracy of Samsung Galaxy smartphones in stationary measurements. *PLOS ONE*, *14*(4), e0215562.

Taylor, P. J. (June, 2013). *How Technology is Revolutionizing Our Understanding of Human Cooperation* (inaugural lecture). Twente University Press.

Tomko, R. L., McClure, E. A., Cato, P. A., et al. (2019). An electronic, smart lighter to measure cigarette smoking: A pilot study to assess feasibility and initial validity. *Addictive Behaviors*, *98*, 106052.

Twenge, J. M. (2019a). More time on technology, less happiness? Associations between digital-media use and psychological well-being. *Current Directions in Psychological Science*, *28*(4), 372–379. 0963721419838244.

Twenge, J. M. (2019b). Stop debating whether too much smartphone time can hurt teens, and start protecting them. *TIME*. http://time.com/5555737/smart phone-mental-health-teens/.

UK Parliament (2018). *Science And Technology Committee: Impact of Social Media and Screen-Use on Young People's Health Inquiry*. www.parliament.uk/business/commit tees/committees-a-z/commons-select/science-and-technology-committee/inqui ries/parliament-2017/impact-of-social-media-young-people-17–19/.

Van Rooij, A. J., Ferguson, C. J., Colder Carras, M., et al. (2018). A weak scientific basis for gaming disorder: Let us err on the side of caution. *Journal of Behavioral Addictions*, *7*(1), 1–9.

van Smeden, M., Lash, T. L., & Groenwold, R. H. (2020). Reflection on modern methods: Five myths about measurement error in epidemiological research. *International Journal of Epidemiology*, *49*(1), 338–347.

Venkatesh, V., Thong, J. Y. L., & Xu, X. (2012). Consumer acceptance and use of information technology: Extending the unified theory of acceptance and use of technology. *Management Information Systems Quarterly*, *36*(1), 157e178.

Venkatesh, V., Thong, J. Y. L., & Xu, X. (2016). Unified theory of acceptance and use of technology: A synthesis and the road ahead. *Journal of the Association for Information Systems*, *17*(5), 328e376.

Waithira, N., Mutinda, B., & Cheah, P. Y. (2019). Data management and sharing policy: The first step towards promoting data sharing. *BMC Medicine*, *17*(1), 80.

Wellcome (2020). *What Researchers Think about the Culture They Work In*. Available from https://wellcome.ac.uk/sites/default/files/what-researchers-think-about-the-culture-they-work-in.pdf.

Wiederhold, B. K. (2019). Should smartphone use be banned for children? *Cyberpsychology, Behavior, and Social Networking*, *22* (4), 1–2.

Wilcockson, T. D. W., Ellis, D. A., & Shaw, H. (2018). Determining typical smartphone usage: What data do we need? *Cyberpsychology, Behavior and Social Networking*, *21*(6), 395–398.

Yarkoni, T. (2019). The generalizability crisis. *PsyArXiv*. DOI:10.31234/osf.io/jqw35

Index

For EU product safety concerns, contact us at Calle de José Abascal, 56–1°,
28003 Madrid, Spain or eugpsr@cambridge.org.